POLITICAL EDUCATION

POLITICAL EDUCATION

NATIONAL POLICY COMES OF AGE

THE UPDATED EDITION

CHRISTOPHER T. CROSS

Foreword by Richard Riley and Ted Sanders

Teachers College, Columbia University
New York and London

To Allyson Marie Goodall,
granddaughter extraordinaire,
who will inherit
the educational system that
my generation has shaped.

Published by Teachers College Press, 1234 Amsterdam Avenue, New York, NY 10027

Library of Congress Cataloging-in-Publication Data

Cross, Christopher T.
  Political education : national policy comes of age / Christopher T. Cross ; foreword by Richard Riley and Ted Sanders—the updated edition.
       p. cm.
  Includes bibliographical references and index.
  ISBN 978-0-8077-5151-0 (pbk. : alk. paper)
  1. Federal aid to education—United States—History—20th century. 2. Public schools—United States—Finance. 3. Education—Political aspects—United States—History—20th century. I. Title.
  LB2825.C76 2010
  379.1'210973—dc22
                                        2010025873
ISBN 978-0-8077-5151-0 (paper)

Printed on acid-free paper

Manufactured in the United States of America

17 16 15 14 13 12 11 10   8 7 6 5 4 3 2 1

Contents

Foreword

IN THE LAST DECADE OR SO we have seen K–12 education emerge in public opinion polls as one of the key issues for attention by the federal government, a stark contrast to what we saw in similar polls in earlier decades. In this book, Christopher Cross does an excellent, even-handed job of tracing the evolution of federal policy during the later half of the 20th century. Cross brings to the book his own experience of 32 years in Washington, combined with research done in several presidential libraries and interviews with more than 20 people who held key positions during that time.

What emerges is a highly readable chronicle of how the federal role has been transformed from a time when education could command hardly any attention in Washington to a period where both political parties engage in battles to see who can lay claim to the title of being most responsible for reforming and supporting our public schools. While those of us who participated in shaping the federal role during the last 20 years may not always agree with the points that Cross makes, we believe that this book makes an important contribution to understanding how education has achieved this transformation.

In 2004 we will see political races at the national, state, and local levels across the nation. Education will surely be a topic of importance in many of those races, as will the role of the federal government. If we are to make intelligent choices about where the nation is headed, if we are to choose between competing approaches, it is important that we understand how and why we have come to where we are today. *Political Education* provides one lucid account of what happened. Cross also infuses his writing with an important human dimension by noting and tracing the contributions of key figures, Democrat and Republican, educator and politician, across the years.

In his final chapters, Cross captures several important lessons gleaned from his research and makes some interesting suggestions about where we may be headed in the years to come. While we may disagree on the details of what he suggests, the value of this volume will lie in educating the reader about our history and provoking a dialogue about our future.

Clearly education is today a national issue. That genie can never be put back into the bottle. We must move forward, making decisions based upon both good information and a profound respect for our children.

There is no issue more important to each of us and to future generations.

Richard Riley
U.S. Secretary of Education, 1993–2001

Ted Sanders
President, Education Commission of the States

Preface

THE STORY OF HOW THE FEDERAL ROLE in K–12 education has evolved since World War II is, in most respects, also an examination of how the influence of the federal government has grown and evolved in American society. Education as a federal issue had its humble beginnings in the chorus of relatively minor issues in the Truman-Eisenhower era. By the time of Bill Clinton and George W. Bush, education had become a headliner, sharing top billing as a national domestic issue.

The development of the federal role in K–12 education is multifaceted. This book explores the development of education policy within the legislative and executive branches of the federal government. Although there are places where the impact of federal judicial decisions become intertwined with legislative and executive policy development—and are therefore treated accordingly—for the most part, that is another story.

Before this journey of 50-plus years is embarked on, a bit of historical background is provided. Then policy development is treated chronologically, because it is simply impossible to see the development of the federal role without understanding how the actions of one era affect the next. Key players and how they shaped federal policy are also discussed, because policy development is woven of personalities, events, and timing.

THE "WHYS" AND THE "WHATS"

Some readers may ask why the history of federal policy is important and what difference federal policy has made. This book demonstrates how federal policy has been—for better or worse—a constant influence on what states and local districts do, especially with respect to students most at risk. It also shows the steady and logical progression in the influence of federal policy. Indeed, by 2003, as this manuscript was being finalized, issues about how to comply with provisions of the most recent incarnation of the Elementary and Secondary Education Act—known as the No Child Left

Behind Act of 2001—were clearly driving questions of policy and practice in almost every state and in the majority of the nation's 15,000 school districts in ways that were unimaginable in earlier decades.

Federal policy has made a positive difference, especially in the education of our most at risk students. Children who are poor, who are from racial or ethnic minorities, or who are disabled have all been profoundly affected by federal law and by the way in which federal law has driven state law and local practice. While policies have sometimes been naive, and even misguided, on balance the federal presence has been a net positive.

Concurrent with the expansion of the federal role have come bureaucracies that seem to just grow like Topsy; reporting requirements that are often overwhelming; and federal audits, rules, and regulations. In the first seven chapters we will explore the history, the rationale, and the resulting policy changes that tell the story of how federal policy has been transformed. In chapter 8, we will discuss what can be learned from these 50-plus years. In the final chapter, we will examine where federal policy may lead in the future.

It is important to evaluate the impact of federal policy because it will only become more important in the coming decades. The genie is, indeed, out of the bottle. Future policymakers and practitioners need to have an understanding of the history of U.S. education as they enter this new era of federal influence. A historical perspective will also help all of us—policymakers, parents, voters—in evaluating proposals that will emerge as candidates for national office debate policy options in 2004.

This book explores the development of federal policy for K–12 schools, primarily through the various iterations of the Elementary and Secondary Education Act (ESEA) and, to a lesser extent, the Individuals with Disabilities Education Act (IDEA). It also examines the creation of the U.S. Department of Education. Although many other federal agencies—such as the National Science Foundation, the Department of Agriculture, the Federal Communications Commission, the National Endowments for the Arts and Humanities—also affect schools, they are not central to this narrative, because on a daily basis they have far less to do with the overall teaching and learning mission of schools.

In writing this book, I researched books and articles published over the 50-year period, visited several presidential libraries, and studied materials stacks of the Congressional Research Service and the National Library of Education. I interviewed 20 people who are or have been involved in the making of federal education policy. I called upon my own experience in both the executive and the legislative branches of the federal government, my several years of working with federal policy as president of a state board of education, my work with the business community, my position as an officer in firms doing business with the federal government, and my service on many federal policy and advisory committees.

Acknowledgments

T HERE ARE MANY PEOPLE whom I must acknowledge for their contributions in making this book possible and for the impact that they have had on my life in education policy over the course of the past 35 years.

I begin by paying tribute to two people who have been my inspiration and mentors: Al Quie and Elliot Richardson. Each shaped education policy in profound ways and each was a wonderful role model of intelligence, perseverance, and integrity.

Financial support was provided by the Atlantic Philanthropies. Alan Ruby and Angela Covert have been wonderful supporters of my efforts to tell the story of how federal policy has evolved.

Readers will also note that one of the chapters is written by Paul Manna. In the course of my research, I met Paul, who was in the midst of conducting fieldwork for his Ph.D. dissertation. After discovering our mutual interests, I asked Paul to write the chapter on No Child Left Behind, as it was an important element of his work. Paul joined the government department at the College of William and Mary in the fall of 2003.

There are many professional colleagues over the years for whom I developed enormous respect. John F. Jennings, with whom I dueled for many years, is quite simply one of the best in the business.

Carole Saltz of Teachers College Press and her colleagues Catherine Bernard, Lyn Grossman, Amy Kline, and Ami Norris were invaluable to me in preparing the book for publication. I am also very grateful to the staffs of the several presidential libraries, each of which greatly assisted my work, as well as the staff of the National Library of Education in Washington, D.C. A special thanks to Wayne Riddell of the Congressional Research Service at the Library of Congress for providing access to the extensive document collection at CRS. Very special thanks to my old friend and colleague Marty LaVor for his superb photographs, pictures never before published that illustrate the tensions, the victories, and the inner workings of the political process.

Finally and most important, my wife, Dee Dee, has both suffered with me and guided me as she provided invaluable assistance with the editorial skills that she acquired during her own career. She has been patient, supportive, and editorially demanding, not a set of skills easily managed.

Introduction

A Policy Primer

A BRIEF TUTORIAL ON HOW FEDERAL education policy is developed may be useful as a guide through the chapters that follow. For the most part, policy recommendations emerge from the executive branch, generally in the form of a message from the president to the Congress. This message is generally preceded by months of staff-level negotiations involving both career and political appointees in the affected agencies. In our case these agencies are the U.S. Department of Education (and, before its creation, the Department of Health, Education, and Welfare), the Office of Management and Budget (formerly the Bureau of the Budget) and various White House offices. Outside interest groups are consulted, as well as key leaders of the president's own party in Congress. If a new administration wishes to move quickly, consultations with agency staff, interest groups, and Congress may be minimal. Such was the case in 2001, with George W. Bush, and with some of the early Ronald Reagan proposals.

Once a bill or an administration proposal is sent to Congress, the action shifts. Unless the White House has large majorities of its own party in power or can create a truly bipartisan consensus, control passes to the committee or subcommittee chairs. Most action originates in a subcommittee.

Committees and subcommittees can kill a bill by simply never reporting it: voting not to send it on up the line or taking no action on it. Most presidential initiatives at least get to the stage of being considered by a full committee.

HEARINGS

Hearings are a very important part of the process, whether held on Capitol Hill or in the field. Many an important education issue has been shaped by members' personal exposure to issues, especially through visits to schools and through field hearings on programs.

It is at this stage that lobbyists have their greatest influence. Education associations, such as the National Education Association and the National School Boards Association, are often called upon to produce witnesses, frequently with the understanding that these witnesses will support the position taken by the chair. The minority party is given one day in which they can schedule witnesses, but the majority may have a dozen days for their witnesses. In addition, of course, lobbyists will buttonhole staff and members, advocate for special additions or exceptions, and in general try to shape the bill to the liking of their membership. The bill that emerges from a committee is the product of considerable bargaining.

FLOOR CONSIDERATION

In the House of Representatives, all major bills must then get a rule—a resolution that governs under what conditions that bill will be considered on the floor of the House. The Rules Committee also has the power to kill a bill by simply never granting it a rule. There are ways around this potential roadblock, but they are rarely invoked.

In the Senate, once a committee passes a bill, it will be called up for consideration by the full Senate, but only if the majority leader agrees to schedule it. The Senate leadership can also take a bill off the floor, even after debate has begun, if its members believe it is taking too much time.

The Senate also uses a rule of cloture: If 60 senators agree, debate on a bill will end after a fixed period of time, technically giving each senator time to speak. Without cloture, a bill can be filibustered to the point that the leadership pulls it from consideration.

RESOLVING DIFFERENCES IN LEGISLATION

After both the House and Senate pass a bill on the same subject—assuming that there are differences between the two bills—a conference of the two bodies is held, with each side getting one vote. Conferences can take days or months. However, some never finish before the end of a 2-year congressional session; in this case, the entire process must start all over again.

Once a single language is agreed upon and incorporated into the bill in conference, both the House and Senate must accept the agreement reached in the conference. Finally, the bill is sent to the president, who has 10 days (excluding Sundays and holidays) to sign or veto it. If vetoed, the bill goes back to Congress and a two-thirds affirmative vote of both House and Senate is required to enact the bill without the approval of the president.

A further complication is that this whole process must be repeated every year for the appropriations that fund each agency. Authorization bills are generally for at least 3 years; appropriations bills are enacted each year.

If the Congress and the president cannot agree on funding levels, a continuing resolution is enacted, an event that generally maintains funding at the level of the previous year.

Bills that authorize programs or establish policy in other ways, such as Title IX of the Higher Education Act or Section 504 of the Rehabilitation Act, also require the preparation of regulations. Regulations are prepared by a team of attorneys and program staff in an agency. It is quite common for it to take 6 months to 2 years for the final regulations to be issued. Most program recipients receive their guidance and direction from the regulations, not the law itself. Since the very process that created the law is one that values ambiguity, the regulation-writing process offers an additional opportunity to influence policy.

The Millennium Decade

Bush and Obama

THE DECADE OF *NCLB* AND *NCLB* ANGST

The first decade of the 21st century was a turbulent time for federal education policy. It began with the election of George W. Bush and ended with a Race to the Top proposed by Barack Obama and his education secretary, Arne Duncan, the former chief executive officer of the Chicago Public Schools. This level of attention seems to confirm that national leaders believe they must act to fill what they perceive as a vacuum in state leadership, especially in light of the advances other nation's have made in education quality and student performance.

Although those were key events, the decade will probably always be noted as the No Child Left Behind decade. Whether you loved it or hated it, NCLB dominated the education agenda during that time and will certainly remain a major issue in the early part of this decade.

In Congress, the decade was marked by several major transitions, most important the death of Massachusetts Senator Ted Kennedy, which ended an era of Kennedy influence over national education policy that began with John F. Kennedy's election to the House in 1946. The decade also saw the elevation of John Boehner, another one of the "Big Four" leaders who crafted NCLB, as he moved into the House Republican leadership post and the departure of Sen. Judd Gregg from his position as ranking Republican on the Senate Health, Education, Labor, and Pensions (HELP) Committee. By the time the second session of the 111th Congress opened in January 2010, only California Representative George Miller remained in a key post affecting reauthorization of K-12 education policy. These changes, coupled with the increasingly divisive politics that enveloped Washington and the angst that accompanied the implementation of NCLB, created a political dynamic in which the coalescing of a majority in either the House or the Senate to produce a bill to reauthorize ESEA/

NCLB—which had been due to take place in 2007—became increasingly difficult.

The decade was also marked, quite predictably, by battles over funding. It began with issues around the full funding of NCLB and Individuals with Disabilities Education Act (IDEA), and ended with the Federal government infusing the education system with unprecedented resources through legislation intended to stimulate the economy following the near-collapse of the nation's financial system. The attendant decline in state revenues created a fiscal challenge that will make maintaining this new level of federal support a crucial issue when the stimulus funds run out after FY 2011.

NCLB IMPLEMENTATION

NCLB became law in January 2002, but it took many months for regulations to be issued and even longer for accurate information to make its way down to the school and classroom level. It is now apparent that few school people understood at that time just what a major impact the law would have on their daily lives.

As regulations were released, school officials' anxiety increased about implementing the law. Questions were raised about issues ranging from the delivery of supplemental services, to the ability of schools to handle transfers, to the alleged narrowing of the curriculum, to teaching to the test, to—most vexing—how to determine who is a highly qualified teacher. In the first Bush term, there was little deviation from a hard-line, strict-constructionist interpretation of the law, or at least the White House interpretation of what it meant. Despite this attitude, wide variation emerged among the states on such matters as (a) the minimum size of the group in a school that would be required for purposes of reporting student data, (b) what assessments were used, and (c) how a state defines the level of student achievement required to achieve proficiency.

The first Bush education secretary, Rod Paige, had his every action closely monitored by a White House team led by Margaret Spellings, who would become secretary in Bush's second term, and a core of tough and vigilant watchdogs both within the department and in the Washington policy community. Interestingly, that group ranged across the spectrum from the far left (EdTrust and the Citizens' Committee on Civil Rights) to the center (The Business Roundtable) to the far right (Heritage Foundation). Although each seemed to have different motivations, all had a strong commitment to closing the achievement gap, holding schools accountable and improving the overall quality of American education. Unexpectedly, after she became secretary in 2005, Spellings permitted a number of waivers and deviations from the law that were widely applauded by the education community, including the limited use of value-added measures to determine which schools achieved AYP (Adequate Yearly Progress) and variations in sanctions that permitted tutoring services to be offered before school transfers were required for schools not making AYP in multiple consecutive years.

THE HILL

Although NCLB should have been reauthorized in 2007, it was clear that no consensus existed on what should be done. This lack of consensus resulted from a split government and a fragmented constituency: Congress was in the hands of the Democrats and the White House was held by the Republicans and there were widely different views of what should occur. Moreover, various interest groups had their own very different agendas. In the summer of 2007, George Miller, chair of the House Education and Labor Committee, and Buck McKeon, the ranking Republican, released a "discussion draft" that was the product of a great deal of work at both the staff and member levels. Almost immediately, various interest groups began to shoot it down, and Miller and McKeon stepped back and acknowledged that consensus could not be reached. (In 2004, a reauthorization of IDEA was signed into law; it did adjust some of the areas of conflict with NCLB and moved schools away from the IQ-based discrepancy model to one of early intervention.)

The realities of the forthcoming 2008 presidential election then took over and each party saw advantage in waiting for a new administration, so nothing significant happened in Congress. On the Senate side, the politics were complicated by the fact that three members of the Senate authorizing committee (Dodd, Clinton and Obama) were running for the presidential nomination and none was anxious to see education become a divisive factor in the campaign. Despite the efforts of the Gates and Broad foundations to make it a central focus, education was so minor an issue in the presidential campaign, it was not even mentioned until the final presidential debate on October 16, when moderator Bob Schieffer used his last question to raise the issue.

A NEW ADMINISTRATION

Despite the lack of attention to education in the 2008 campaign, Obama quickly placed a focus on it by nominating Arne Duncan as Secretary of Education. Confirmed on inauguration day, Duncan got off to an extraordinarily fast start, boosted by the inclusion of almost $100 billion in the American Recovery and Reinvestment Act (ARRA), which was signed by President Obama a few short weeks later.

Although much of the money from ARRA went to states to compensate them for lost tax revenues (state fiscal stabilization), over $25 billion was allocated to states to supplement Title I and IDEA, and $5 billion was allocated to the secretary so that he could hold a competition for states to "Race to the Top." This unprecedented act dwarfed the discretionary funds reviously made available to an education secretary; it was a clear attempt to use incentives as a way to achieve federal goals, moving away from the strict compliance mentality that had governed federal education efforts since the 1960s. After setting aside $650 million of the $5 billion for a competition for new assessments and $350 million for an innovation competition, $4 billion became the bait to lure states into accepting a federal agenda that called for them to expand charter schools, create measures of teacher effectiveness, turn around low-performing schools, and adopt common standards and assessments.

On January 19, 2010, 365 days after Obama's inauguration, 40 states and the District of Columbia submitted applications that required the signature of state chiefs, governors, union officials, and school boards. Winners— Delaware and Tennessee—were announced in April and a second round of the competition will take place later in the year. No matter who wins the race to the top, it is clear that the Obama administration has skillfully used the enticements of incentives, offered at a time of severe decline in tax revenues, to spur action as significant as anything that has happened since Lyndon Johnson in opened the doors to federal funding of education in 1965.

President Obama's first State of the Union address, in late January 2010, promised another several billion dollars for education, partly contingent on the passage of the reauthorization of ESEA. When the 2011 budget was released in early February it became clear that this administration, like virtually every other one in the past 40 years, was proposing to eliminate or consolidate 44 programs. That proposal, however, puts Obama and Duncan at odds with a number of interest groups and their supporters in Congress, setting up a certain battle focused on many of the same issues that will resurface in any reauthorization. The budget cycle also provides Sen. Thomas Harkin (D-IA) with some unusual powers. As chair of both the Senate authorization committee and the appropriations subcommittee that funds the Departments of Education, HHS and Labor, Harkin has the ability to change the course of ESEA/NCLB by, for example, prohibiting the use of funds for enforcing AYP or the highly qualified teacher provisions.

Despite the March 13, 2010 release of the Obama blueprint for reauthorization, it is likely that even valiant efforts to gain passage before the end of this Congress in December will fail. The Obama administration has too many issues of greater urgency for the Congress to deal with—such as jobs, health care and taxation—and while there is general consensus at the 30,000 foot level on the Hill, various constituencies, such as the teachers unions, have grave reservations. Moreover, the battle over health care reform has left a legacy of partisanship that will take time to heal and there is simply no political advantage to having a contentious battle on education before the November elections.

1

Setting the Stage

The Early History

Today, EDUCATION IS A VITAL national issue, capturing the attention of presidents, presidential wanna-bes, and congressional leaders. The evolution of the federal role in education, however, is a study in American politics.

Federal interest in education goes back to the creation of the nation, when the military academies were established, and later, when the Northwest Ordinance in 1787 provided that land be set aside in each township to be used for the support of education. Indeed, right after the Civil War, Congress created a non-cabinet-level federal Department of Education. With a staff of three, it lasted less than 2 years before it was merged into the Department of the Interior. Also enacted during the Civil War and in its aftermath were two bills, the first and second Morrill Acts, providing support to land-grant colleges in every state.

As Munger and Fenno note in their 1962 book, *National Politics and Federal Aid to Education*, attempts were made in the 1870s to create national schools in states where there were none. Although the bill passed both House and Senate at various times, never did both houses pass it in the same Congress (p. 2).

To provide a context for the expansion of education's importance in the United States, at the dawn of the 20th century, the nation had about 15 million students enrolled in K–12 public schools; today, that number approaches 47 million. In 1900, only 6.4% of 17-year-olds were graduating from high school. A century later, it was more than 72%.

Except for laws to support vocational education—the Smith-Hughes Act of 1917—not much happened in federal education policy in the early part of the 20th century. The Smith-Hughes Act passed largely because by 1917 the percentage of 14- to 17-year-old children enrolled in schools had grown in less than 30 years from 7% to almost 30%. And during World War I, the military discovered that 25% of inductees were illiterate, and many were unable to speak English. Schools were searching for an educational program that was not tailored to the elite class, which characterized most of those enrolled in high schools in the 19th century.

Even today, the Smith-Hughes Act is considered a landmark, as it was the first legislation to provide direct federal program support for schools. Yet financially, the federal investment was negligible. Three years after the Congress enacted Smith-Hughes, the federal government was providing only .3% of support to elementary and secondary education; more than 83% was provided by local funding, the remainder by the states.

The bad news about literacy also led to a flurry of other legislative proposals. Bills were introduced to create a U.S. Department of Education (upgraded from the bureau level in the Department of the Interior), to fund literacy and financial equalization aid and to train teachers. Even with the support of then U.S. president and former Princeton University president Woodrow Wilson, nothing was enacted. As had happened soon after the Civil War, one house or the other would pass a bill but never in the same Congress or for the same purposes.

Finally, in 1929, President Herbert Hoover asked his secretary of the interior to appoint a large commission to study the federal government's role in education. Although this National Advisory Committee on Education recommended a coherent federal policy, the elimination of special programs, and the creation of a general aid program based on fiscal adequacy, nothing came of the report because it came in the dark days of the Great Depression.

This committee reported that it found it impossible to provide a comprehensive list of formal federal educational activities (Report of the National Advisory Committee on Education, 1931). The committee pointed out educational programs ranging from the direct operation of schools on Indian reservations and on military bases abroad, to research programs in the Department of Agriculture.

By 1934, almost 40,000 teachers across the nation were being paid directly with federal funds through general relief aid provided to state and local governments as part of Franklin D. Roosevelt's depression-era efforts. In the mid-1930s, Congress voted $48 million to hire unemployed teachers and allocated $75 million through the Reconstruction Finance Corporation for loans to pay overdue teacher salaries. In addition, some funding from the Public Works Administration was used to construct school buildings.

In the last few years prior to World War II, although many bills were passed by either the House or Senate to expand support by making temporary assistance permanent, none succeeded. All were of a general support nature and lacked a clear, education-related, federal rationale for support other than fiscal, which was simply not sufficiently compelling to gain approval.

Although further legislation was introduced during World War II, nothing passed except the Lanham Act (1941), which supported schools heavily affected by the war effort. Today, that program, known as the Impact Aid Act, continues to assist a number of school districts with general support funds.

ERAS OF REFORM SINCE WORLD WAR II

The end of World War II was a watershed for American society. The GI Bill provided support for veterans to attend college or receive vocational or technical training. This program transformed the federal government's role in education and, in the process, transformed American society by expanding opportunities for higher learning to hundreds of thousands of veterans and their families. A corner was turned. This new era would develop in erratic and unpredictable ways over the course of the following several decades.

As education historian Diane Ravitch chronicles so well in her landmark book *The Troubled Crusade* (1983), education since World War II has seen the ebb and flow of many eras—some would say fads. While not the subject of this book, an overview of these eras gives the reader a perspective of the contextual environment of federal policy.

In the decade after World War II, the Progressive movement reigned in the public schools. Although it was never formally defined, it included such things as active learning, cooperative planning, the elimination of competition for grades, the merging of subjects, and "effective learning" (as opposed to learning for knowledge) (Ravitch, 1983, p. 44). An outgrowth of this was the Life Adjustment Movement, which advocated the idea that the schools were to provide people with skills for living rather than subject matter knowledge. Lawrence Cremin (1961, p. 22) said that progressive education was "a many-sided effort to use the schools to improve the lives of individuals."

This movement began to sputter in the mid-1950s; it was eclipsed in the later part of the decade by the Cold War and the launch of Sputnik. These "crises" led to an emphasis on content knowledge, especially in math, science, and foreign languages. Although the progressive movement persists today through such efforts as cooperative and project-based learning, it never again gained the dominance that it enjoyed in the post–World War II era.

The 1960s was the time of the Open Education movement, with its emphasis on tearing down classroom walls. During this period the radicalism created by the Vietnam War was beginning to be felt. The idea of a core curriculum was abandoned and students were urged to enroll in whatever courses they wished to take, whether or not they had any academic merit.

From the mid-1960s—following passage of the Civil Rights Act in 1964—through the 1970s, public education was characterized by pressures from groups on the left and right who sought special programs or a special curriculum in everything ranging from bilingual education, to women's studies, to African American studies, to prayer in the classroom. This was also a period when the courts were extremely active in their rulings, especially with respect to desegregation, school prayer, and affirmative action.

During this time, schools and teachers also changed. In 1945, only a few teachers, mostly those in urban districts, were represented by collective bargaining units. There were 100,000 school districts. Thirty years later, districts numbered fewer than 20,000, and most teachers belonged to unions. Even in the right-to-work states, where the powers of unions were legally limited, unions gained enormous influence.

The 1980s were heavily influenced by reports of the demise of the American education system. Schools responded by increasing efforts to establish minimum-competency exams and by raising the number of units required for a high school diploma. Although calling this the back-to-basics era would be an overstatement, the pendulum had begun to swing back to the idea of more rigorous content and holding students accountable.

In the 1990s, standards, testing, accountability, and school choice took center stage, on the basis of the notion that all students can learn at much higher levels and that adults must be held accountable for what students learn. This decade was one of systemic reform, with all the elements of teaching and learning strongly interrelated and interdependent. Although it is too early to evaluate the period since 2000, strong efforts are being made to improve the quality of both teachers and teaching. Time will tell.

2

The Truman and Eisenhower Years

Impact Aid and NDEA Pass; Construction Support and General Aid Fail

AFTER THE END OF WORLD WAR II, with one military-related exception, it took years (until 1948) for any legislation for federal aid to elementary and secondary schools to even get past the committee approval stage in the Senate, and a decade (until 1955) before that happened in the House.

The one exception was in 1950. With the pressure of the military buildup during the Korean War, a new law was passed—the Impact Aid Act—making permanent the concept of the Landrum Act of 1940, which provided general aid to school districts "impacted" by the presence of federal land and employees. Because no local property tax revenue came from federal land, the impact on local school enrollment and finances was often major.

A different kind of pressure was felt by most other school districts—the need to build more schools to accommodate the increase in enrollment caused by millions of GIs coming home, marrying, and starting families. With this new reality, the focus shifted dramatically, from general aid and special programs to construction support.

When the baby boom children reached elementary school age in the early 1950s, public school enrollment soared, and space was at a premium. In fact, in the 1950s, enrollment increased by more than 11 million students—from 25.1 million to 36.4 million—imposing a crushing burden on facilities and also contributing to an enormous shortage of teachers.

Predictably, the result of the enrollment crush was a cry from governors, school superintendents, and teachers for federal support for school construction. The issue was made all the more important by the fact that even in normal times, poor states had a very difficult time raising money to build schools. While organizations such as the National Education Association (NEA) continued to push for general aid, there was agreement that construction should be given higher priority. In addition, the chairs of the congressional education committees were mostly from states that were heavily affected by the classroom shortage, a fact that led directly to general aid being pushed aside in favor of construction support (Munger & Fenno, 1962, p. 12).

One of the most outspoken supporters of construction aid was Kentucky Republican senator John Sherman Cooper. In the Senate, Cooper was joined by Ohio Republican senator John Bricker and Minnesota Democratic senator Hubert H. Humphrey. Although most characterized construction support as a temporary or emergency measure, others felt that this would provide the opening for general aid. As we shall see, the baby boom issue would continue to loom large at the national level (Sundquist, 1968, pp. 158–160).

During this same postwar period, Ohio Republican senator Robert A. Taft, the conservative intellectual leader of the Senate and later Dwight D. Eisenhower's opponent for the 1952 GOP presidential nomination, came out clearly in support of general-aid dollars to schools to be used for whatever purpose they chose. The NEA was the biggest advocate of this position—they knew that about 80 cents of every dollar spent went to salaries, and saw general aid as a way to assure that teachers would be better paid.

Taft's position in 1948 was in substantial opposition to that of other leaders of his own party, and he went further than most congressional Democrats of the time. Taft became a cosponsor of the 1949 Senate education bill, proposed to provide general aid. Although the bill passed the Senate, the House took no action and it died at the end of that Congress. What Taft said in 1948 would hold true for decades to come, even though the idea of general federal aid would fade away within a few years.

> Four years ago I opposed the then pending Bill on this subject [federal assistance to education]; but in the course of the debate it became so apparent that many children in the United States were left without education, and then it became apparent, upon further study, that that was not the fault, necessarily, of the States where they lived, but rather, of the financial abilities of the States, that I could see no way to meet the condition which now exists regarding illiteracy in the United States and lack of education in the United States without some Federal assistance, particularly for those states which today are considered below the average of wealth in the United States. ("Statement," 1948)

At about this same time, a subcommittee of the House Committee on Education, chaired by North Carolina Democrat Graham Barden, reported a bill that would specifically deny any federal aid, including transportation, for students to attend private schools. As Munger and Fenno (1962, p. 2) note, Catholic groups led by the Knights of Columbus and New York's Cardinal Francis Spellman, attacked the bill. This incident ignited an exchange between Spellman and former first lady Eleanor Roosevelt that cast both in an unfavorable light and made the bill simply too hot to handle. It never even made it out of the full House committee.

Although it appeared to be an isolated incident, this bill set the stage for an issue—aid to religious schools—that would plague attempts to get federal aid enacted for the following 15 years.

THE EISENHOWER YEARS: SETTING THE STAGE

The 1952 presidential campaign featured education as a key issue. Dwight Eisenhower, who as president of Columbia University had opposed the 1949 Senate general aid bill, spoke about the classroom shortage in a speech in Los Angeles, where he noted, "This year 1,700,000 American boys and girls were without any school facilities," and that "the American answer" should be federal aid (Sundquist, 1968, p. 155). Sundquist wrote that Eisenhower compared school construction aid to help that the federal government had given states to support roads, hospitals, and mental institutions. Ike also believed that federal control was simply not an issue, since the money could only be used to build classrooms, thereby keeping the federal government away from the issue of what was taught or who would teach.

Although both major party platforms talked about education in 1952, the Democrats called for support of construction and maintenance, teacher salaries, and fellowships. The GOP platform stressed local control.

Surprisingly, as Sundquist notes, although Eisenhower talked about education in his first State of the Union address in 1953, he failed to pursue the subject with the Congress, even though Republicans controlled both the House and Senate. There were those in his administration who saw classroom construction as something states should provide. They were also reluctant to get the federal government into the issue of sorting out which states would get how much, thereby creating clear political winners and losers.

Others, however, took matters into their own hands. When a bill dealing with oil leases on federal land came before the Senate, Senator Lister Hill, a senior Democrat from Alabama, added a rider placing the oil lease revenues in a trust fund for educational support. In spite of the fact that Hill carried the Senate, he lost the amendment in conference with the House. Although it was not enacted, the Hill amendment was symbolic of the often unorthodox attempts that education supporters made to find ways to support public schools.

Thus ended 1953: many attempts, a few hits, but no victories.

THE *BROWN* DECISION

In 1954, two major events took place. One would forever shape the course of education in the nation; the other was a stalling tactic on the part of Eisenhower.

The first was the decision of the Supreme Court in *Brown v. Board of Education of Topeka*, which declared the segregation of children in schools unconstitutional and in direct violation of the 14th Amendment to the Constitution. On May 17, 1954, Chief Justice Earl Warren announced the unanimous decision of the court in *Brown*. The case dealt specifically with de jure segregation: dual school systems in many states—one for Whites, the other for Blacks—and the inequitable resources that they were provided, resulting in most Black children receiving a poor education.

The *Brown* decision would affect the course of federal education policy by creating a series of legislative and procedural issues that would impede passage of legislation. It also fundamentally changed school districts in every state in the South. Many northern districts, like Boston, where segregation was present as a matter of housing patterns—de facto segregation—also experienced court-ordered desegregation.

THE 1955 WHITE HOUSE CONFERENCE ON EDUCATION

The second event was Eisenhower's decision to call for a White House conference on education, to be convened in 1955, and to be preceded by conferences in each of the states. Although Eisenhower professed that this would provide wide input on the part of the American people, both congressional Democrats and Republicans saw it as a delaying tactic.

The administration's action, or lack of it, was especially frustrating in light of testimony on the effects of the baby boom from Health, Education and Welfare (HEW) secretary Olveta Culp Hobby. (The Office of Education had been made a part of HEW when the latter was created as one of Eisenhower's first acts in 1953 and was headed by Commissioner Sam Brownell.)

As documented by Sundquist, at an April 1954 Senate hearing on the bill to create a White House conference, Hobby and Brownell testified to a national shortage of 340,000 classrooms, estimated to increase to more than 400,000 by 1960, with a total construction cost of at least $10 billion. Hobby said that the problem belonged to the states, a direct contradiction of what Eisenhower had said in his campaign in 1952. In 1955, Secretary Hobby returned to tell a House hearing that the administration now estimated that the shortage by 1960 would be "only" 176,000 classrooms, a remarkable decrease over the figure of one year earlier. Needless to say, Hobby's credibility suffered (Sundquist, 1968, p. 163).

The intransigence of Hobby and Brownell on the construction issue contributed to a tense hearing; in the end, however, the Senate and House proceeded, while the White House remained silent on the construction bill.

The administration's backpedaling over the construction issue, fueled by the administration's own witnesses and their failure to propose a direct response to the overcrowding issue, led to enormous frustration. Senator Cooper was both chair of the Senate Education Subcommittee and from Kentucky, a state where many classrooms had 60 children and where more than 10,000 classrooms would be needed in the following 5 years.

The Senate's frustration at the Eisenhower administration's failure to act led, in July 1954, to the Senate committee unanimously reporting out the Cooper bill. This bill called for $500 million in construction aid over a 2-year period. Probably because of White House pressure, as well as that of Georgia senator Richard Russell, the bill was not placed on the schedule until one day before adjournment, effectively keeping it from being considered in the Senate during that Congress.

By 1955, the administration had changed its tune. Although Sundquist declared that this was because of Eisenhower's personal insistence, it is easy to imagine that officials in both the secretary's office at HEW and in the Office of Education promoted a change. Unfortunately, the overly complicated bill that emerged from the administration depended largely on loans and would have required legislative action in every participating state. It's interesting to note that it was Nelson Rockefeller, then serving as undersecretary of HEW, who designed the plan, in collaboration with investment bankers from New York and without the benefit of consultation with educators or legislative leaders.

At this point, the issue became more politically complicated, when civil rights proponents in both chambers, encouraged by Clarence Mitchell of the National Association for the Advancement of Colored People (NAACP), moved to attach language to the bill; this language required, in accordance with the principle of the *Brown* decision, that each state receiving funds certify that their schools were desegregated. Given that the two committees with jurisdiction were chaired by southerners (Hill in the Senate, Barden in the House), ways were found to delay consideration of this legislation in 1955, 1956, and 1957.

In one of those moments in history that many would rather forget, when the Cooper bill was being considered in 1956, a coalition of organizations, led by the American Federation of Labor and Congress of Industrial Organizations (AFL-CIO) and the NEA, lined up to oppose the desegregation amendment. All these groups were opposed to what became known as the (Adam Clayton) Powell amendment. They were joined in that opposition by both Eisenhower and Adlai Stevenson, Eisenhower's Democratic opponent in both 1952 and 1956. Although their motivations varied, many were willing to sacrifice civil rights considerations to obtain federal support.

Debate in both the House and Senate became heated. In the Senate, Richard Neuberger, a liberal Democratic senator from Oregon, declared that the amendment would provoke "a bitter and hopeless debate." In the House, Powell, who represented Harlem and would later chair the House committee, countered by saying, "Negro people have waited many, many years for this hour of democracy to come and they are willing to wait a few more years rather than see a bill passed that will . . . build a dual system of Jim Crow education" (Sundquist, 1968, pp. 165–166). Proponents of the legislation felt that this was their best chance to get federal support and they knew that adoption of the Powell amendment would doom the bill by forcing southern members of Congress to vote against it. This was 2 years after the *Brown* decision and one year before Arkansas governor Orval Faubus stood at the door of Little Rock Central High in defiance of the 1,100 federalized National Guard troops, whom Eisenhower had sent to enforce the court's decision (Patterson, 2001, p. 110).

When the House version of the Cooper construction bill went to the House floor in July of 1956, Powell offered his amendment and a coalition of big-city Democrats and Republicans supported him. The amendment passed 225-193, but then the entire bill was defeated by a vote of 224-194. Howard Baker, a Tennessee Republican, was the only southerner to support final passage. Many who had supported Powell voted no on final passage.

Democrats, among them Senator Hubert H. Humphrey, attacked Eisenhower for not producing Republican votes to secure passage. It is likely that Eisenhower's silence on the matter was a strategic decision made in the White House and reflected the division among his advisers on the construction issue.

Some saw what had taken place in the House as a cynical plot, with many Republicans supporting Powell on his amendment but planning to then turn around and vote against the bill after his amendment had been adopted. Although there was certainly some truth to that, many Republicans turned against the bill because a GOP amendment to modify the allocation formula to target poorer states was defeated by a wide margin. Only nine Democrats had supported the formula modification. *New York Times* writer James Reston called it all "racial politics," and noted that the outcome was the result of a "combination of fierce emotional feeling among southern Democrats and determined Republican action to win back the Negro vote" (Sundquist, 1968, p. 167).

That vote in 1956 on the construction aid bill turned out to be a landmark. It would take almost another 10 years before enough support could be mustered to overcome the issues that had killed the 1956 bill. States would limp along in building new schools, most never able to keep up with the demand. The result was that millions of children in the 1950s attended schools that were old and dilapidated, crowded far beyond capacity, with classes of 40 or more students.

In 1957, following the November 1956 elections, the House tried again to pass a construction bill. This time the administration, led by the assistant secretary of HEW, Elliot Richardson, worked with the House committee to formulate a compromise bill, one that would be acceptable to both the Congress and the White House. Richardson would become secretary of HEW 13 years later.

Unfortunately, when the bill came to the House floor in July, chaos reigned, largely because of the lack of a clear signal from Eisenhower on several major issues, including a Republican amendment to again alter the formula to aid poorer states. Again, a "Powell" amendment was offered and adopted, although not by Powell, who was absent. Suddenly, Virginia Democrat Howard Smith moved to strike the enacting clause, effectively killing the bill. The motion was adopted on a roll call vote of 208-203. House leaders had tried in vain to reach Eisenhower to get a clear White House signal of support to save the bill. Later Eisenhower would claim that he was unaware of those attempts (Sundquist, 1968, pp. 172–173).

SPUTNIK: EDUCATION MEETS NATIONAL DEFENSE

Ten weeks later everything changed. On October 4, 1957, the Soviet Union launched into space a small satellite named Sputnik. As a partial response, in a nationally televised address, Eisenhower talked about the nation's shortage of qualified scientists and engineers. The construction issue dissolved and interest in general aid diminished. The focus became a series of crash programs, mostly at the college level, supporting math, science, and foreign-language instruction. This was at the height of the Cold War. The USSR was investing mightily in its military establishment, while schools in the United States engaged regularly in atom bomb attack drills. The United States was feeling vulnerable to the Soviet bear. The idea of losing the "space race" caused political leaders, supported by the public, to mobilize behind several actions to meet this new challenge.

On January 29, 1958, an administration bill called the Education Development Act of 1958 was introduced. On January 30, Senator Lister Hill, chair of the Senate committee, introduced the National Defense Education Act (NDEA). Although similar to the administration bill, Hill's proposal provided greater financial support. Hill had made a calculated decision that in light of the Soviet threat, his colleagues would not dare to oppose the bill. Both bills were designed to get more students to study math and science by subsidizing loans for tuition and assisting schools and colleges in the development of science and language laboratories. Hill's actions were in the best tradition of using a critical moment to achieve a previous objective.

Not all the interest groups agreed with this new emphasis, but the deal had been made. For the first time since 1917, a major education bill would be enacted that was not strictly for the support of military issues, even though it took the aura of national defense and a space race crisis to get it passed.

Amazingly, when the bill came to the House and Senate floors for consideration, the Powell amendment was offered, but was limited to students receiving aid to attend college. It did not apply to public schools, states, or school systems; Southerners were off the hook and could vote for the bill. In fact, the Senate voted 62-26, the House 233-140. Many border and southern House Democrats who had voted the previous year to kill the construction bill were recorded in favor, since the limitations on the Powell amendment made the bill acceptable.

In the Senate, two of the committee members—Strom Thurmond and Barry Goldwater—were dissenters. In his minority views, Goldwater said, "If adopted, the legislation will mark the inception of aid, supervision, and ultimately control of education in this country by federal authorities." Senate Majority Leader Lyndon Johnson called the bill "an historic landmark," one of the most important measures of this or any other session (Sundquist, 1968, pp. 178–179).

Elliot Richardson, who had been the lead negotiator for HEW and had helped guide the bill through Congress, said, "Discussion no longer centers on the question of whether there will be federal aid. Rather, the debate has shifted to the two factions who agree that there should be federal aid but who divide sharply over the form in which it is to be provided" (Sundquist, 1968, p. 180). By this he meant short-term aid for specific purposes, like NDEA, or the permanent sharing of costs as proposed by the NEA and some others.

Each of these statements contained elements of truth. Even though NDEA affected both K–12 and higher education, it did change the nature of the debate for public school aid. Support for education programs was now clearly a matter of federal policy, whereas the political momentum for construction was gone. However, it would be another 7 years before there would be a second major breakthrough in securing passage of new legislation.

The decade of the 1950s closed with a final attempt to get a construction bill, as NDEA had done nothing to solve that problem. In fact, in January 1959, Robert Maynard Hutchins, president of the University of Chicago, was quoted in the *New York Times* as saying, "History will smile sardonically on the spectacle of this great country's getting interested, slightly and temporarily, in education only because of the technical achievements of Russia and then being able to act as a nation only by assimilating education to the cold war and calling education a defense bill" (Sundquist, 1968, p. 180).

During the 1958 congressional elections, Eisenhower had campaigned against Democrats as big spenders. The result was that all departments were ordered to hold down spending for the following year, a year that would precede the next presidential election. Recognizing that the Republicans must have a program on education, HEW secretary Arthur Flemming and Elliot Richardson set out to fashion a bill, one that used long-term financing to lessen the immediate budgetary impact of construction assistance. It was reported that it only became an administration initiative because of the intervention of Vice President Richard Nixon, who was able to get it past Eisenhower (Sundquist, 1968, p. 181).

However, the administration bill was viewed as inadequate, and Democrats led by Congressman Lee Metcalf of Montana introduced their own bill to provide support for construction and, with the avid endorsement of the NEA, support for teacher salaries.

Although the House committee reported the bill on a largely party-line vote, the Rules Committee refused to clear the bill for floor consideration in the House, in part because of the opposition of Catholics who viewed the failure to include private and nonpublic schools as a fatal flaw.

In March 1960, a West Virginia Democrat, Cleveland Bailey, chair of the House Education Subcommittee, cobbled together a 3-year temporary construction assistance bill. It eventually cleared the House by a vote of 206-189, even though it did not have administration support.

Meanwhile, in the Senate, matters became very complicated and even more political when Pennsylvania Democrat Joe Clark offered a floor amendment to the construction bill to permit states to use the money for teacher salaries. The vote among senators was a tie, 44-44. Presiding officer and vice president Richard Nixon was forced to cast the deciding no vote, an act that would contribute to the NEA's support of John F. Kennedy in 1960—the first time the NEA would enter national politics—even though a formal endorsement was not made. That vote would haunt Nixon throughout the 1960 campaign.

Following the defeat of the Clark amendment, the Senate adopted a scaled-back version of the original construction proposal. At this point, once the House had finally adopted its version of the construction bill, the normal course of events would have been to send the bill to a joint House-Senate conference committee. In the House, even that action requires approval of the Rules Committee. Although the committee had approved House consideration of its bill by the narrowest of margins, two members changed their positions when it came to allowing the bill to go to conference. By a 15-7 vote, the Rules Committee refused to permit the appointment of conferees. Apparently, Southerners concerned about the Powell amendment joined with Republicans, who did not want to see an Eisenhower veto in an election year. The bill died as Congress adjourned for the 1960 campaign.

By the end of the 1950s, it appeared that securing enactment of general aid, or even major program support, was simply not possible as long as the twin issues of race and religion remained unsolved. Indeed, those two issues blocked every attempt that decade to secure support for education, save the single instance of the NDEA, when the pressures of the Cold War and the fear that the Soviets would surpass the United States technologically fueled the passage of a bill.

The politics of Congress, along with the failure of several presidents to pursue the issue of education support with vigor, conviction, and muscle combined to make the decade one of frustration. The only two federal actions of any significance for public schools in the legislative arena were both tied to national defense, NDEA, and Impact Aid. However, interest and support for education was growing and legislative actions were becoming more frequent. In addition, education groups, especially the NEA and its smaller rival, the American Federation of Teachers (AFT), were becoming more vocal and active in politics.

A new decade was about to unfold, and a new president would soon be in the White House. The 1960s would begin with a new sense of optimism.

3

The Kennedy and Johnson Years

Failure and, Finally, Success

In the 1960 presidential election, education returned as a major issue, with John F. Kennedy making education aid a major factor in his campaign. Kennedy charged that Richard Nixon was willing to support federal aid only for construction, whereas Kennedy wanted aid for teacher salaries as well. Nixon's position was, of course, also affected by the vote Nixon had cast against expanding the Senate bill calling for the addition of teacher salaries to the construction assistance proposal. Nixon and the Republicans were now tagged as being anti–federal support. That gave Kennedy, and later Johnson, Jimmy Carter, and Bill Clinton, the opportunity to "own" education as a signature issue for Democrats. With minor exceptions, that situation persisted for 40 years, until the campaign of 2000.

The 1960 campaign was significant for two other reasons. It was the first time that a major party had selected a Catholic (Kennedy) as a candidate, and it was the first campaign during which there were televised debates between the candidates.

When Kennedy formally announced his candidacy early in 1960, he listed improving science and education as the third of his six priorities. Although Kennedy continued to pound Nixon on his negative vote in the Senate, Nixon achieved a tactical advantage with the release—virtually on the eve of the first broadcast debate—of a comprehensive program in education. For the K–12 schools, he proposed construction assistance aimed at freeing dollars to increase teacher salaries. Nixon saw this as a mechanism to keep at bay federal control over what went on the classroom. In another harbinger of what was to come, Nixon also proposed a "national clearinghouse" for education research, demonstration, and dissemination. That idea would emerge again a decade later as a proposal by Nixon for a National Institute of Education (Graham, 1984).

As Sundquist (1968, p. 187) notes, in the very first debate, Kennedy said, "We want high teacher salaries; we need high teacher salaries." Nixon, who had been called by Kennedy for his tie-breaking vote, retorted, "But we also want our education to be free of federal control. When the federal government gets the power to pay teachers, inevitably . . . it will acquire the power to set standards and to tell the teachers what to teach." In the year that Nixon died (1994), the very issue of who would set standards became a major political issue (Sundquist, 1968, p. 187).

The religious factor became intertwined with the education issue in such a way that Kennedy found himself the first presidential nominee to specifically disavow aid to parochial schools. Since that issue, along with the assurance that federal funds would go only to schools that had desegregated, was one of the major stumbling blocks in enacting federal aid in the 1950s, the stage was set for a confrontation.

Kennedy's stand as a presidential candidate and as president was in sharp contrast to his position in 1949, when in his second term and as a member of the House Education and Labor Committee (one of his fellow committee members was Richard Nixon), Kennedy introduced a bill to provide federal support for transportation, health services, and textbooks in both public and parochial schools. The Kennedy proposal was based on a Louisiana law providing that supplemental pupil services, like libraries, were open to all.

Although Kennedy's 1949 bill went nowhere, a Senate general aid bill, cosponsored by conservative Republican Robert Taft of Ohio, did reach the House. When Kennedy failed to get his amendment to pay half the transportation costs for both public and private schools, he voted in the committee against reporting the bill, thereby providing the deciding vote to kill it (Graham, 1984, p. 4). How ironic that a dozen years later a similar battle would be played out with Kennedy on the opposite side of the church-state issue.

Throughout the campaign, education continued to be a significant issue and Kennedy worked hard to gain the support of teachers. Almost on the eve of the election, Kennedy promised that with the support of a Democratic Congress, legislation to support both construction and teacher salaries would be quickly enacted. Although at that point the NEA was not yet making formal endorsements, it was widely reported that Kennedy had the support of this powerful teacher union (Graham, 1984, p. 9). Given the razor-slim margin of the final vote, the NEA could easily argue that Kennedy owed his election to the education issue and the support of teachers. In that same election, the Democrats actually lost seats in both the House and Senate, giving the coalition of Republicans and conservative Democrats significant leverage and undermining Kennedy's mandate.

THE HOVDE TASK FORCE

Following his narrow election victory, president-elect Kennedy created a Task Force on Education as one of 13 high-level, high-visibility groups to address major issues. The six-member education group was headed by Frederick Hovde, president of Purdue University. The group included both Francis (Frank) Keppel and John Gardner, two men who were to figure prominently in education policy during that decade. The Hovde task force submitted its report just prior to Kennedy's inauguration. The report called for several legislative and administrative actions; the major ones affecting public schools were as follows:

- A flat grant of $30 per student to be sent to the states for transmission to local school boards. Funds were to be used for construction, teacher salaries, or any other purpose related to educational improvement. States and districts were required to maintain their effort. Total cost was estimated at $1.2 billion annually.
- A grant of $20 per child to go to states where the personal income was below 70% of the national average. The same uses and requirements would pertain. The task force estimated that about one fourth of the states with about 7 million students would benefit. The total cost was estimated at $140 million annually.
- A grant of $20 per child to be made to cities with populations of 300,000 or more. The funds were to be used for research and experimental programs, construction, and guidance and employment programs for students over 16 years of age. The task force estimated that 6 million students would benefit, at a cost of $120 million annually.
- Amendments to the National Defense Education act to enable more students to become teachers (*Proposed Federal Aid to Education*, July 27, 1961).

The price tag was stunning, calling as it did for spending of almost $9.5 billion over a period of just under 5 years, far higher than the price tags for even the most generous of Congressional proposals and at a time when the non–Social Security U.S. budget was less than $100 billion.

Finally, and in accordance with Kennedy's campaign statements, the task force recommended that funding be used only for public schools. That provoked New York's Cardinal Spellman, who had sparred with Eleanor Roosevelt on the same issue more than a decade earlier, to now denounce the Kennedy-appointed task force (Graham, 1984, p. 13).

This last issue, the question of aid to parochial and private schools, was one that generated deep, powerful feelings. Organizations like Americans United for Separation of Church and State were prepared to fight fierce battles to keep public money out of the hands of nonpublic schools, citing the Constitution and its prohibition against the support of religion. They were joined in their opposition by most of the mainline Protestant churches and by representatives of the non-Orthodox Jewish faith.

Catholic schools were equally as strong in their support of federal aid. In many big cities, like Philadelphia, New York, and Boston, these schools educated large numbers of students. Without parochial schools, most of these students would have to be educated in the public schools. Catholics saw it as an issue of fairness and it became an issue that would not go away.

The stage was set for yet another church versus state showdown—one of the prime issues that had thwarted all previous attempts to enact a federal aid bill for public schools.

The start of the Kennedy administration also saw the reemergence of the role of the Bureau of the Budget (BOB) (known today as the Office of Management and Budget [OMB]), a part of the executive office of the president that had achieved substantial influence in the area of program planning in the Roosevelt and Truman administrations.

The BOB reacted very strongly against the Hovde task force recommendations, declaring them too focused on urban areas and too targeted to K–12 education when the biggest growth would occur at the college level in the 1960s. In place of the task force recommendations, BOB had its own complicated proposals and, most significant, lumped them legislatively with extensions of both the impact aid and vocational education programs, both very popular with Congress (Graham, 1984, pp. 13–18).

In the end, Kennedy sided with neither the Hovde task force nor BOB. On February 27, 1961, he sent his first elementary and secondary education proposal to the Congress. Although it did contain the prohibition on aid to nonpublic schools, it was surprisingly nothing more than a somewhat smaller version of the construction/teacher salaries bill that had passed the Senate the previous year. The submission of the bill caused the National

Catholic Welfare Conference to declare its opposition to the bill (Sund-quist, 1968, p. 189).

Oregon Democratic senator Wayne Morse managed the president's bill to passage in late May 1961, by a vote of 49-34, almost identical with the vote on the construction bill that the Senate had passed in 1960.

In the House, the situation had become even more contentious than in 1960. The opposing views taken by the two presidential candidates the previous year now locked members into opposing camps. So extreme had positions become that Powell, who now chaired the House Education and Labor Committee, did not even offer his own desegregation amendment, in an attempt to pave the way for passage of the bill. Peter Frelinghuysen, a moderate New Jersey Republican, offered the Powell amendment, but it lost in the committee on a party-line vote.

Again, the black hole of education bills in the House—the Rules Com-mittee—became the burial ground for the new president's first attempt to achieve an education victory. The margin of defeat in the Rules Committee came from Democrats Thomas P. O'Neil of Massachusetts and James Dela-ney of New York, both of whom represented heavily Catholic districts. The Republicans were aligned in solid opposition to the Kennedy bill. An attempt had been made by the secretary of HEW, Abraham Ribicoff, acting in con-cert with White House staffers Ted Sorensen and Lawrence O'Brien, to save the Kennedy bill by amending NDEA to make nonpublic schools eligible for loans, but that attempt was too little too late. The die had been cast earlier; attempts to mollify the Catholic opposition were a failure (Graham, 1984, p. 21). Blame for the loss was quick and pointed. A *New York Times* edito-rial blamed what it saw as inept White House leadership.[1] Others also blamed Kennedy for his failure to get a bill enacted, although it is not clear what he could have done, considering the presence of both the church-state issue and the ever present tension over desegregation and the Powell amend-ment, whether offered by Powell himself or not. Kennedy's own status as the first Catholic president would have made it almost impossible for him to have taken a position of active support of parochial education.

The following year, 1962, saw a focus on higher education, and the result was very similar. Although bills for college construction support and student aid passed both the House and Senate, the final conference report was defeated in the House for reasons tied to religion and integration. Leg-islation to support K–12 public schools never even reached the floor in either the House or the Senate. The fact that it was an election year kept both sides from wanting to cast votes that might hurt some of their col-leagues in November. The twin issues of religion and desegregation (race) succeeded yet again in limiting the federal role in support of public schools.

The extent of the animosity over the church-state issue was so extensive that in June 1962, five of the major elementary and secondary education organizations, representing teachers, chief state school officers, and administrators, took the unprecedented step of coming out against the House higher education bill because it provided construction loans to private colleges. They feared that this would set a precedent for aid to Catholic elementary and secondary schools. That action, combined with a late June Supreme Court decision against school prayer, doomed the bill. The intervention of the K–12 lobby into legislation for higher education aid created deep fissures that would take years to heal.

As the 1962 session of Congress ended, the Bipartisan Citizens Committee for Federal Aid for Elementary and Secondary Education began a campaign for a truly "radical" approach to federal aid, one that would, at least in that group's view, put aside the church-state issue. Composed of a remarkably diverse set of people (two former HEW secretaries, two former commissioners of education, Walt Disney, William Menninger, Walter Reuther, James Conant, and Howard K. Smith), the committee proposed simply giving money to the states whereupon it would become state money, hence subject to state law in all things, including aid to private and parochial schools. This was a concept that would be revisited often over the years, usually in the guise of grant consolidation (Graham, 1984, pp. 40–41).

Of course, the BOB hated the idea. In what would become an oft-quoted line, the BOB saw this as the equivalent to "putting the money on the stump and running"—an idea abhorrent to the federal mavens of fiscal responsibility.

A CHANGING OF THE GUARD

At about this time, two major administrative changes took place in HEW: Secretary Abraham Ribicoff and Commissioner of Education Sterling McMurrin, both widely regarded as ineffective, resigned; Ribicoff to successfully run for the Senate. Their replacements were Anthony Celebrezze as secretary and Frank Keppel as commissioner. Celebrezze, a prominent Italian politician, was mayor of Cleveland, and politically very important to Kennedy. Keppel was dean of the Harvard School of Education and had been a member of the Hovde task force two years before his appointment. McMurrin was unknown to Kennedy. In fact, when the papers reported his resignation in the form of a letter to his Utah congressman, Kennedy is alleged to have said, "I never heard of the fellow!" (Graham, 1984, p. 45), a telling comment and probably the inspiration for the selection of Keppel, whom Kennedy knew personally, though not well, through his Harvard connections. Significantly, Keppel saw his first task as healing the wounds created by the intervention of the public school lobby in helping to kill the 1962 higher education bill.

To keep everyone singing from the same song sheet, the administration crafted a 24-part omnibus bill that included something for everyone except the Catholic and private school lobby, who only benefited from some minor parts of the bill. Titled the National Education Improvement Act of 1962, this bill provided construction loans for colleges—both public and private—and aid to public schools to be used for everything from teacher salaries to construction to special projects to "improve urban and rural education quality" (Graham, 1984, p. 45).

Although the bill was hailed by *New York Times* education columnist Fred Hechinger as the first major aid-to-education bill since the end of World War II not tied to national defense and the Cold War, momentum quickly collapsed. The House committee, under the leadership of Adam Clayton Powell, moved to break the bill into four pieces, largely to satisfy the egos and jurisdictions of his senior education subcommittee chairmen, Edith Green of Oregon and Carl Perkins of Kentucky. That single action effectively killed, yet again, the elementary and secondary education bill in the House. The battles of the past over race and religion were not to be repeated in 1963.

When Wayne Morse, the Oregon Democrat who chaired the Senate committee, saw what was happening in the House, he gave up trying to herd a single bill through the Senate and focused on the higher education bill and vocational education expansion. With a very poor record of earlier successes, both houses worked very hard to enact a higher education bill, and by mid-November it was on its way to the White House. Also passed were extensions of impact aid and vocational education and the first small program of assistance for educating disabled children.

In an interesting footnote to history, 3 days before John Kennedy left Washington for that tragic trip to Dallas, he called together the NEA leaders from across the nation to the White House Rose Garden to thank them for not creating another battle over religion in the higher education bill.

THE JOHNSON ADMINISTRATION AND THE GREAT SOCIETY

Following Kennedy's assassination, all three bills were signed by Lyndon Johnson in his first few weeks in office. In his December 16 comments at the White House, Johnson urged that Congress return in 1964 to complete the Kennedy legacy by passing an elementary and secondary education bill.

Johnson's words were empty rhetoric. He was up for election in 1964 and he did not want the political landscape clouded by battles that could only serve to divide the constituency that he needed in November. In fact, so little attention was given to the issue that Johnson, soon to be hailed as the greatest education president of all, did not even bother to send an education message to Congress. As a result, 1964 was a year of quiet. The only actions taken were rather routine extensions of impact aid and NDEA and some minor portions of the National Education Improvement Act pertaining to library services. Another year went by without any real effort being made to secure federal support.

Of course, among Johnson's priorities in 1964 was congressional enactment of the Civil Rights Act, a measure that would forever shift the debate over education from aid to segregated schools to desegregation assistance, open countless doors for African Americans at every level of society, and usher in an era of battles over school busing for desegregation purposes. Moving resolution of this issue away from the education arena would prove to be critical in gaining passage of Johnson's Great Society programs in 1965. Religion, however, remained a divisive issue, a challenge to be overcome if a successful school aid bill was ever to reach the president's desk.

THE GARDNER TASK FORCE

In 1964, Johnson put in motion a variation on the Kennedy task forces, which would play a very significant role in shaping the programs of the Great Society. The variant was secrecy. Whereas the Kennedy groups had been publicly appointed and great fanfare had accompanied their reports, Johnson wanted none of that. As befitting his image as a master of political strategy, he wanted control. Although Johnson claimed to his cabinet that these task forces would not supercede normal planning roles, they in fact became *the* planning mechanism for his administration.

Bill Moyers, now known for his public television work, directed the task force operation in the White House. On the 14 different task forces were 124 people—only five were women, few were minorities, none were from organized labor, 46 were academics, and, surprisingly, given Johnson's disdain for the Ivy League, half were from the Ivy League (Graham, 1984, p. 62). Each task force was assigned an executive secretary, most of them from the BOB.

In education, the most important task force was that chaired by John W. Gardner, president of the Carnegie Corporation of New York. William

Cannon was the executive secretary, Emerson Elliott his alternate. Gardner and the 12 members were all men. Ten (including Gardner) were either school officials or academics. Others were the mayor of St. Louis, the editor of *Time* magazine, and the president of Polaroid. Of the school officials, two would become commissioners of education in the Nixon administration—James Allen, New York State commissioner, and Sidney Marland, Pittsburgh school superintendent. Among the academics were Clark Kerr (University of California), David Riesman (Harvard), and Jerold Zacharias (MIT). Commissioner Frank Keppel was the sole federal member and the only person who had also served on the Hovde task force for Kennedy. Richard Goodwin, later to marry historian Doris Kearns, was the White House liaison. Kearns was herself a White House Fellow.

The task force met with the president on July 21, 1964. They had been directed by Moyers to submit their reports in early November, giving them but 4 months to deliberate and reach consensus. Cannon, chief of the BOB's Education, Manpower, and Sciences Division, was a central player— he had drafted the initial paper for the task force, then served as its full-time staff.

Rather than rehashing approaches to general aid for public schools, the task force seemed to quickly settle on aid to poor and disadvantaged children as their major theme. In a phrase that would return in a very politically charged way in the Clinton administration 30 years later, the task force talked about "opportunity to learn."

In opening its report, the task force used language that could easily have been used by Clinton or George W. Bush at the end of the century:

> This is a fateful moment in the history of American education. For almost a decade, we have been engaged in a lively, argumentative reappraisal of our schools and colleges, and a search for new paths. The years of appraisal and innovation are just beginning to pay off in a clearer understanding of where we have failed and a surer notion of what our goals must be.
>
> And now the President of the United States has said explicitly and repeatedly that education is at the top of the Nation's agenda. . . .
>
> It follows that education will be at the heart of the Great Society. And it will be education designed to serve the high purposes of that society—education that will enable every child to develop his talents, that will liberate and enhance every man and woman, that will create a moral and political community. (*Report of the President's Task Force on Education*, 1964, p. i)

The report goes on to discuss "The Opportunity to Learn," in language that foreshadows the rhetoric that accompanied proposals in both the Clinton and Bush administrations:

Access is a major theme of this report. . . . Generations of Americans have
preceded us in this concern; indeed it is the most powerful theme in our educational history. Yet even today, children of disadvantaged background are de-
prived of normal access to educational opportunity . . .

Theoretically, a child in rags should be as teachable as a child in tweeds.
But most poor children are to be found in our rural and urban slums, and
those slums breed conditions that do in fact diminish the teachability of the
child. . . . The schools are very probably inferior in quality, and it is not easy
for them to attract good teachers.

Thus in those areas where the children need more intensive educational
services than other children, they often get less. For too many of the poor,
educational experience has been a series of failures, each failure reinforcing
the lesson of failure so that education is for them an habituation to despair.
(pp. ii, 6)

That language would lay the groundwork for Lyndon Johnson's proposal
for Title I of the Elementary and Secondary Education Act (ESEA). In fact,
the language of the Gardner task force in this regard helped shape the
language of the Great Society strategy, even though major issues dealing
with such factors as fiscal equalization, allocations, and governance were
not addressed in the report.

Although the Gardner task force also called for some programs in
higher education, such as the expansion of university-community extension
programs to include areas like urban planning, as well as programs for
student assistance and support of the humanities. The second priority for
K–12 education was for a program of matching grants to create supplementary educational centers to provide services such as remedial education—reading assistance was specifically mentioned—and for programs for
the disabled. These centers were seen as either community- or school-based
and as being locally designed to meet specific community needs. The centers alone were estimated to require one billion dollars a year in federal
support.

The task force clearly stated that federal funds should not replace any
state or local funds already used for such purposes. This recommendation
would finally emerge as Title III of ESEA, and the issue of who controlled
that funding would become the subject of a major fight in 1967. The concept of Title III would later be called the greatest contribution made by
the Gardner-Cannon task force by policy leaders such as Samuel Halperin
(Samuel Halperin, personal communication, November 10, 2002).

The Gardner report also called for the creation of a nationwide network of large-scale National Educational Laboratories to conduct basic
research on learning and to "speed the dissemination of improved methods
and practice" (Report, 1964, p. iii). The task force envisioned 18–20 of

these institutions, spread across the nation and modeled in part on work already being done at places like the University of Oregon and the University of Wisconsin.

This recommendation led to the creation of a series of regional education laboratories and the establishment of research centers on various issue topics. Although all the research centers are today located at universities, most of the labs are freestanding institutions. And whereas they have never achieved the vision of the Gardner task force (largely because funding was never sufficient), they are another example of the report's powerful ideas. The labs and centers would become Title IV of the Johnson bill. They exist today in the law that governs the educational research division of the U.S. Department of Education.

Three other sections of the task force report are worth particular attention. Largely because of the presence of Commissioner Keppel on the task force, special concern was given to strengthening state departments of education. As Keppel notes in his oral history in the Lyndon Baines Johnson Library, he knew that the Office of Education was in no position to manage grants and relations with 25,000 or so school districts. Far better to shore up state agencies and deal with 50 entities (actually more than 50, since they also worked with the District of Columbia, Puerto Rico, the Virgin Islands, and other nonstate jurisdictions) than to try and staff and organize at the federal level on that scale.

State education agencies in the early 1960s were notoriously weak and ineffective. Keppel and the task force wanted to see them strengthened with specialists, planners, and statisticians. The result is that even today, in many state agencies the salaries of a majority of the staff are paid for by federal programs, which they manage exclusively. States escaped the need to finance strong agencies since the feds did it for them. Keppel's advocacy on this issue prevailed, and Title V of ESEA became support for state departments of education. Because of opposition from the BOB—especially from Cannon, who did not believe the states were capable of acting—Title V was never well funded. Only $25 million was appropriated in the first year (Samuel Halperin, personal communication, November 10, 2002).

The task force also called for general aid to education, almost as an afterthought. Although the members endorsed the idea, and urged that any such program provide for some sort of fiscal equalization, given the disparity in the ability of states to support education, the task force said that they did not want a church-state fight over general aid to derail their other public school recommendations. Members used that section of the report to again urge that there be aid for disadvantaged areas. Emerson Elliott, a BOB staffer who worked with Cannon, recalled in an interview that Wilbur Cohen, assistant secretary for legislation at HEW and an ardent supporter of general aid, felt that ESEA was "the wedge to general aid," which would be created by merely altering the Title I formula. Cohen's theory was not to be realized, in large part because the protective lobbies that would grow up around Title I were not willing to see general aid emerge unless Title I was adequately funded.

As a matter of legislative strategy, Gardner and company urged that these new initiatives be accomplished by amending the always popular Impact Aid Act, known as P.L. 81-874, a strategy that Morse had tried earlier. This time the legislative strategy was successful. Even though nobody was really fooled, amending an existing law with wide support made it more palatable than starting from scratch (Graham, 1984, pp. 61–68).

Finally, the task force talked about governance. To deal with the federal-control/state-relations issue, the creation of a presidentially appointed committee to study federal-state-local relations and to explore the possible creation of a "permanent Commission on education that would be wholly under the jurisdiction of the States" (*Report*, 1964, p. v) was proposed. Although a committee was never appointed by Johnson, with Gardner's assistance from the Carnegie Corporation and money from the Ford Foundation, the Education Commission of the States (ECS) was created. This was an idea that James Bryant Conan, the retired president of Harvard, had talked about in his 1964 book. Within a year, ECS came into existence and continues today as a valuable forum for states on issues of policy.

The task force also addressed governance at the federal level, urging the creation of an independent (not in HEW) Office of Education at the presidential level, similar to the Office of Economic Opportunity (OEO). This office would carry out and coordinate programs and develop federal education policy. Drawing on the example of the Council of Economic Advisors, the task force also called for the creation of a "Council of Educational Advisors" to conduct a "continuous review of American education, identifying needs and setting national goals" (*Report*, 1964, p. vi). Although neither an independent agency nor the council was ever created, the notion of setting national education goals would reemerge when another Texan, George H. W. Bush, became president in 1989, a quarter century later.

THE 1964 ELECTION

In the presidential election campaign in the fall of 1964, education was a significant issue, but was focused mainly on supporting students attending colleges. Significantly, the Republican platform reversed direction from 1960, when construction aid had been endorsed.

The 1960 election was a landslide victory for Johnson over GOP candidate Barry Goldwater, a senator from Arizona. Johnson also helped increase the Democrats' margin in the Senate by two seats, and assisted his party in picking up 38 more House seats. Operating in secrecy throughout the summer and fall, the Gardner task force delivered its report to the newly elected president on November 15. By the end of the month, Johnson had given a general OK to move forward.

Although passage of the Civil Rights Act in 1964 had taken the desegregation issue off the table at least temporarily, the church-state issue remained a major obstacle. Keppel knew that this posed the greatest threat to getting a bill to Johnson. Working with the leaders of the National Catholic Welfare Association, Keppel was able to convince them to concentrate on "supplemental services" and not ask for support for teacher salaries.

As Keppel notes in his Johnson Library oral history, the final political compromise had many forebears. John Brademas, an Indiana Democratic congressman, in an interview tells of his role in convening the leadership of the NEA and the National Catholic Welfare Association at a very private dinner meeting—by coincidence, the key leaders were all from Indiana and had strong ties to Brademas. By the end of the evening, the notion of the "child benefit theory" (the money is to aid the child, not the school or religion) had emerged (Keppel, 1972, p. 8). That became the basis for the most important political compromise that would be achieved to ensure passage of ESEA, which was, at that time, the most comprehensive and far-reaching public school bill in the history of the country.

Johnson, too, had a legislative strategy in mind. As Keppel relates, Johnson believed that he had to move quickly. Although he had won in November by a 16-million-vote majority, he believed that his leverage would diminish. "It doesn't make any difference what we do. We're going to lose them at the rate of about a million a month." In vintage Johnson style, he told those assembled, Keppel and Celebrezze among them, "I want this coonskin on my wall" (Keppel, 1972, p. 7).

Johnson, a former teacher, was a passionate believer in equity and in the power of education to help pull people out of poverty, having himself been raised in a poor family and having succeeded in life, he felt, largely because he had received an education—one that had been entirely in public schools. Johnson also knew the way that Congress worked better than most of those serving on the Hill. He had been an extremely effective leader in the Senate and knew exactly how to get things done; and he saw education as key to winning the War on Poverty.

Johnson also believed that with the swing of 76 votes in the House (through the election of 38 more Democrats), combined with the politics of the Senate, he had to find a way to avoid the graveyard of the House

Rules Committee on any conference report. To do that he had to get quick passage in the House and then get the Senate to accept the House bill with no amendments, to avoid a potentially fatal conference.

Johnson sent the ESEA bill to Congress, along with his education message, on January 12. It was introduced that same day in the House by Democrat Carl Perkins, chair of the Elementary and Secondary Education Subcommittee, and in the Senate by Wayne Morse, Democrat and chair of the education subcommittee.[2] With much fanfare and very few alterations, the House passed the Perkins bill on March 26 with a margin of 110 votes, 263-153. Every one of the 38 new Democrats voted for the bill, exactly as Johnson had predicted. Two weeks later, the identical bill passed the Senate by a vote of 83-18. LBJ had in 87 days accomplished what others over decades had failed to do. With an authorization level of one billion dollars, ESEA was certain to change the face of American education, and it did (Graham, 1984, pp. 76–78).

ESEA BECOMES LAW

As a sign of how anxious he was to sign the bill, Johnson did so on Palm Sunday, April 11, in a photo-op ceremony in front of his old one-room schoolhouse in Texas. With typical presidential hyperbole, Johnson said, in part:

> By passing this bill, we bridge the gap between helplessness and hope for more than five million educationally deprived children in America.
>
> We put into the hands of our youth more than thirty million new books, and into many of our schools their first libraries.
>
> We reduce the terrible lag time in bringing new teaching techniques into the nation's classrooms.
>
> We strengthen state and local agencies which bear the burden and the challenge of better education.
>
> And we rekindle the revolution—the revolution of the spirit against the tyranny of ignorance (Johnson, 1965).

Of course, not everyone was so euphoric. In the House, Howard Smith, a Virginia Democrat, said, "We apparently have come to the end of the road as far as local control over our education in public facilities is concerned" (Sundquist, 1968, p. 215). John William, a Democrat from Delaware, said, "This bill . . . is merely the beginning. It contains within it the seeds of the first Federal education system which will be nurtured by its supporters in the years to come. . . . The needy are being used as a wedge to open the floodgates and you may be absolutely certain that the flood of Federal control is ready to sweep the land" (Sundquist, 1968, p. 215). As we will see, similar language would be repeated over the decades as new federal education legislation was enacted.

The local-versus-federal-control issue was, of course, an extension of political divisions that began with the founding of the country, when those who saw the nation as primarily a federation of states were pitted against those who supported a stronger central government. In education, this battle continued to rage, largely because the Constitution never mentioned education as an issue, although there are those who believe that the phrase "provide for the common welfare" surely includes education. Because the Tenth Amendment leaves to the states all those things not enumerated in the Constitution, the states-rights/local-control people believe that the federal government must stay out of the schools, even though none took issue with the Northwest Ordinance of 1787, which had made admission as a state contingent upon the creation of grants of land in every community to support schools.

During the course of considering the bill on the Hill, Keppel reports that Senator Robert F. Kennedy, the New York Democrat who would run for president in 1968 and be assassinated in Los Angeles during the primaries, raised a serious objection to the lack of any language evaluating Title I. Keppel reports that Kennedy said, "Look, I want to change this bill because it doesn't have any way of measuring those damned educators like you, Frank, and we really ought to have some evaluation in there, and some measurement as to whether any good is happening" (Keppel, 1972, pp. 9–10).

Keppel reported that he agreed with Kennedy and urged that such an amendment be made by the Congress, or else he (Keppel) would hear "bloody-murder" from his fellow educators. So as not to upset the "no Senate amendments" strategy, House committee member John Brademas inserted some rather vague language on evaluation on the House side. As discussed later, the failure to be clear and specific about evaluating Title I would remain a major issue for decades and Robert Kennedy's words would come back to influence his younger brother, Edward, in the year 2001.

Samuel Halperin, a senior education staff person in HEW in the 1960s, had the responsibility of working with Keppel and the White House to guide the bill through Congress. He said in an interview, "In 1965, everyone had a naive view of education. We felt, in the words of Senator Wayne Morse, educators were all good people and that all you needed to do was give them some tools and some dollars and good things would happen. They didn't need a lot of specifics. Not much thought was given on how to assess what they had done; it was assumed that the right thing would happen" (Samuel Halperin, personal interview, May 7, 2002). Barry White, an OMB career official who would later head the division that included education, commented in an interview, "In the 1960s, it was more important to get money into low-income areas than to do anything that was educational or accountable. The belief was that money was the end game. It didn't work, dropouts weren't eliminated, kids didn't learn" (Halperin, personal interview, May 7, 2002).

Halperin and White's recollections are borne out by reading the hearings in the House and Senate and the committee reports that accompany the bills. The burden was to be on the state plan to spell it all out, and as Halperin notes, "state plans are seldom disapproved." The only guiding language was that programs had to be "of sufficient size, scope, and quality," and all these decisions rested with the states (Halperin, 1969, p. 7). As would be later learned from General Accounting Office (GAO) reports and from a number of private watchdog organizations, good intentions were not enough. There were isolated instances of abuse—of swimming pools built, toilets constructed, and lots of audio-visual equipment purchased (often, never used)—all in the name of Title I.

Indeed, the House committee report on ESEA failed to even address the issue of what was to be done. It first called attention, as did the Gardner task force, to "the close relationship between conditions of poverty and lack of educational development and poor academic performance." How to accomplish that was dealt with by saying that educators "provided evidence that there is no lack of techniques, equipment, and materials which can be used or developed to meet this problem" (*House Report 143*, 1965, p. 2). As Halperin noted, his office drafted the report and they were not going to prescribe how the money was to be spent (White, personal communication, November 10, 2002).

By the end of the century, there was such dissatisfaction with what had been achieved with the federal investment in Title 1—more than 150 billion dollars—that a very different approach emerged relative to the role of states and local districts. That new law, based upon a legislative strategy that began to develop in 1988 and was enhanced in 1994, became the No Child Left Behind Act of 2001. The emergence of this dissatisfaction can be attributed largely to the fact that over the years the concept of Title I as a funding stream to schools was replaced with the concept that Title I was a program to overcome educational disadvantage among poor children.

These two conflicting motivations were never reconciled, with one view advocated by liberals out of the Kennedy-Johnson tradition, the other by moderate and conservative leaders, such as Clinton and George W. Bush. What was certain was that Johnson had very effectively used the issues of poverty and civil rights to break a decades-old deadlock on federal aid to education. The issue was shaped by the times, just as criticism of Title I's success in later years would be shaped by a new perspective about what federal aid should accomplish.

RESHAPING THE OFFICE OF EDUCATION

Even as Johnson was signing the ESEA bill in Texas, the White House remained very concerned about the ability of the Office of Education to administer the vast increase in responsibility mandated by ESEA, and later, the Higher Education Act of 1965. Indeed, one of the other 13 task forces set up by the White House in 1964 had been on government reorganization. Chaired by Don Price, the dean of the Harvard Graduate School of Public Administration, the task force had reviewed a memo prepared by the BOB, which read, in part:

> In addition to operational shortcomings, it is alleged that the Office of Education suffers from an almost complete lack of creativity and innovative capacity ... the office ... has generally been viewed as the willing captive of school administrators and education associations. (Graham, 1984, p. 88)

The Price task force, operating in accordance with the Johnson mandate for secrecy, proposed the creation of five new cabinet departments: education was number 2 on their list, with only transportation given a higher priority. Although Johnson did move to create the Department of Housing and Urban Development in 1965 (also a Price recommendation) and the Department of Transportation in 1966, he never did propose a Department of Education. Indeed, it would be another 15 years before that agency came into existence, and then largely because of the support that the NEA gave Jimmy Carter in making its first formal endorsement in 1976 and his reciprocal support for one of the NEA's major goals. In the intervening years, until legislation made education into a new cabinet agency, many internal battles would be fought over how best to organize HEW and how education would be treated under those schemes.

On April 12, 1965, one day after signing the ESEA bill, Johnson approved a recommendation presented to him by Douglass Cater, the White House education advisor, on behalf of several White House senior staff aides, as well as Keppel and Celebrezze, to create an intergovernmental task force on education. Johnson quickly agreed, and Dwight Ink, a senior official with the Atomic Energy Commission, was named chair. As Ink notes in his oral history interview, when he was called by the White House to serve, no mention was made of the fact that the report was to be done in 60 days. After he had accepted the assignment, he read about that re-quirement in the newspaper—apparently not an uncommon occurrence in the Johnson administration (Ink, 1969, p. 8).

By June 14, the four-person group had submitted its report. Ink later became a high-level official in the BOB's successor agency, the OMB. The Ink report, formally known as the Report of the White House Task Force on Education, called for the creation of four bureaus to handle elementary and secondary education, adult and vocational education, higher educa-tion, and research. The report also urged major reform of the agency's grant review process, the "vigorous" recruitment of additional professional staff, and clarification of the roles of advisory panels and consultants (*White House Task Force on Education*, 1965).

With the Ink report in hand and a deputy who was willing to be the hatchet man, Keppel sanctioned major personnel moves. As Bailey and Mosher report in their book on the implementation of ESEA, morale was shattered by the speed and methods used by Henry Loomis, Keppel's dep-uty. People quit when they were uncertain if they had jobs, phones didn't connect people, jobs went unfilled, work went undone. Loomis demanded 50 new high-level (supergrade) positions from the White House; he got 23 (Ink, 1969, p. 10). The administrative-support starvation that began in 1965 would remain a fact of life for the following 4 decades.

The struggle over just how strong to make the federal bureaucracy had begun in earnest. It remains unresolved even today. As a result, the number of people charged with administering federal programs has never kept pace with the growth of expectations. The result is that technical assistance and support to states and local school districts is extremely limited and the ability to hire new people with new talents and different expertise has be-come a major problem. This has made it easy for educators and politicians to criticize those at the federal level.

In his oral history, Ink notes that the reorganization had not been carried out as he wished. He cites the "elevation" of Keppel and the depar-ture of Loomis as having halted momentum for reorganization. Although many changes were made, few would argue that the U.S. Office of Educa-tion had become a well-managed, efficient, productive agency (Ink, 1969, p. 10).

MORE LEADERSHIP CHANGES

By this time, Celebrezze had become a federal court judge and John Gard-ner had replaced him as secretary of HEW. Soon thereafter, Keppel was kicked upstairs to the new and mostly ceremonial position of assistant secretary of education, in no small measure because of his showdown with Chicago mayor Richard J. Daley on the issue of school desegregation. Harold "Doc" Howe II became the new commissioner.

The Daley-Keppel clash is an excellent illustration of the tensions that exist between states and the federal government. States want support, but not many restrictions. Federal officials are loath to dole out money without accountability, and often use federal funding to leverage state and local policy, as Keppel attempted to do with Chicago.

Personnel changes were also about to be made in the White House, although totally unrelated to the Daley-Keppel clash. As Hugh Davis Graham notes, Johnson and the White House staff had become addicted to the use of task forces (Graham, 1984, p. 110). After Moyers was moved by Johnson to replace George Christian as press secretary in 1965, Joe Califano, a brash young aide to Defense Secretary Robert McNamara, became the White House task force czar. This job gave him a central role and unquestionably was key to his elevation a dozen years later to secretary of HEW under President Carter; in that role he would engage in a determined battle to keep education within HEW, even as Carter supported the creation of education as the 13th cabinet-level agency.

Califano was seen by some in HEW as "arrogant, uninformed, bright but spread exceedingly thin." Douglass Cater, another White House aide, was generally held in high regard, but he was outranked and often eclipsed by Califano and his staff of assistants. "Califano gave the impression that he would deal with only department secretaries or God Almighty—and then only grudgingly. Califano went to great lengths to make the decisions" (Halperin, 1969, p. 10).

In 1965, the task force mechanism focused heavily on interagency matters. In fact, there were but four outside task forces in 1965, compared with 13 that focused on internal matters, and all were composed entirely of senior federal officials. One of the outside task forces—on international education—was chaired by Dean Rusk. Although it did produce recommendations that formed the basis for the International Education Act of 1966, no money was ever appropriated to implement its programs; ironically, this was partly because it became a casualty of the Vietnam War and the strained federal budget.

Although Moyers had begun the 1965 task force process, Califano took over that summer, adding members and instructing the Keppel task force to produce position papers on eight topics. Although many of the items were related to higher education, for K–12 education, two are particularly important—the development of a year-round preschool program and the redefinition of Title I to reach more disadvantaged children and with a greater focus on remediation (Graham, 1984, p. 115). The latter was significant because to get ESEA enacted in 87 days, Johnson had to agree that the authorization would be for only 2 years. Keppel responded with his own list of topics, headed by the development of a program for a National Assessment of Educational Progress (NAEP), an idea that John Gardner had advocated while at the Carnegie Corporation. Keppel saw it as a way to determine what the investment in ESEA had produced in the way of improved learning.

Formally created several years later, NAEP would become known as the "Nation's Report Card." In 2000, NAEP would become a core element in the proposals for Title I reform by presidential candidate George W. Bush.

As Keppel had predicted, educators were very nervous about what they saw as "national tests," even though for the first 2 decades, these tests produced only data by region of the country; even today, they provide data that is reliable only for states and some large districts. Individual student scores remain impossible to either compute or obtain.

Keppel's other priorities were less ambitious and dealt with school personnel and facilities and higher and international education. Keppel's ideas for other K–12 programs may have been tempered by the fact that the Civil Rights Act of 1964 had mandated a study of equal educational opportunity, an assignment undertaken by sociologist James Coleman, then a faculty member at Johns Hopkins University, and federal policymakers were anxious to see those results before moving forward. When Coleman did deliver his report in 1966, it turned out to be not only important but one of the few social science reports whose findings would endure over time.

On October 8, 1966, just weeks before he was "kicked upstairs," Keppel sent the report of the Interagency Task Force on Education to Califano. Although recognizing that major needs remained in areas such as preschool and construction, the Keppel task force did not explicitly advocate new programs; instead it—along with many other task forces—identified 1966 as a year of coordination and consolidation. Unquestionably, spending on the Vietnam War was also a major factor. After all, 1965 had seen an eightfold increase in the assignment of American troops to Southeast Asia, with defense spending at about one half the federal budget of about $115 billion. In classic fashion, Johnson was trying to support both guns and butter.

In 1966, the administration was also faced with the need to reauthorize ESEA, and the realization that the 1965 formula—the one that had helped insure passage—meant that 95% of all school districts received funding. Thus many well-funded suburban districts were getting money, not what Johnson had had in mind.

Johnson's budget request was somewhat meager for a Great Society program—it actually asked for significantly less than the amount of the previous year. Therefore the issue became money, not program changes, although criticisms of the latter were heard all around. In the end, Congress voted for a 2-year extension at authorization levels significantly higher than those sought by the president. The year ended with no real policy changes. That November, in the off-year elections, Johnson lost some of his legislative clout in Congress as Democrat majorities eroded.

The year 1966 was also notable as the year in which the Coleman report was released. On the basis of an extensive examination of data, Coleman (1966) concluded:

> Schools bring little influence to bear on a child's achievement that is independent of his background and general social context; and that this very lack of an independent effect means that the inequalities imposed on children by their home, neighborhood, and peer environment are carried along to become the inequalities with which they confront adult life at the end of school. (p. 325)

For decades to come, arguments and academic studies would abound on just what the Coleman report meant. Often the report was misinterpreted as implying that since "schools don't make a difference," spending on education was wasted. Several scholars who later reanalyzed the Coleman data would claim that the original findings of the report were wrong. Even today, arguments continue over just what the Coleman data say about education, the family, the social environment and resources.

Ever the planner, back in the White House, Califano established, in 1966, another 11 outside task forces, largely because Johnson wanted new proposals—even if they couldn't be sufficiently funded. Two task forces were important for education: one on government reorganization, led by Ben Heineman, a Chicago businessman; and one on child development, led by Joseph Hunt, a psychologist from the University of Illinois, which included noted academics Jerome Brunner of Harvard and Uri Bronfenbrenner of Cornell (Graham, 1984, p. 137).

When the Hunt task force reported in January 1967, it was far too late to coordinate their report with Johnson's budget presentation for 1968—Johnson's last full year in office. In making its case, the Hunt report combined some very useful data; for example, the federal government was spending in excess of 15 times more per senior citizen than per child. The report also noted that seniors voted and children did not. In other ways, the report was extremely naive politically (Graham, 1984, p. 144).

Although supporting earlier intervention for children with services like Head Start, the Hunt report advocated the establishment within HEW of a federal Office of Children, with a leader equal in rank to those in charge of the "H," the "E," and the "W." That person was to serve as a federal ombudsman for children, able to make grants at the local level for community and neighborhood commissions on children, commissions whose members would in turn serve as ombudsmen for children. Also contained in the Hunt report was the idea of income maintenance grants for mothers, and one-stop social- and medical-service centers in communities. Both of these ideas would reemerge in the Nixon administration.

Of course, the cost estimates for all these proposals were enormous, and the Vietnam War was escalating both in terms of troop commitment and dollars. This, combined with what many saw as the Orwellian nature of several of the recommendations, meant that the Hunt task force report was effectively buried. All that emerged was a Johnson proposal to create "Follow Through," a program for children who had been in a Head Start program. Although it was enacted and funded, Follow Through was never more than a slim shadow of Head Start and far from what Hunt and his 16-member committee had recommended.

In talking about the work done on education and other social programs in the Johnson administration in 1967 and 1968, Halperin said:

> [It was] of great haste, great superficiality. . . . We were overextended, overtired and the morale left a lot to be desired . . . there was a little too much gimmickry for my taste in some of these legislative proposals. There were too many under-funded small starts rather than an overall philosophy that would be built on from year to year. Every year we started de novo trying to figure out . . . what do we do (under Califano's lash) for kicks this year? (Halperin, 1969, p. 15)

THE QUIE AMENDMENT

In the following year, 1967, it was time to begin consideration of yet another reauthorization of ESEA. This time, things did not go so easily. The Congress, especially the committee leadership—Carl Perkins in the House and Wayne Morse in the Senate—were most upset with the meager budget increase that Johnson had submitted for education programs. In addition, a senior Republican on the House committee, Al Quie, proposed an amendment to ESEA that panicked the White House and eventually led to the adoption of an amendment by Edith Green, a senior Democratic House member from Oregon. This amendment would undo a great deal of what Gardner-Cannon had tried to achieve in the 1965 law in giving the Office of Education the ability to direct resources.

Quie, a hardworking, well-liked moderate, was very supportive of federal aid for public education. He was nonetheless upset with many aspects of what had been enacted to that point. In his LBJ Library oral history, Quie said:

> I have felt that we were proliferating federal efforts in education . . . school systems had to hire a person just to concern themselves with federal programs, hunt them up and see if they could qualify to receive money under them. You could greatly simplify all of the red tape and give more flexibility to the local schools if we consolidated programs. (Quie, 1969, p. 24)

In addition, Quie had concerns about the Title I formula, which he felt was not equitable. His idea "caught fire down in the White House." Suddenly, the administration feared losing face, and the power of the White House was mobilized. As Commissioner Howe (1969, p. 4) recalled in his oral history, "There was a knockdown, drag-out fight between the administration and most of the Democrats, on one hand, and a few conservative Democrats and the Republicans, on the other." Johnson did not want anything to upset what he felt was a carefully constructed political balance in the law. Quie felt that the formula wasn't a good one both in terms of how the money was allocated—he favored the use of educational, not economic, disadvantage—and how it was apportioned among the states.

Later, Quie would express some astonishment at how much White House energy was thrown into the battle when, as he said, "there weren't that many Republicans around." The Johnson forces' argument, which turned out to be very powerful, invoked the church-state issue as a defense against change, noting that most states prohibited aid to nonpublic schools and that if federal money were administered under state law, parochial schools would lose out in those states. Also at issue was that under the Quie amendment, a number of border and southern states would lose Title I money.

The stakes were so high that in a speech at a school in suburban Maryland, Johnson personally attacked the Quie amendment by name as being detrimental to poor states, poor children, and the cities. Quie, for his part, was working closely with then House GOP leader Gerald Ford to mobilize outside support. Six years later, Ford would become president when Richard Nixon resigned. Chief among the Quie supporters from the education community was the Council of Chief State School Officers (CCSSO); most of the other education groups supported the Democrats.

Although the Quie substitute for the committee-approved bill eventually lost—by fewer than 30 votes—the controversy created an opportunity for Democrat Edith Green, the fabled "Gentle Lady from Oregon," to enter the fray with her own set of amendments. One of these amendments stripped the U.S. commissioner of all his discretionary authority under Title III (supplementary centers and innovative programs) by sending all the money directly to the states. Green was also successful with her amendment requiring that school desegregation be equally enforced in all states—a move largely seen as favorable to the South, which felt that its school systems (de jure) were being unfairly targeted, while systems in the North (de facto) were being ignored (Graham, 1984, pp. 152–155).

In arguing for her Title III amendment, Green (1985, p. 32) later recalled, "I had come to the conclusion that the tremendous bureaucracy that we had in Washington . . . was not what we needed . . . all of the brains and wisdom . . . do not reside on the banks of the Potomac." Commissioner Howe, in explaining the Johnson defeat at the hands of Congresswoman Green, would explain that he felt that the tension over civil rights enforcement affected the Title III decision with the Congress: "Whereas we are willing to continue the categorical aid system, we don't want this direct relationship from the federal government to the local school district" (Howe, p. 5).

In the Senate, consideration of the ESEA reauthorization bill saw the emergence of the first small program for bilingual education, championed by Texas Democrat Ralph Yarborough. Although the Johnson people argued that such programs could be supported under existing authority, the advocates won and a new Title VII was added to ESEA. Bilingual education would provoke controversy for decades to come, with some arguing that its purpose was to prepare children for an English-speaking world, and others arguing it was to preserve the language, culture, and heritage of non-English speakers.

Because of various delays, including debate in the Senate over civil rights enforcement issues, the 2-year ESEA extension was not signed until January 1968, during a time when Johnson was preoccupied by the Vietnam War. Instructive in the ESEA reauthorization is that two old issues—religion and race—were again decisive factors, and two new issues, grants consolidation and state control, emerged, issues that would remain potent forces over the following decades.

The final year of Johnson's term, 1968, saw no real activity in legislation or policy concerning public schools. Higher education issues, including the extension of the 1965 Higher Education Act, were before the Congress. As had become the Johnson tradition, there was a task force on education, but it was an interagency group and most of their agenda consisted of examining proposals made in 1967 by a task force led by University of North Carolina president William Friday. The Friday report contained some dramatic suggestions, including a "moon-shot" style assault on urban education, but the timing was bad. Money was not available, Johnson was not devoting time and attention to domestic issues, and the country was in turmoil.

The Johnson administration, which had started with a bang, ended with a whimper. In his oral history, Howe (1969) noted:

> Few people foresaw in the early enthusiastic days of the passage of LBJ's education legislation the difficulties of this job. And now the frustrations have set in because the job is difficult.
>
> President Johnson really had to go all out to get this great legislative program through and so say, "We're going to solve this problem . . . through education." And then two and a half years later the problem still exists. Halting efforts have been made to solve them, I think with inadequate amounts of money. (p. 12)

Howe's words, the concerns of people like Dwight Ink about the organization and capacity of the federal government, and the concerns expressed by Al Quie, Samuel Halperin, and Edith Green would ring true for decades to come, but would remain unresolved. Those same concerns would continue to be expressed over and over by political leaders in both parties, and often by educators at the local and state levels.

THE 1968 NIXON-HUMPHREY ELECTION

In late March 1968, Lyndon Johnson announced that he would not run for nor accept a second term. The nation was already in turmoil, with riots in cities and on campuses over the Vietnam War. Within a week, Martin Luther King Jr. was assassinated in Memphis, and cities like Baltimore and Washington erupted in flames. Robert Kennedy, then a senator from New York, and Hubert Humphrey, Johnson's vice president, sought the Democratic presidential nomination. Richard Nixon was favored to be the GOP candidate in November. Three months later, Robert Kennedy was assassinated in Los Angeles, on the night of the California primary. The war and the state of civil disruption in the country dominated the campaign that fall. Education, except for issues of school busing and desegregation, was not a major issue.

In November, Nixon won his long-sought presidential prize, beating Humphrey in a close election. During the transition, Graham reports that although Johnson was in general quite cooperative with the new team, he refused to allow Califano to share any of the still-secret reports of the dozens of White House task forces that operated during his administration (Graham, 1984, p. 200). As one of his last acts, just days before his term ended, Johnson released both his economic report and his budget proposals, proudly highlighting the education accomplishments of his administration. It was his swan song for an administration that had forever changed the financing and governance of education in the United States.

The passage of the Civil Rights Act of 1964, along with the creation of the child benefit theory, had temporarily mitigated the issues of race and religion. Both would reemerge in future decades, but for now it was possible to declare a battlefield victory. Education had finally emerged as a national priority. Whereas in the 1940s and 1950s education had been tied to national defense, in the 1960s it was hitched to a new wagon—the War on Poverty. A new strategy had emerged, even if it was still linked to other, more politically powerful forces.

4

The Nixon, Ford, and Carter Years

From Trust to Nailing Everything Down

Wℎᴇʀᴇᴀs ᴛʜᴇ 1950s ꜰᴇᴅᴇʀᴀʟ ᴛʜᴇᴏʀʏ of action was based on national defense and the Cold War, and aimed at "fixing" math and science education as a cure to education's woes, the 1960s theory was based on fighting poverty in a new type of war. Policymakers, from Johnson on down, believed that if money got into the right hands, students would be better educated and everything would improve. The 1970s saw another theory of action, one based on distrust of almost everyone. The result was greater specificity in law and regulation, more reporting, and the creation of more federal programs in the belief that without these targeted efforts, areas such as services for the gifted would not be adequately provided by states and local districts. Although many of these programs, such as bilingual education, were based on the equity argument that drove the Great Society, many others were not. Each seemed even more proscriptive than the one before.

SCHOOL BUSING BECOMES THE DOMINANT EDUCATION POLICY AS VIETNAM WAR PROTESTS CONTINUE

As noted, not even a simple extension bill for ESEA was passed in 1969, the first year of the Nixon administration. An extension bill did pass in 1970, but the White House was concerned that it was not the Nixon plan and that it contained unrealistically high authorization levels (Memorandum from Harper to Cole, 1970).

The White House had promoted Special Revenue Sharing, a form of block grants that would replace many of the existing programs. Representative Carl Perkins, who had succeeded the deposed Adam Clayton Powell as chair of the House Committee on Education and Labor, led the fight against the Nixon proposals, seeing them quite correctly as a way to eviscerate many of the Johnson-era Great Society programs. Robert Finch, a major Republican political leader in California who had served as Ronald Reagan's lieutenant governor and was a close friend of Nixon's, was Secretary of HEW. Finch was unsuccessful in convincing Congress of the merits of the Nixon plan and left HEW in mid-1970 for a White House post.

After that fight, which Nixon lost, the administration spent most of its energy promoting the proposed Equal Educational Opportunities Act. Aimed at restricting the still extremely volatile issue of busing school children to achieve racial balance, the Nixon bill contained language assuring equal opportunities for all children. The bill proposed directing the courts not to deny the assignment of a child to a neighborhood school, a provision meant to keep White children from being bused out of their neighborhoods. There was also language to protect school districts from being sued if they did not achieve racial balance.

Although the new administration did have several other education initiatives, many of them were administrative, not legislative. The political agenda was dominated by the Vietnam War, campus riots, and urban unrest. In 1969, even the appropriations bill for HEW did not pass, which created the all-too-frequent use of a mechanism known as the continuing resolution—a legislative device that allowed agencies to spend money only on existing programs and only at the level of the previous year. The use of continuing resolutions would become a staple of education funding in the 1970s, 1980s, 1990s and into the new century.

The administrative actions taken by the Nixon White House were quite innovative, though they were not perceived as so at the time. Three are especially worth noting.

The first was a program funded by the OEO to test the feasibility of school vouchers. Although several sites were considered, the only one finally funded was the Alum Rock School District near San Jose, California. At the time, this program was considered daring; in reality, it was a test of public school choice, since no private schools were included. At its peak, 18% of children took advantage of the vouchers (Ascher, Fruchter, & Berne, 1996). As Denis Doyle, the person in charge of the Alum Rock study would later say, "Alum Rock looked like nothing so much as a district made up exclusively of charter schools [a term that didn't exist then]. . . .

Each school . . . acquired its own distinctive personality and enrollments ebbed and flowed just as voucher theory predicted" (Denis Doyle, personal communication, December 12, 2002).

The OEO director who authorized the voucher demonstration was Donald Rumsfeld. A former Illinois congressman, Rumsfeld would serve as White House chief of staff and secretary of defense under President Gerald Ford, and would return to Washington in 2001 as secretary of defense under President George W. Bush. His deputy at OEO was Frank Carlucci, who would serve as secretary of defense in the Reagan administration. His chief of staff was Richard Cheney, secretary of defense under Reagan, and later vice president in the George W. Bush administration.

The second administrative action was the Experimental Schools Program. Designed in the Office of Education and later transferred to the National Institute of Education (NIE), this program was conceived as a way to test new designs in education. Whereas it funded many interesting ideas, the program eventually faded away. In many ways, it was an early attempt to bring about what came to be known as New American Schools in the 1990s.

The final effort, also destined to fade away, but illustrative of federal concern over an issue in which the government could exercise enormous leverage, was a study of school finance. Chaired by Neil McElroy, CEO of Proctor and Gamble, the President's Commission on School Finance was conceived of as an examination of the structures and taxes that financed public schools. Daniel P. Moynihan, then serving as a counselor to the president, urged that the commission encourage every state to conduct such a study (Letter from Moynihan to McElroy, 1970).

While all these administrative actions were taking place, there was no education issue more pressing for the new administration than school desegregation. Within a month of Nixon's inauguration, South Carolina Democrat Strom Thurmond, chair of the Senate Armed Services Committee, wrote to express his concern:

> Nor has there been any apparent change in their [HEW and Department of Justice's] paramount interest in achieving racial integration without regard to the consequences to education. As a result, the public school system, itself, in the South is endangered, to the detriment of all school children, because of the loss of confidence in the system by the public. (Letter from Thurmond to Nixon, 1969)

The pressures and concerns around school integration led the Nixon administration in May 1970 to propose the Emergency School Assistance Act (ESAA). In his statement transmitting the bill, Nixon proposed aid to assist de jure districts in the 21 dual-system states with their special needs for facilities, personnel, and training in order that they could achieve unitary status. He also asked for money for districts where de facto segregation existed, as well as for financing "innovative techniques for providing educationally sound interracial experiences for children in racially isolated schools" (Nixon, 1970).

This was a clear instance in which federal education policy relative to financial support was being driven by reaction to judicial decisions, an entirely appropriate role given the nature of the issue and its political importance. Nixon also believed that providing support was a better strategy than cutting off federal aid, an action that he believed would only harm the affected children (Patterson, 2001, p. 155).

To get the effort started while awaiting congressional action, the administration decided to put together a holding action by using a provision in the Economic Opportunity Act to create a temporary program called the Emergency School Aid Program (ESAP). This was accomplished by having OEO director Rumsfeld sign a delegation of authority memorandum in August 1970 to the secretary of HEW giving HEW authority to operate a program (Office of Economic Opportunity, 1970). The Economic Opportunity Act, a remarkably broad law that provided for substantial administrative powers, had been one of the first bills passed in 1964 in Johnson's War on Poverty. Although neither the Congress nor the executive branch had ever envisioned use of this act for this purpose, it was a creative solution that all sides accepted as a stopgap form of aid.

Because it took 2 years to get ESAA put into law, this temporary authority, provided through the OEO legislation, assisted by providing support to reward districts that had desegregated, as well as providing aid to stimulate voluntary integration. Under this temporary authority, more than 1,300 districts were eligible for support; by November 16, 1970, 898 had applied and 731 had been funded, for a total expenditure of $46 million (Memorandum to the president from Ehrlichman, 1970). Although the number of districts affected was less than 10% of those in the nation, they were all in the South. Southerners controlled the leadership of the Democrats in Congress and Nixon needed their support to enact his agenda. Media attention to what was taking place in schools in these 21 states also contributed to the need for immediate action.

In a remarkable triumph of will and politics over bureaucracy, secretary of HEW Elliot Richardson established a 36-hour decision cycle for grants in a process that involved both the OE and the Office for Civil Rights (OCR). Until early 1970, OCR was headed by Leon Panetta, who would later serve as a congressman from California and then as chief of staff to President Clinton. Panetta resigned from HEW in February 1970 to protest Nixon's Vietnam War policies. The Office of Education program was administered by Greg Anrig. Anrig would soon leave federal service to become Massachusetts's state superintendent of education and, later, president of the Educational Testing Service.

As noted, although in 1970 and again in 1971 the Nixon administration proposed legislation to assist school districts with the additional costs related to school desegregation, the language used would also have prohibited the busing of children for integration purposes, until all legal appeals had been exhausted. With civil rights organizations in solid opposition to these provisions—largely because of the controversy over busing—in neither year was Congress able to muster support for passage. The race issue that had blocked federal aid in the 1950s and the 1960s was back, and only the temporary expedient of using OEO's legal authority kept this delay from becoming a crisis.

NIXON EDUCATION PROPOSALS IN 1970: BEYOND BUSING

The Nixon administration produced its first non-busing-related proposals for education in 1970. Aimed at amending the Higher Education Act, the bill also including a proposal to create a National Institute of Education (NIE), an idea that recast a Nixon proposal from the 1960 campaign. Congress held hearings, but it took no real action in the first session of the 92nd Congress.

The White House architect of these proposals was Harvard professor Daniel P. Moynihan, who had previously gained fame for his controversial report for the Department of Labor on the state of African American families. In 1969, he came to the White House as a domestic policy advisor to President Nixon. His ultimate effectiveness was severely compromised when in 1970 his private advice to the president to exercise "benign neglect" when confronted with the political agenda of the more radical Black leaders was leaked to the press (Patterson, 2001, p. 170). Moynihan would later become a Democratic senator from New York.

Having come from academia, Moynihan was seen by his former colleagues as a conduit of ideas to the White House. Ted Sizer, then the dean of the Harvard Graduate School of Education, wrote to Moynihan in April 1969 to offer his suggestions on what might be done to improve education. He, rather inelegantly, addressed the letter to Moynihan in the "West Wing Basement," perhaps an apt description—in the West Wing, but low in influence (Letter from Sizer to Moynihan, 1969).

Sizer said that more money was very important, but so was experimentation. In an internal memo to Moynihan, Richard Nathan, assistant director of the Office of Management and Budget (OMB), reacted to Sizer's ideas by using language that is eerily similar to what would be said more than 30 years later:

> My view is that experimental programs in education need to be viewed together and stressed—Follow Through, Experimental Schools, and a stronger Head Start R&D effort.
>
> We must get rid of bad R&D (thesis writing) and put strong effort into selected and intensive experiments such as above. When we get some answers, we've got to disseminate in a way which supports and stimulates what leadership there is among educators. (Memorandum from Nathan to Moynihan, 1969)

Another assistant to the president at that time was Arthur Burns, later to become chair of the Federal Reserve System. In a memo to Nixon, Burns made an argument that is also echoed today and was then consistent with Nixon's proposal for NIE. Speaking about an issue of school finance, Burns said, "The clearest conclusion for the Federal government to come out of all of this is that education needs a much greater investment in hard research. . . . Such research needs to be designed far more rigorously than any yet undertaken, but it badly needs to be done" (Memorandum for the President, 1969).

Moynihan stayed with the administration less than 2 years, having been badly hurt by his "benign neglect" advice (Patterson, 2001, p. 170). In one of his final memos before departing, Moynihan wrote about his experiences to Chief of Staff Bob Haldeman:

> As I get ready to leave the Nixon White House after having been around long enough to have some sense of our patterns of behavior, I would like to send you one or two memos on subjects that you can usefully keep an eye on.
>
> Almost number one is the question of support for the President from members of his Administration. There just isn't enough. Just as important, nobody goes to the aid of anyone who gets into trouble by supporting the President.
>
> As an example, which I would hope will not seem too personal, I have been doing my best to call attention in circles where it would be regarded as a good thing to the unprecedented success of the Administration in disestablishing the dual school system of the south. There has been more change in the structure of American public schools in the past month than in the past 100 years.
>
> Seriously. And Nixon did this by thinking hard about how it could be successfully done. This included a strategy of not drawing too much attention to the matter in advance. But in the aftermath we have every right to speak about what is practically a national secret. Every time I have done so, I have

got the stuffings kicked out of me. (Memorandum from Moynihan to Haldeman, 1970).

Earlier that year, in a note to H. R. Haldeman and John Ehrlichman, one of Moynihan's assistants passed along these comments on the subject of the White House staff that came from a phone conversation with Moynihan:

> I don't object to White House staff people lying to me—as in the reference to my leaking those memoranda and the Urban Affairs Council minutes. Lies at least are purposeful.
>
> But I do get alarmed when fantasy enters.
>
> There is no great harm in having a few character assassins on the White House staff, but we should keep the number of madmen to a minimum. (Memorandum from Klebanoff to Haldeman and Ehrlichman, 1979)

While Moynihan had been the chief administration architect of NIE, the chief congressional proponent was John Brademas, later to become president of New York University. Brademas chaired a House education subcommittee and was joined in supporting NIE by Republican congressman Al Quie.

By this time, 1971, relationships between the executive and legislative branches had deteriorated substantially. The Nixon administration was engaged in an active battle with Congress over withholding appropriated money and Congress reacted by becoming more specific in law and leaving less discretion to the executive branch. At another level, the Office of Education began writing regulations that were much more detailed and directive, partly because of abuses in spending Title I money that had been uncovered by watchdog organizations, HEW auditors, and the media. An era of overprescription and tighter regulations had begun, one that would prevail for the remainder of the decade.

This was also an era of divided government. For the following 8 years, the White House would be held by Republicans, while both houses of Congress would be firmly in the control of the Democrats. For the previous 8 years, the Democrats had controlled both the legislative and executive branches. The Vietnam War was consuming the nation, and unrest existed on campuses, in cities, and especially in Washington. In most large and many smaller cities, the pressure to integrate schools was growing and federal court orders to compel busing were common, almost as common as the protests against them.

By the time the second session of the 93rd Congress convened in January 1972, the Nixon administration had decided to again seek congressional support for a formal program to financially assist in desegregating public schools. This was, after all, a presidential election year and financial support in southern cities, as well as many in the North, would be a plus.

One of the chief architects of the administration's education bill was Paul O'Neill, an associate director of OMB. O'Neill, who began as a career civil servant, would leave the deputy directorship of OMB in 1976 and later become CEO of Alcoa. While at Alcoa, he chaired the President's Education Policy Advisory Committee for George H. W. Bush. In 2001, O'Neill became secretary of the Treasury in the administration of President George W. Bush.

EDUCATION AMENDMENTS OF 1972

By early 1972, Congress was well into the process of passing a new higher education bill, one that would contain the first authorization for the Basic Educational Opportunity Grant (BEOG) program, now known as Pell grants. Because the higher education bill was now a train leaving the station, the Emergency School Aid authorization bill (to assist desegregating schools) was tacked on as an additional boxcar.

Also tacked on to this bill was a seemingly minor title authored by Congresswoman Edith Green that barred gender discrimination in educational activities and programs paid for with federal funds. Known as Title IX, it was modeled on language in the 1964 Civil Rights Act that barred racial discrimination. Although many who supported it expected it to be applied to only a small cluster of activities, increasingly expansive federal court decisions would broaden Title IX's provisions to include virtually every aspect of education. Supporters would particularly note the impact of Title IX on opportunities for women in athletics.

Because Title IX was added to the bill without either House or Senate hearings, the legislative history of congressional intent is exceedingly sparse, consisting primarily of a short section in the committee report, a statement by Congresswoman Green, and some dialogue on the House floor during debate on the overall higher education bill. That absence, though not entirely unusual, would be a key part of the controversy surrounding Title IX, and its application over the following 30 years. In fact, the debate about Title IX and its impact led President George W. Bush in 2002 to appoint a high-level commission to examine the impact of Title IX.

Given the controversy over school busing, especially in the more populist House, the higher education bill became a magnet for antibusing amendments. By this time, Representative Carl Perkins was chair of the House Education Committee. A remarkable legislator who had the perseverance and stamina of an athlete, Perkins served as chair until he died in office, in 1984, while on a trip to visit constituents in his eastern Kentucky coal mining district. Perkins never had to raise a cent in election contributions and never spent more than a few hundred dollars of his own money to win reelection.

The Senate full committee was chaired by Harrison Williams of New Jersey. Claiborne Pell of Rhode Island chaired the education subcommittee. Jacob Javits of New York was the ranking Republican on the full committee and Vermont senator Winston Prouty was ranking Republican on the subcommittee in the Senate.

Debates on the floor of the House and the Senate were lengthy and acrimonious. A conference committee met for weeks, finally emerging with a compromise, after Perkins, who chaired the conference, kept the conferees in session until 5:30 a.m. The final bill retained both the NIE and the ESAA provisions.

Debate on the conference report was equally emotional and also consumed a great deal of time in both Houses. The bill reached the White House in mid-June, giving the president 10 days, not counting Sundays, to act. As fate would have it, the bill was signed without any ceremony on June 23, 1972, shortly before the "smoking gun" conversation of Watergate fame took place in the Oval Office. Less than 26 months later, the recording of that conversation would be instrumental in leading to the first and only resignation of a president in U.S. history.

Elliot Richardson, secretary of HEW, was called to the White House on the morning of June 23, along with this author, who was then deputy assistant secretary for education legislation at HEW, to participate in a press briefing. Neither Richardson nor I knew until we were ready to walk down to the press briefing room whether the president had signed the bill. We were told by Domestic Policy Chief John Ehrlichman that the president had signed it that morning. In a twist of fate, Richardson would later become attorney general, and in October 1973 would resign in protest over the president's order to fire Watergate special prosecutor Archibald Cox in the infamous "Saturday Night Massacre." As closely as can be determined by an examination of the records, Richardson and I were waiting in Ehrlichman's second floor West Wing office at about the time of the smoking gun conversation in the Oval Office. As a sign of how distant the Office of Education was from the action, Sidney Marland, the commissioner, only later that day learned of the signing when he saw a newswire story.

This bill and its signing created considerable internal intrigue in the White House. Most staff had strong opinions about the busing provisions, whereas they had not much to say about the rest of the bill.

Some argued that the president should sign the bill and then go on television to denounce the busing provisions. One of presidential assistant

Charles Colson's staff said, "The second part of the bill i.e. the anti-busing amendment should be exposed to the hilt. Congress has succeeded in sweeping the busing issue under the rug. My blue collar people are not sharp enough to see this. Our only hope is that the President be credited with exposing a Congressional fraud and defending the common man" (Memorandum from Balzanno to Colson, 1972).

Other staff took the opposite view. In a memo summarizing the views of Dick Cook and Tom Korologos of the congressional relations staff, Todd Hullin tells H. R. Haldeman, "Cook and Korologos are against having a signing ceremony in that it puts the President in the awkward position of signing a bill that he's 'blasting.' . . . They also caution against using members of the education community as a platform from which to make an anti-busing statement. This would be blatantly political and 'they wouldn't let us get away with it'" (Memorandum from Hullin to Haldeman, 1972).

Although the 1972 bill put in place the most significant set of higher education programs ever enacted, the White House statement that day was all about school busing, as were the press stories that followed. Almost no attention was paid to any of the programmatic aspects of the bill. Again, issues of race—this time in the guise of school busing—had eclipsed content. Nothing was said of Title IX.

In a press conference held the day before he signed the bill, when asked if he would sign it, Nixon said:

> It is one of the closest calls that I have made since being in this office. . . . I have mixed emotions about it. First, as far as many of the strictly educational provisions, they are recommendations of this Administration. . . . On the other hand, the Congress, as you know, did add a provision, section 803, with regard to busing. It was certainly a well-intentioned position, but from a legal standpoint it is so vague and so ambiguous that it totally fails to deal with this highly volatile issue. (Nixon Press Conference No. 24, 1972)

We see in the matter of school busing that the president seemed both to use the bully pulpit and to shy away from using it, as Moynihan's first memo illustrates. The internal conflicts within the Nixon administration were enormous, with first one side and then the other seeming to gain the upper hand.

The period of 1969–1972 is another excellent illustration of the conflict between politics writ large, as in the issue of school busing, and how that conflict overwhelms educational issues, as in the case of the early ESEA amendments, the 1972 higher education bill, and the attempts to raise new ideas, such as on school finance.

ESEA IN 1974 AND THE 1975 SPECIAL EDUCATION LAW

The 94th Congress, which began in January 1973, was scheduled to consider the next reauthorization of the ESEA. Al Quie had become the ranking Republican on the House committee, John Ottina was the U.S. commissioner, and Casper Weinberger the secretary of HEW. Sidney Marland had left to become president of the College Board. Terrell (Ted) Bell would succeed Ottina in 1974, leave to return to Utah in 1976, and come back to Washington in 1981 as secretary of education in the Reagan cabinet.

Richardson had left HEW to become secretary of defense, a post he would hold for a few months before being named attorney general. His successor at HEW was Weinberger, who had most recently served as director of OMB, where he had earned the title "Cap the Knife" for his efforts to cut domestic spending. Whereas Richardson had enjoyed reasonably good relations with the Hill, Weinberger had a much harder time. In fact, Carl Perkins so disliked him that when Weinberger testified before his committee, Perkins experienced an intentional slip of the tongue and addressed him as "Captain Weinburglar." The education lobbyists in the audience loved it.

Hearings in 1973 on the reauthorization were lengthy and detailed. By this point, results of the 1970 census were out and the extent to which the population had shifted since 1960 was quite evident. The big gainers were southern and western states; the losers the Rust Belt and the Northeast. Because the 1965 Title I formula was based largely on 1960 census data related to low income, these shifts created major financial stakes for state delegations. In addition, Al Quie, long unhappy with the assumption that being poor equated with being poorly educated, was preparing his next move to allocate Title I funds within a district based on the academic needs of students.

The entire consideration of the 1974 amendments took place in the long shadow of Watergate. The degree of tension and distrust between the legislative and executive branches was at a level not seen in decades. Although Nixon had won reelection in a landslide over George McGovern in 1972, Nixon's mandate quickly melted away as the press and congressional investigators revealed more and more of the story of the break-in and of a cover-up that would bring down a president.

As action proceeded in both the House and the Senate, issues of Watergate and school busing created an atmosphere far different from that which had existed in 1965 or during subsequent reauthorizations. Civil rights organizations issued reports showing that money was still being misspent; parent organizations were upset that they were not being consulted on the use of Title I dollars. Other groups came forward to make their claims on the need for new categorical programs for the metric system, gifted children, community schools, career education, consumer education, women's equity, and arts education. All would end up with new programs—often with new and separate offices in the Office of Education and a token authorization that, even if fully funded, would amount to less than 50¢ per child if allocated across the entire national school population. Each program was to fund some demonstration projects that, theoretically, would spur states and local districts to spend their money. Few did and most of these programs withered away, having achieved very little.

In the end, Title I amendments would constitute 15 pages of the 130-page bill. Seven pages were devoted to a new National Reading Improvement Program, a favorite of Marland and a program built on the Right to Read Act proposals of James Allen, Marland's predecessor at the Office of Education in the Nixon administration. This same issue—reading—would emerge on a somewhat larger scale in both the Clinton and Bush administrations; the reading problem still not solved.

During the hearings in the House subcommittee, in the full committee, then again on the floor, Quie pushed his concept of helping those most in academic need, whether they were in a high poverty school or not. Although he lost at every turn, by mostly partisan votes, his advocacy for a focus on academic need rather than on the assumption that poverty and academic deficiencies were inextricably linked was relentless.

Ultimately, the formula fight for Title I became ugly, as all sides resorted, for the first time, to using detailed spreadsheets produced by the Congressional Research Service of the Library of Congress to predict who would win and lose under certain scenarios. Almost nightly during mark-ups, new numbers were produced, numbers that were based on some variation designed to either maximize or minimize the effects of use of the 1970 census. Politics had discovered the power of the computer, and no fight over the allocation of federal funds would ever be the same again.

Not surprisingly, the final decision was based on the use of the 1970 census, with provisions that mitigated the impact of the decline in dollars for states losing population. The administration had little impact on the result, as various blocks of states did most of the negotiating, with Congressional leadership from Perkins and Quie in the House, and with Williams, Javits, and Prouty in the Senate.

The progress of the 1974 act had some relationship to Watergate. During the fall of 1973, while hearings on the ESEA amendments were being held, the Watergate legal crisis reached a crescendo with Nixon's firing of Archibald Cox, the Watergate special prosecutor; Elliot Richardson and William Ruckelshaus then resigned from the Department of Justice, in the above-mentioned Saturday Night Massacre. As 1974 opened and Watergate hearings were being planned, the ESEA bill moved forward, coming to the House floor in March for 3 days of consideration, with busing again a major theme of debate. Senate consideration came in May, with the bill on the Senate floor on 6 different days. The conference on the bill was relatively uneventful, except for issues of busing. The White House continued putting pressure on the busing issue, largely to curry favor with southern senators and congresspeople so as to try to keep them on its side on Watergate issues.

On August 9, just after the conference report passed both houses (in late July), Nixon resigned and Gerald Ford became president, the nation's first to serve without having been elected to the office. Ford, appointed vice president in 1973 upon the resignation of Spiro Agnew, signed the ESEA bill on August 21st as one of his first acts. The signing took place in the auditorium of the HEW headquarters building and was a major event for the media and for the education community.

Two months later, Ford pardoned Nixon for his actions, sparing the nation a continuing agony, and in a single stroke of the pen paving the way for the election of Jimmy Carter in 1976.

EDUCATION FOR ALL HANDICAPPED CHILDREN

In his 1987 book, *The Politics of Education: Conflict and Consensus on Capitol Hill*, John Brademas, then president of New York University, described the era of the mid-1970s as the time when a resurgent Congress was driven by the confrontational actions of both Nixon and Ford. Fueling that fire was the frequent use of vetoes and budget impoundments; countering these executive branch actions was the expansion of Hill staff, both personal and committee, and the creation of the Congressional Budget Office.

One of those vetoes came in 1974, when Richard Nixon vetoed the child development bill that had been written by Brademas, who chaired a House subcommittee, and Minnesota Democrat Walter "Fritz" Mondale, chair of a counterpart Senate subcommittee. The veto, as Brademas explained in an interview in 2002, left him angry and in need of a new challenge. In meetings with his staff, they came up with the idea of a vast expansion of services for disabled children, with strict requirements for placing children in what came to be known as "the least restrictive environment," and detailed procedures to ensure that children were appropriately identified and placed (John Brademas, personal interview, January 21, 2002).

In 1974, Congress passed, after two presidential vetoes, an extension of the Vocational Rehabilitation Act. Section 504 of that act contained a provision banning discrimination against the disabled, using language very similar to that contained in the Civil Rights Act and in Title IX of the 1972 act, which banned discrimination based on gender. Marty LaVor, a senior aide to House Republicans during that time, recalled that section 504 helped set the stage for the special education law in 1975. He also noted that although section 504 was only 43 words long, the regulations enacting it were more than 40 pages long (not uncommon), and they were written by the OCR with little input from the program office (Marty LaVor, personal interview, September 16, 2002).

The first draft regulations provoked a firestorm when they were published, as they proposed banning discrimination against an alcoholic or drug addict. Soon thereafter the definition of *disabled* was amended to eliminate this problem. The notion of an airline not being able to take action against an alcoholic pilot or a hospital not being able to deny privileges to an addicted doctor was not well accepted by the public (LaVor, personal interview, September 16, 2002).

Section 504 would soon find its way into the schools as a device for providing services to children with special needs without using all the compliance requirements of Public Law 94-142, the Education of All Handicapped Children Act.

After deciding to push forward with special education legislation, Brademas met with Quie, then the ranking Republican, who had long been a proponent of better services for special needs children; they cosponsored the bill. As Jack Duncan, Brademas's subcommittee staff director, reported in an interview, the subcommittee staff met with lobbyists from the Council for Exceptional Children, an advocacy organization of parents, who became their research staff. HEW staff, both political and career, were opposed to the bill (Jack Duncan, personal interview, May 9, 2002). They foresaw a vast expansion of services and cost, both of which did indeed come to pass. Many states were also opposed.

When the bill emerged from the subcommittee in 1975, the formula was straightforward. Funds were to be allocated to states based on the count of all school-age children. Duncan reports that committee chair Carl Perkins refused to consider the bill in full committee until the formula was amended to include a factor of 50% of the state's average per public expenditure—because that would parallel the Title I formula. In the view of Perkins and his staff, this would make it easier to eventually get general aid at that level for all students, whether in federal programs or not. In conference with the Senate, that figure was cut to 40%, with a phase-in over several years.

The concept had been that the federal government would share in supporting the excess cost of educating children with special needs, recognizing that these children, like those disadvantaged students under Title I, were a national concern and that many states and districts did not have the resources to pay for special services. In addition, the law mandated a series of processes, including an individualized education plan for each student, which were not a part of Title I or any other federal education law.

Unfortunately, the research available to support an excess-cost approach was not consistent. In a book published a year after passage of this act, Joseph Marinelli of the Florida State Education Agency summarized several studies made on this point (Marinelli, 1976, p. 151). Marinelli found that excess cost estimates for speech disabilities ranged from 1.18 to 5.97 times the cost of educating non-special-education children. For emotionally disturbed children, the range was 2.61 to 3.95 (p. 169). The result was the enactment of a general formula not tied to any special costs for services—a formula that used 40% of average per pupil expenditure as a proxy measure.

For the following 25 years, states would argue—as would many congressional and interest-group supporters—that the 40% figure represented an entitlement and that the federal government was betraying its obligation by not fully funding what was seen as a promise. In separate interviews, Brademas (personal interview, January 21, 2002) and Duncan both said that there had never been any hearings on this figure and that to the best of their knowledge, no legislative history existed to support it. In fact, Duncan in his interview expressed considerable dissatisfaction with the fact that states are still seeking increases in federal funding rather than accepting the reality that the education of all children is a state obligation. He also expressed the view that what was known as Public Law 94-142—and later became the Individuals with Disabilities Education Act (IDEA)—had not led to any real advances in accountability for the improvement of education for students in special education because of its focus on process rather than outcomes (Duncan, personal interview, May 9, 2002).

Once the House had passed the Brademas-Quie bill in early 1975, the Senate passed similar legislation. This time, the conference was not contentious and the bill reached the White House in due course. Despite initial White House opposition, tempered in the end by the close relationship between Al Quie and Gerald Ford, Ford signed the bill. Quie's influence with Ford stemmed from their close working relationship in the House and from Quie's role as a major force in engineering Ford's ascension to the Republican leader's post when a group of "young Turks" banded together to overthrow Illinois's Charles Halleck and replace him with Ford (Albert H. Quie, personal interview, April 10, 2002).[1]

In 2001, the special education law became the focal point of a controversy that literally changed the balance of power in the Senate: Vermont

Republican senator James Jeffords cited as one major reason for his leaving the party and becoming an independent, the failure of the Bush administration to pledge to fully fund IDEA. Jeffords's departure shifted control of the Senate to the Democrats. Jeffords had been a freshman on the House committee when P.L. 94-142 had passed in 1975. The lack of a rationale for the 40% figure has apparently been of little concern to those who have argued its entitlement-like nature in the intervening years, while never making the parallel argument for Title I, which contains the identical concept, although not the process requirements.

The special education law, today widely known as IDEA, is significant for the degree to which it and the accompanying regulations mandate both what and how schools and school districts must do with respect to serving children with special needs. The approach contained in the law represented the dissatisfaction of Congress with both the executive branch and schools. The moving personal stories about how special needs children had been denied an education were enormously compelling to the Congress. As always, personal stories told by ordinary citizens were more compelling than testimony given by any official from either the states or the federal government.

Public Law 94-142 was an illustration of what LaVor characterized as "time and circumstances" (Marty LaVor, personal interview, September 16, 2002). The bill reached the White House after the Nixon resignation, the stories of how children were denied services were heartrending, and relations with Congress were far too fragile. There was simply no way the bill could have been vetoed in that climate.

1976: THE BATTLE FOR A DEPARTMENT EMERGES AS A POLITICAL ISSUE

In what would become the final year of Ford's brief presidency (he served for 30 months), the major education program legislation would be an omnibus bill to extend the Higher Education Act, the remaining titles of NDEA, the Vocational Education Act, and several smaller programs. In a model of congressional efficiency, both the Senate and House passed the bill in late August, they passed the conference report in September, and the bill was signed by the president on October 12, in time to be used as sign of progress in the November elections.

In 1976, a little-known southern governor, Jimmy Carter, emerged as the Democratic presidential candidate to challenge Republican Gerald Ford. Carter had built a careful network of supporters across the country, often relying on teachers and using his own interest in, and record of support for, education in Georgia as a major issue in state primaries.

That year was also the first year that the NEA formally endorsed a candidate. Carter worked hard for that endorsement. His running mate was Walter Mondale, the junior senator from Minnesota. Mondale's brother was an official of the NEA.

One of Carter's major proposals was that he would support the creation of a cabinet-level Department of Education by breaking up HEW, an agency that had only come into existence in 1953. The NEA and Carter argued that education was too important to be lost in the third tier of HEW, and that the higher echelons of HEW were almost always consumed by issues of health, social security, and welfare. Creation of a cabinet-level agency had long been a goal of the NEA. The NEA's emergence as an open supporter of candidates, along with the fact that Ford's position had been weakened by the Nixon pardon and that he had never been elected to the presidency, all combined to ease Carter into the White House, albeit by a narrow margin.

The situation for the NEA was perfect. The group had openly supported Carter, he had won with a strong commitment to create a new federal education agency, and he had won by a margin small enough that the NEA could legitimately claim they had made the difference in getting him elected.

Because inflation was soaring and the stock market was flat, the campaign focused on the economy. Education was not a major issue, aside from the question of whether or not to create a new agency. Ford, predictably, was opposed to the idea, as was the GOP platform, which always tilted against larger government.

Once elected, Carter moved with neither speed nor energy to carry out his campaign promises on education. Members of his own team were less than enthusiastic about the concept; among them was Joseph Califano, the former Johnson White House staffer, who became Carter's first secretary of HEW.

Carter had also promised during the campaign to create a new federal Department of Energy—a reaction to the "oil shock" that had caused long lines at the gas pumps a few years earlier. When he became president on January 20, 1977, energy trumped education as an issue for immediate action.

However, in the proposal for a new cabinet agency for education, Carter had an instant ally in the Senate, someone perfectly positioned to assist him: Abraham Ribicoff, who as governor of Connecticut had helped get John Kennedy elected. As a reward, Ribicoff was given a wide choice of job options, and had chosen to serve as John Kennedy's first secretary of HEW. He would later tell almost everyone that he hated that job. He found the agency too big, too diverse, and impossible to manage. As a result of that experience, Ribicoff himself introduced bills through his Senate career to create a U.S. Department of Education. Until Carter was elected, no president had expressed any real interest in the idea.

Carter had promised to pay attention to government management and organization, and he had appointed Harrison Wellford to head a reorganization team in OMB. Wellford, with a staff of more than 100 people, was in charge of the President's Reorganization Project—identified by the official-sounding acronym PRP.

As talk of a Carter proposal surfaced, it became clear that not only Califano was against the new department. The AFT, rival to the NEA, was as outspoken in its opposition as the NEA had been in its support. More important, the AFT had a leader, Al Shanker, who was bigger than life, had a regular paid column in the Sunday *New York Times*, and was an officer of the AFL-CIO. Just as opposed was the U.S. Catholic Conference, which feared that Catholic schools were bound to lose out because of the influence that the NEA had over Carter. Religion, not much of a factor in U.S. education policy for a decade, would reemerge as a major issue in the saga that led to the creation of the department. Also opposed were almost all the associations representing higher education, which saw no advantage to a new department.

Throughout 1977, the administration did little publicly about the department. Carter was often asked if he still favored the idea. Although he said he supported it in general, he often qualified his support with comments about further study. In the meantime, Ribicoff, believing the department's creation would be a cinch and that Carter would soon send a bill forward, introduced his own bill on March 14 with 34 cosponsors—most were Democrats, but the group included four moderate Republicans. In the fall of 1977, Ribicoff held several hearings, but the House, faced with other issues, did nothing.

Within the administration, there were many battles. In February, Wellford hired Pat Gwaltney, who held a master's degree in public administration from Harvard and who had worked in HEW earlier in her career, to head the team that would manage the education study and process in OMB. By May, she was still pulling her team together. Many issues remained to be explored, including, What should be in this new agency? How should it be organized? What impact would these decisions have on other agencies? How could support be built for whatever decisions would be made? How could the opposition be neutralized?

All these concerns were put aside in the Carter White House when the issue of Bert Lance began to dominate the news. A close confidant of Carter, Lance had been a Georgia banker; after Carter was elected, one of his first appointments was to make Lance director of OMB.

Seven months after Lance began his job, stories began to emerge casting doubts on some ethical issues surrounding Lance's service as a bank president. Soon, the Congress was embroiled in investigations—most originating in the same committees charged with the Department of Education bill—and the White House was overwhelmed by the Lance issue. By the end of September, Lance had resigned and Ribicoff announced that hearings would begin—at last—in mid-October.

The Lance affair had another impact on the Department of Education bill. The original OMB plan was to propose options for the next steps in an interim decision memo to the OMB director and the president by mid-August. That schedule was abandoned when it became clear that the Carter administration would not be ready to testify during the first set of hearings.

Ribicoff and his staff arranged an impressive set of witnesses for the hearings, including several former commissioners and HEW officials. Among the witnesses was Ted Bell, who had been commissioner in the Ford administration. In his statement, Bell said, "The Commissioner is a . . . level V in the governmental structure and in HEW is one of the lowest forms of human life. . . . I did not have the clout in that huge organization. . . . You come to the job and you are soon disillusioned about it" (quoted in Heffernan, 2001, p. 110).

WHAT WAS IN? WHAT WAS OUT?

In fact, the interim OMB decision memo did not reach the president until Thanksgiving. By then, Jim McIntyre had replaced Lance at OMB, while Califano was continuing to pull every string he could to derail the dismantling of his agency—antics that would be among the major reasons that would lead Carter to fire him in the summer of 1979.

At this point, Califano tried working through his connections with the very sectarian Catholic Church, the very secular *Washington Post*, and the leadership of the higher education groups to derail the effort. Califano's influence with the *Post* stemmed from his social connections and because of his earlier legal work, including that related to the *Post*'s decision to publish the Pentagon Papers.

The option advocated by the opponents was to re-create HEW along the lines of the Department of Defense, which has departments within a larger agency. Education would become a "department" within HEW, headed by an undersecretary at an elevated rank, much as the navy operates within Department of Defense (DOD). Barring that option, Califano wanted the president to propose a broad department, a proposal that would do the most to elicit opposition from organizations not wanting to see their familiar turf disturbed and, thereby, sink the whole idea.

Across the mall, Shanker and the American Federation of Teachers (AFT) were working with the AFL-CIO to ensure their continued opposition to breaking up HEW. In their 16th Street offices five blocks from the White House, the NEA continued to believe that Carter would fulfill his campaign promise and Congress would comply. As events unfolded, the NEA realized that the campaign promise would cause them more trouble than they had imagined: editorial writers, senators, and congresspeople lashed out at the idea as being nothing more than a campaign payoff. As a result, NEA leaders had to work hard to convince others to take the lead while they stood in the shadows providing resources and logistical support.

But before anything could be done within the administration, Carter had to decide what would be transferred to the new agency. In her decision memo to McIntyre and Carter, Gwaltney and her staff identified 267 programs in 24 agencies with a total budget of $25 billion, about 10% of all nondefense spending as potential candidates for transfer. These programs included everything from veteran's education benefits and internal personnel training to promotion of the arts and culture. Gwaltney later confirmed that she and her team favored the broader concept of a department (Patricia [Gwaltney] McGinnis, personal interview, September 17, 2002).

In the end, Gwaltney and McIntyre recommended three options for Carter's consideration.

1. A narrow department, largely based on bringing the *E* out of HEW, but possibly including a few other programs
2. A department combining education and human development. This would not include all the 267 identified programs, but would include Head Start and some programs authorized by the Social Security Act that provided services such as foster care and adoption assistance
3. A reorganization of HEW along the lines proposed by Califano ([Gwaltney] McGinnis, personal interview, September 17, 2002)

Under any of these options, the staff would come back to Carter in a few months with a detailed plan and recommendations on personnel, programs, and operations.

Finally, on the Monday after Thanksgiving, in a large White House meeting, Carter gave general directions to go for a broad, but still undefined, department. He said that he would permit Califano to do some reorganization within HEW in the interim. In short, almost everyone in attendance thought that their position had been adopted.

It was not until April 1978, on the eve of McIntyre's scheduled appearance before Ribicoff, that Carter decided to support the Ribicoff bill, although by that time there was enough opposition to some parts of it that even Ribicoff did not support all its provisions. The Ribicoff bill, now with Carter's support, moved Indian education programs from the Bureau of Indian Affairs, as well as the Arts and Humanities endowments, into the new department. Constituencies for these and other programs, like the nutrition programs in the Department of Agriculture, had raised such a clamor that Ribicoff had agreed to reconsider these transfers. Now he was caught between the interest groups, their supporters, and the president.

By mid-July, Ribicoff had completed action in his committee. Indian education would remain in; Head Start was out; vocational rehabilitation programs were in; commodity food programs were out, as were the Arts and Humanities endowments. The committee was unanimous in reporting out the bill. The proponents thought that 1978 would be the year of passage. But it was not to be.

In the House, Chair Jack Brooks opened hearings on July 17, one day before the Ribicoff committee finished deliberations. By this time, the clock was on the side of the opponents. Because 1978 was an election year, everyone wanted some time back home in August to campaign, so the leadership agreed to end the session in early October.

The usual parade of witnesses appeared before Brooks's Government Operations Committee. However, in contrast to the positive mood in the Senate, the mood here was far from supportive—members from both sides of the aisle raised concerns, complained about big government, and voiced their fear that this new agency would jeopardize local control of schools.

Behind the scenes, the opponents were busy. Shanker and the Catholic interest groups worked together in a classic case of the odd couple. Califano worked his contacts, and an unusual coalition of committee Republicans and Democrats banded together to cause mischief. The leaders of the coalition were John Erlenborn, a conservative Illinois Republican, and Leo Ryan, a liberal California Democrat. Erlenborn was the second-ranking Republican on both the Government Operations Committee and the Education and Labor Committee. Neither Erlenborn nor Ryan had any love for the NEA, and both felt that the bill should not be enacted.

On August 3, Brooks started his markup, expecting to finish in a few days. By the time every delaying tactic had been used by Erlenborn, it was

August 15 and everyone was exhausted. When the final committee roll call came, the vote was 27-15 in favor—far from the unanimous Senate vote. With seven of the 15 no votes cast by Democrats, it was now evident that Carter could not hold his own party together in the House.

In September, the bill reached the Senate floor. After several days of consideration and many votes trying to move programs like the DOD schools and Indian education out of the bill, on September 28, the Senate passed it by a vote of 72-11. Indian education and child nutrition programs were out; DOD schools stayed in.

In the House, when it looked as though the Rules Committee would again be the black hole of education legislation, the White House leaned on several members and a rule was granted.

Two days after the Senate vote, the House leadership called up the rule that would authorize consideration of the bill. This time, the dirty work was done by Ryan, who used every possible procedural obstruction tactic on the House floor until the leadership pulled the bill from the schedule.

With the clock ticking and Congress faced with many more bills than they could handle before adjournment, the bill was scuttled. Carter did not list it as a high priority, and because Erlenborn and other opponents had filed more than 100 amendments, the leadership knew that they could not afford the time the bill would take on the floor. Furthermore, the vote count was quite uncertain; Carter could easily have lost one of his important initiatives. The year 1978 ended with no bill reaching the president.

In a bizarre and tragic footnote to history, one of the main opponents of the Department of Education was killed late that year. Congressman Leo Ryan made a trip to Guyana to visit a cult leader who, it was claimed, was holding some of his constituents against their will in a jungle camp. The cult leader was Jim Jones. Ryan was murdered while trying to board his charter plane in Jonestown to return with several cult members to the United States. Jones then ordered his followers to commit mass suicide by drinking poisoned Kool-Aid. That day, 913 people, including 276 children, died. The nation and the world were in shock.

In addition to personal tragedies having occurred that day, the House had lost a fine congressman, and department opponents had lost an important leader. The narrowness of the vote the following year is a testament to how intertwined seemingly unrelated historical events can become.

1979: A NARROW VICTORY

By early February, Carter had made some decisions; instead of reacting to other legislation, the administration sent a bill forward—Ribicoff and

Brooks both introduced it, even though Ribicoff also had his own bill. The opponents worked overtime. Editorials opposing the department appeared in almost every major publication, led by the *New York Times*, the *Washington Post*, and the *Wall Street Journal*. In a headline, the *New York Times* described the creation of the department as "The High Price of Cheapening the Cabinet" (1978) and took particular aim at the NEA.

At this point, Carter chose to narrow the department's scope, realizing that every transfer out of another agency would create more opponents. The administration backed away from the transfer of Head Start, child nutrition, and Indian education programs (Patricia [Gwaltney] McGinnis, personal interview, September 17, 2002). Still in, and important to Carter's strategy, was the transfer of the DOD-operated schools at U.S. military installations abroad and on a few bases in the United States. Although the dollars here were not significant, the number of people was. In fact, these DOD schools accounted for the majority of personnel in the Carter proposal, thereby enabling him to claim that it was a "major" department. Without those teachers, the staff for the department would be about the smallest of any cabinet-level agency, thereby giving credence to opponents' charges that this was all about a political debt, not substance (Patricia [Gwaltney] McGinnis, personal interview, September 17, 2002).

Given the ease with which the bill moved through the Senate in 1978, Ribicoff had an easy time in 1979 holding a few days of hearings, then moving the bill to a markup in his committee on March 14. It passed in less than an hour, but this time it was not unanimous. Freshman Maine Republican William Cohen, who would later become secretary of defense in the Clinton administration, was the only vote against it in committee.

The opponents of the DOD schools transfer were relentless. They argued it didn't make sense to have one agency operating a significant support service within the bounds of—and for the benefit of—another agency. Because it was recognized by Congress that such a transfer would take time, the actual transfer was scheduled for several years after passage. Well before that time, however, House opponents on the Armed Services Committee added an amendment to another bill repealing the transfer and it never took place. Ironically, 20 years later, data from the National Assessment of Educational Progress would show the DOD schools to be a model for educating children of all races and incomes.

Two weeks later, on March 26, Brooks opened hearings in the House and the opponents had a field day. With informal counts showing that the bill might not pass through the committee, the NEA and its supporters moved into high gear. They enlisted some key business leaders in support of the bill, as well as Vernon Jordan, president of the National Urban League. The opponents then produced New York senator Moynihan, who said, in part, "[This] . . . is being done for political purposes. . . . It is being done to win the next election . . . this is institutionalizing politics in education." Shanker asked why, if the idea was so great, no one outside of the "E" in HEW wanted to have their programs or agencies included. Finally, Marian Wright Edelman, head of the Children's Defense Fund, testified against separating education from health and social services. A week later, at the final House hearing, opponents included Stanford University president Richard Lyman, the executive director of the local school boards association in Pennsylvania, and Brookings Institution scholar David Brenneman (Heffernan, 2001, pp. 350–355). The antidepartment forces had turned out an impressive array of witnesses.

Although things did not go quite as smoothly this time for the proponents in the Senate, the bill passed by the end of April—with 72 votes in favor. This time, however, there were 21 votes in opposition. To achieve passage, Ribicoff had been forced to accept a number of amendments, including one to establish an office of bilingual education, advocated by Texas Democrat Ralph Yarborough, who was in a tight reelection campaign.

Back in the House, Brooks was ready for markup and he scheduled it to begin May 2, knowing that the vote counts were too close to predict the result. Again, there were amendments that passed, but this time there were fewer amendments to transfer programs out, because Brooks was using the Carter bill, which stripped the department to the bare bones. One of the amendments that did pass required that the new agency reduce its staff by at least 400 people and hire no more than 50 new people a year thereafter; with no reference made to tying any increase to growth in programs or appropriations. Late on May 2, a vote on reporting the bill was called. It passed on the narrowest of margins, 20-19. This time the number of Republicans supporting it was cut in half—to two—and a sizeable number of Democrats joined the majority of Republicans in opposition.

Finally, on June 7, the bill having passed through the House Rules Committee, debate began; scores of amendments were printed in the *Congressional Record*, as the rule required. Amendment after amendment passed—dealing with prayer, busing, and racial quotas. Stricken were the transfers of some student aid programs for those entering the health professions and of the Bureau of Indian Affairs (BIA) schools. Still, it was anyone's guess as to the final outcome.

After several days of floor debate in June, the Speaker pulled the bill and scheduled it to come back for consideration after the Fourth of July break. Finally, on July 11, Speaker O'Neill called for the final vote on passage. When it was announced, the ayes were 210, the nays 206. A shift of only two votes would have killed the bill. McGinnis believed that the deciding factor in the vote was a highly complex chart showing the number of HEW offices involved with making education decisions (Patricia [Gwaltney] McGinnis, interview, September 17, 2002).

A week later, Carter fired Califano, four other cabinet officers, and another 30 top aides. Newspapers reported that one of the major reasons Califano was fired was because of his efforts against the Department of Education bill. The *Washington Post*, in an unseemly reference, called it a "political Jonestown" (Heffernan, 2001, p. 472).

Although a brief meeting of the House-Senate conference committee took place before the August recess, it was mid-September before the conference was concluded. Although some of the controversial amendments on issues such as prayer were removed, others, like that on quotas, were modified and retained.

Usually, once a bill goes to conference, the vote on the conference report itself is routine. In this case, when the Senate took up the conference report on September 24, there were three fewer votes (69) in favor than there had been in April. Three days later, the House accepted the conference report by 215-201. On October 17, in a media event in the East Room of the White House, Jimmy Carter signed the bill.

Within 2 weeks Carter had nominated Shirley Hufstedler, a federal judge from Los Angeles with no previous experience in education, to be the first secretary of education. On May 7, 1980, the new United States Department of Education came into being. Almost exactly 6 months later, Carter lost the election to Ronald Reagan and the NEA was confronted with the prize it had helped create falling into the hands of those who had opposed its creation. Such are the fortunes of politics.

In reading the bill, one is struck with how prescriptive it is. In the fashion of the times, everything was nailed down. Even though both the legislative and executive branches were controlled by the Democrats, relations were not good. Having started down the road to greater specificity during the Nixon and Ford administrations, Congress kept at it. Everything from the composition of certain advisory committees to the titles of assistant secretaries was specified. The days of trust were long gone.

Even today, a discussion about the creation of the department brings strong reactions. Bill Morrill, a former assistant secretary for planning and evaluation at HEW, called it madness, claiming that HEW was far better at seeing across issues like economic disadvantage. That function now falls to the budget people in OMB and to the political people in the White House (Bill Morrill, personal interview, April 12, 2002).

Ted Sanders served as undersecretary of education in the first Bush administration, and for several months as acting secretary. In an interview, Sanders said, "It [the department] was not a good idea. I never saw a cabinet meeting where education was discussed. Education would have been far better served to have had a National Foundation, along the lines of Ted Bell's proposal." (Bell made his proposal in 1982, when Reagan was trying to abolish the department.) (Ted Sanders, personal interview, April 19, 2002).

Milt Goldberg, who served as executive director of the National Commission on Excellence in Education (which produced the *Nation at Risk* report in 1983) and who later served in several capacities in the research part of the department, commented that it "created more fragmentation, more bureaucratic levels" (Milton Goldberg, personal interview, May 8, 2002).

Others, such as Samuel Halperin, who had been a key figure in the Office of Education in the Kennedy and Johnson administrations, felt that creating the department was a long overdue acknowledgment of education's important role in American society (Halperin, personal interview, May 7, 2002). Jack Duncan, a key aide to John Brademas in the 1970s, felt that the creation of the new department "[has] certainly led to more money for education" (Duncan, personal interview, May 9, 2002).

Pat Gwaltney, the OMB staff person in charge of the Carter plan, said that the inception of a bully pulpit for education was the most important reason to create the department. She noted that the debates and attention to education at the national level since that time would likely not have occurred if education had remained as a small part of HEW ([Gwaltney] McGinnis, personal interview, September 17, 2002).

Although the creation of the department did not immediately have any substantive impact on the federal role, it did set the stage for placing education more at the center of national concerns and policy and for what would be a substantial expansion of the federal role in later years. It is impossible to imagine that education would have become the major issue it did in the presidential campaigns of the 1990s had it remained unchanged within HEW and had its leader remained "one of the lowest forms of human life," as Ted Bell had put it in the Ribicoff hearings in 1977.

The counter argument is that after the creation of the department, education became a much more political issue and the failure to consolidate more programs into the new agency contributed to the fragmentation of education policy, especially in areas like math and science. In reality, there is truth in both sets of views.

ESEA: THE NEXT CHAPTER

In 1978, while legislation for the department was being hammered out, the education committees, which had no role in those proceedings, were work-

ing on the next reauthorization of ESEA.[2] Once again, there would be formula fights over how the money would be allocated, and again, an amazing
number of new programs would be created.

The legislation to extend and amend ESEA moved fairly rapidly
through both the House and Senate, partly because hearings had been held
in 1977. Since 1977 was the first year of the Carter administration and the
Democrats had not held the executive branch for 8 years, it took a while
for key officials to be appointed and for policy decisions to be made. In
the meantime, the Congress was exercising the independent streak it had
developed during the Nixon and Ford administrations, and simply went
ahead with its work. In fact, Carter did not send his ESEA proposals forward to the Hill for more than a year, until February 28, 1978, at which
point much of the work had already been done on the bill. Nonetheless,
Carter did have some impact on a few provisions—such as the change to
try and concentrate Title I funds more heavily in districts with the highest
concentrations of low-income students.

Marshall (Mike) Smith, who was an assistant U.S. commissioner when
Ernest Boyer was commissioner—and would later serve for more than 7
years as undersecretary and acting deputy secretary of education in the
Clinton administration—characterized the 1978 bill as "[an] attempt to
get better balance. We built on the 1974 program [amendments] of concen-
tration grants, along with a move to school-wide projects. We felt there
was a need to emphasize good practice, professional development, and
cross-age tutoring. The theory was to stimulate whole-school reform and to
encourage states to put more money into compensatory education through
matching" (Marshall Smith, personal interview, April 24, 2002).

Both the House and Senate bills rewrote Title I to make the law's
organization more logical and to further nail down some provisions and
limit the discretion of administrators at the federal, state, and local levels.
The Title I formula was changed to count all welfare children (receiving
support under the Aid for Families with Dependent Children program)
starting in fiscal year 1979, rather than the two-thirds factor then in the
law. Reflecting continued dissatisfaction with using census data, which rapidly became outdated, the final bill also called for using the 1975 Survey
of Income and Education as a factor in adjusting the distribution.

The limits on use of funds was in part influenced by a RAND Corporation report, authored by Milbrey McLaughlin, that detailed the failure
of attempts to evaluate Title I, an issue that would vex policymakers for
decades to come, since Title I was then as much a funding stream as a
program (McLaughlin, 1975).

In her report, McLaughlin notes that Senator Robert Kennedy saw
evaluation as a means of political accountability, giving parents the infor-

mation, and through that, the power to be certain that programs were effective (1975, p. vii). McLaughlin believed that to be effective, evaluation had to be related to incentives at both the state and local levels, to overcome the education system's inherent resistance (p. viii). (As we will see later, Robert Kennedy's theory of action would influence his brother Edward Kennedy in 2001 when yet another reauthorization of ESEA was being discussed. In fact, either Senator Robert Kennedy or Senator Edward Kennedy was a key player in the 1965 ESEA authorization and in every reauthorization thereafter.)

Illustrative of the differing expectations for Title I evaluation was the view of William Gorham, assistant secretary for planning and evaluation in HEW during the Johnson administration—and later, founder of the Urban Institute—who believed that evaluations would yield cost-benefit data that would drive decision making and bring about effective practice.

There were other changes that were significant in Title I. Although parent advisory councils had first been required in the 1974 amendments, the provisions were tightened in 1978 to require that every parent council member receive copies of all federal regulations, as well as audit and monitoring reports. Provisions were added allowing Title I money to be used for the limited travel of parents to meetings, and each school district was required to state in its application how parent advisory council members would be trained.

For the first time, schoolwide projects were permitted if at least 75% of the children in a school were Title I-eligible. Reflecting the advocacy of Al Quie, districts were given the option of ranking schools for service on the basis of either poverty or educational need.

The 1978 amendments also contained several non-ESEA titles. The two most significant were Title XI, which provided for the education of American Indians, Alaskan Natives, and Eskimos; and Title IV, the Overseas Defense Dependents' Education Act, providing for the first time a statutory basis for DOD-operated schools on military installations. These areas—Indians and defense dependents—are the only instances where the federal government actually operates schools at the K–12 level. Although not in HEW, the House committee asserted jurisdiction over these schools and simply tucked the provisions into its ESEA bill. The Senate acquiesced.

The 1978 Act also continued the reading basic skills program that had been created in 1974, and expanded it to cover the acquisition of basic skills in math and communications.

When one examines the 1978 Act, it is startling to notice the vast number of small programs that were either reauthorized or created anew. The list includes the following:

Metric education
Arts in education
Consumer education
Youth employment
Law-related education
Environmental education
Health education
Community education
Preschool partnership program
Correction education
Biomedical education
Population education
Gifted and talented programs
Educational proficiency standards
Women's educational equity
Safe schools
Ethnic heritage programs
Inexpensive book distribution
International Year of the Child
The National Academy of Peace and Conflict Resolution (Education Amendments, 1978)

Each of these programs had an authorization level of between $5 million and $40 million a year; several required the creation of an office within the federal government to administer it. Many of these programs were never funded; even fewer had any lasting impact. Each was a pet idea, usually of a single senator or congressperson. In true logrolling fashion, each was accepted so that everyone could have something special to brag about; after all, 1978 was another election year. There was little attempt to create a rationale for the question, Why this program? and there was never any discussion about whether it was the federal government's role to support an area like law-related education or population education. Indeed, there was never any discussion about whether they should be carried out inside the education agency or by the Department of Justice (for law-related education), or the National Institutes of Health (NIH) (for population education).

This proliferation of programs also made it difficult to articulate a clear federal role. If it was to support programs for children who came to school with some disadvantage (poverty, a disability, lack of English), then where did these small programs fit in? Where did the federal role end and the state role begin? How could funds be concentrated on a few key federal priorities when there were many competing demands for money?

Aimes McGuiness, an official with the Education Commission of the States, in discussing the Carter proposals at a 1978 Institute for Educational Leadership conference, put it this way:

> States are also concerned that the President's proposals seem to be devoid of any thoughtful conception of the federal role in education and the relationship to the responsibilities of states. (*Educational Policy in the Carter Years*, 1978, p. 44)

The 1978 act, which easily passed both the House and Senate, was signed by President Carter on November 1, just before the Congressional elections. As a sign of how relatively noncontroversial it was, the bill was on the House floor on parts of only 3 days in June and July, and went through the Senate in a single day in August. The votes in both bodies were lopsidedly in favor.

Two major education factors that did distinguish the Carter years was the rapid growth in appropriations for education and the fact that the increases requested by the president during this 4-year period were substantially higher each year. In his first budget, Carter requested $9 billion for education programs in HEW—an increase of 32% over the $6.8 billion in Ford's last budget—although only a small increase over the amount actually appropriated in 1977. Each year, thereafter, Carter asked for major increases. By contrast, during the Nixon and Ford era, there were years when a decreased appropriation was sought; and, in one year, 1974, the amount appropriated actually decreased slightly.

The Carter years were seen by many as the best of times. Education got a seat at the cabinet table in the West Wing, federal dollars increased substantially, and a score of new programs were created.

In fact, the seeds of what would become Ronald Reagan's education proposals were sown during these years. As an NEA official said at the time, "I'm not sure we really want a department now that it is in the hands of the 'other side.'" In addition, the very proliferation of programs that so many interest groups had worked to secure in 1978 would create the rationale for the "block grant" proposals that would follow.

The 1970s ended with education having become somewhat of a national issue, even if for reasons that were more political and bureaucratic than substantive. It was also an era marked by almost constant tension between the executive and legislative branches. Having found its wings, Congress began to draw ever tighter circles around the federal executive branch, but also it gave ever more proscriptive direction to states and to local school districts. In turn, the executive branch, often driven by auditors, inspectors general, watchdog groups, and the bureaucratic tendency to cross every *t* and dot every *i*, fashioned ever more detailed regulations for states and local districts to follow, almost all related to process, few to outcomes and results.

5

The Reagan Years

The Bully Pulpit and Loosening the Strings

T HE 1970S HAD BEEN MARKED by a tightening of the strings and an explosion of new programs; the following decade would see the pendulum swing back to grants consolidation, more decision making at the state level, and extensive use of the federal bully pulpit as a way to embarrass and goad schools into improving. It would also mark the zenith of the minimum-competency movement, a movement that would bring its own counter reaction in the 1990s.

The year 1980 was another presidential election year. This time it was a Democratic incumbent, Jimmy Carter, fighting to hold on to the office against a strong challenge by Ronald Reagan, the former California governor, actor, and actors' union president. Reagan had come from far behind the leading national Republican figures Bob Dole, John Connally, Howard Baker, and George H. W. Bush to capture the GOP nomination. There was also a third-party candidate in 1980, John Anderson, a former Republican congressman from Illinois.

Reagan had been governor at the time that student unrest consumed campuses like UC Berkeley, and when conservative educator Max Rafferty had been the state superintendent of schools. Reagan came to the campaign with definite views on education; those views were reflected in the 1980 GOP platform, which called for block grants, the end of forced busing, and the dismantling of the U.S. Department of Education.

The Democrats' platform on education in 1980 was three times as long as that of the Republicans, going to great lengths to point out the many accomplishments of the Carter years and to support every segment of American education, with an emphasis on teacher training (Miller, 1981, pp. 101–109).

The campaign centered on issues of inflation, unemployment, and the SALT II treaty. Reagan scored points in the two televised debates by talking about the "misery index," asking voters if they were worse off in 1980 than when Jimmy Carter had come to office 4 years earlier; Carter had used the term in his race against Gerald Ford.

The issue of the American hostages held at the U.S. embassy in Iran may have decided the election. Reagan received almost 44 million popular votes to Carter's 35 million. In the Electoral College, it was 489-49, one of the most significant mandates in U.S. history, even greater than in Lyndon Johnson's 1964 landslide against Barry Goldwater. For an incumbent president, it was a humiliating rejection.

The "Reagan revolution" was accompanied by a major shift on Capitol Hill. Democrats lost 12 seats in the Senate, and the GOP became the majority for the first time since Eisenhower. In the House, Republicans gained 34 seats, still far from being in power, but large enough to give them an effective working majority on many issues when they were able to align with conservative Democrats. Reagan would take his oath with a mandate for change.

A significant factor in Reagan's election was the virtually unanimous support he received from the religious right. The influence of this faction would be very important in setting the domestic agenda for the administration. Religion was again a factor, but from a far different perspective than we had seen in the 1960s when the issue was how to aid parochial schools. The far right wanted the federal government out of public education, believing that lower taxes and the use of education tax credits and vouchers were the strategies to pursue.

THE REAGAN PROGRAM

Even as Reagan took office, there were clear signs that categorical programs were not working as intended, and that school people were unhappy with the paperwork and requirements of all those small programs.

In a study done for the RAND Corporation in 1979, researcher Paul Hill had reported that many children were in multiple federal programs. In one school, RAND found that 26 or 27 students in one "regular" classroom were in pullout programs most of the day. Typically, migrant Hispanic students were in at least four different pullout programs (Hill, 1979). In a second report, Hill noted that "some schools had so many federal programs that they could not avoid interference, and so little local money that cross-subsidy was the only way to pay for unfunded mandates" (Hill, 1981, p. viii).

Iris Rotberg, the director of research planning at NIE, made this observation:

> The problem basically results from a lack of coordination and clarity in the current system. Students, teachers, and principals must cope with the combined effects of programs that legislators and higher-level administrators deal with separately and in a rather distant setting. The result is that the point of supplementary instruction—to give students extra help in specific areas without replacing the basic educational curriculum—is often lost when students are assigned to several special programs rather than to one of two which best meet their needs. (Miller, 1981, p. 31)

The growth in programs was made very evident by the appropriation for the Department of Education. Whereas in the old HEW of 1960, $465 million was spent on 20 programs, $15 billion was spent on at least 150 programs 20 years later. In a 1981 publication of the Institute for Educational Leadership, Cora Beebee and John Evans, two high-level career staffers in the Department of Education, produced a list of 27 programs aimed at content areas ranging from compensatory education (Title I) to ethnic studies and educational TV (Miller, 1981, p. 42).

In that same article, Beebee and Evans called for a clarification of the federal role, arguing:

1. The federal role in American education is small and likely to remain so . . . about six percent of total national expenditures.
   The federal role is not concentrated, specialized or focused on any consciously selected mission or area of responsibility. Rather it has grown up through a process of ad hoc accretion.
2. There is also much inconsistency and [lack] of clarity about the nature and limits of federal responsibility.
3. Not only does the substance and direction of the federal role lack clear definition, but the pattern also reflects the ad hoc nature of federal involvement in American education. (Miller, 1981, pp. 41–43)

Reagan's arrival gave a major boost to congressional Republicans, who were tired of playing second fiddle and watching the enactment of program after program and what they perceived as a steady erosion of local control. Given the Reagan election mandate, their renewed strength in the House, and their control of the Senate, congressional Republicans were quick to forge a bill to completely redo ESEA through a vehicle known as the Education Consolidation and Improvement Act (ECIA). They had the blessing of the White House, which was spared from having to write its own bill.

In recognition of both its political appeal and necessity, Title I was retained—as Chapter 1 of ECIA. However, many provisions that school districts considered onerous, such as those pertaining to parent advisory councils, were repealed.

The other major education section of the ECIA repealed the authorizations for more than 40 smaller categorical programs, and it consolidated 20 others into a single authorization, with money going to the state to use as it chooses (Education Consolidation and Improvement Act of 1981, pp. 1–4). States were also given wide latitude in how to allocate funds among districts. In all cases, the original authorizations were repealed and the new Chapter 2 merely referred to those purposes. Correction education, population education, youth employment, and a host of others were totally eliminated. Content-specific programs that survived the consolidation included those for desegregation assistance (Emergency School Aid), community schools, and gifted and talented children (Education Consolidation and Improvement Act of 1981, pp. 11–12).

The Republicans in Congress, working with the new director of OMB, David Stockman, a former House member, devised an entirely new strategy to achieve victory. The education bill was one of many that the new administration supported, including a major tax cut and a reduction in the budget. As Stockman put it in his book, *The Triumph of Politics*:

> My counter strategy is to win on the Floor of the House in order to establish Administration control over the Democratic committee chairmen who can murder us in the remainder of the process. (Stockman, 1987, p. 186)

In the case of the House Education and Labor Committee, Stockman knew well that it was dominated on the Democratic side of the aisle by members like Carl Perkins, William Ford, George Miller, and Patsy Mink, all far to the left and all with close connections to organized labor. It was impossible to get a major reform bill favored by the administration and the House Republicans through the committee. Instead, the strategy focused on using an arcane provision of a 1975 law that created the congressional budget process. That law included the requirement that Congress pass a bill each year to "reconcile" spending and income. Once that routine bill came to the floor, the Republicans, working with the conservative "boll weevil" Democrats, were ready.

The rule governing how the bill would be managed on the House floor permitted a Republican substitute that incorporated all the items sought by the GOP, including the Kemp-Roth tax cut and the education consolidation bill, and it carried. To avoid a nasty and prolonged conference that would have given control to the old-line Democrats who chaired the various House committees, Reagan and Stockman persuaded the Senate to merely adopt the House bill, much as Johnson had done in 1965 to get the first ESEA bill enacted.

On June 26, 1981, the ECIA was signed into law as part of the Omnibus Budget Reconciliation Act of 1981. In just a few months, the tide had been reversed; rules had been loosened for schools, paperwork reduced, and states given control over a federal appropriation of almost $500 million for Chapter 2—an amount about 20% smaller than the total of the programs that were consolidated. Although states were pleased with the reduction in red tape, they were most unhappy with the accompanying reduction in federal support. States did get some of flexibility they wanted, however, they had not bargained for a reduction in federal aid as part of the deal.

In fact, the Reagan strategy had three major components: eliminating the federal department, consolidating programs, and reducing spending. The spending reduction part was an element in his economic recovery plan. Block grants, or grants consolidation, were a part of his new federalism approach, a plan that would have the federal government assume responsibility for major welfare programs while "trading" back to the states responsibility for education, along with a reduction in federal dollars and with fewer strings on those dollars. The theory was that fewer strings would mean more efficient use of resources (Verstegen, 1988, p. 10). As will be seen later, Reagan's first priority, elimination of the department, would not be achieved.

In a memorandum found in the Ronald Reagan Presidential Library archives, there is evidence that Reagan appointees had a more complex strategy in mind, a strategy that might have had significant political appeal over the course of the following 2 decades. Because the Reagan administration was so focused on budgetary and social issues, these other elements of the strategy did not get nearly as much attention as they would in later years when advocated by others. The main elements, as contained in a department planning and fiscal guidance policy paper, were as follows:

1. Pursue a consensus that achieving educational excellence is a national goal. . . . The elevation of the quality goal to be as important as the equal opportunity goal will go a long way toward not only achieving other national goals but of achieving social equity.
2. Develop a strong technical assistance and dissemination effort. . . . A lot more is known about how to improve education than is being applied.

3. Focus Federal R&D on improving school effectiveness. . . . Special consideration should be given to research on cost-effective school-wide approaches to improve quality for all students . . . (including) standards in different subjects . . . testing . . . of the higher order skills . . . and [exploring] the development of national competency tests for voluntary use. (White House Staff Files of David Holladay, 1962)

Although these elements of strategy were less visible legislatively— although many were contained within other proposals—Reagan did sent forth legislative proposals for tuition tax credits, Title I vouchers, education savings accounts, and grants in science and math—mostly in the National Science Foundation (NSF). The only initiative that took root came from the Presidential Task Force on Private Sector Initiatives: to create Adopt-a-School programs with the private sector. Since this initiative did not require legislation, it went forward as the Partners in Education Program and was launched by the president on October 13, 1983. The program still exists today, run by a nongovernmental, nonprofit organization, Partners in Education (White House Staff Files of Douglas Holladay and Kevin Hopkins, 1984). Reagan's 1983 voucher proposal was opposed by a majority of Senate Republicans because it was contrary to their belief in the need to support public schools.

A NATION AND A SECRETARY AT RISK

Reagan's secretary of education was Terrell "Ted" Bell. Bell had been the commissioner of education in the Ford administration and had returned to Utah in 1976 to become head of the higher education system. He had earlier served as the Utah's state superintendent of schools (Bell, 1988, pp. 1–6).

Bell's appointment was not without its challenges. First, the administration was on record as wanting to dismantle the Department of Education. Second, Bell was viewed by many conservatives as being too liberal and too much a part of the education "establishment" (Bell, 1988, pp. 40–41, 59).[1] In fact, Bell was the last cabinet member nominated by Reagan and he accepted the job only after being assured that the president would entertain alternatives to dismantling the new department. What Bell had in mind was a restructuring that would create an independent agency of noncabinet status, roughly equivalent to the NSF.

The tension between Bell, the White House, and conservative Republicans is illustrated through some personnel actions. In early April 1982, about 15 months into the new administration's term, Bell was forced to fire Bill Clohan, his number two person, because the White House staff felt he was too liberal ("The High Price," June 11, 1982). A few weeks later, Ed Curren, a conservative with strong ties to many in the White House, and the director of NIE, sent a letter directly to the president calling for NIE to be abolished. Curren sent the letter without Bell's knowledge and Bell demanded that Curren resign or be fired. Within 2 weeks, Curren had resigned.

Although internal tensions remained strained, Bell had shown that he was capable of trench warfare, if need be. Bell would labor throughout his tenure in an environment of sharp ideological divisions between the department's political appointees. For example, one of those appointees was Gary Bauer, later to become a member of the Reagan White House domestic policy staff, then president of the conservative interest group known as the Family Research Council and a candidate for the GOP presidential nomination in 2000. Bell and Bauer had little in common with respect to educational philosophy or political strategy.

The combination of these factors put Bell in a very awkward and uncomfortable position. Despite this, he pushed the White House to have the president appoint a National Commission on Excellence in Education (NCEE). After months of White House delay and indecision, he decided not to wait any longer and to make it a commission that he would appoint, rather than one appointed by the president. To chair the commission, Bell enlisted David Gardner, president of the University of Utah and soon to become president of the University of California system. Other commission members included a former National Teacher of the Year, several college and university presidents (including Bart Giamaitti of Yale); Al Quie (then governor of Minnesota); William Baker (former head of Bell Labs); and two distinguished scientists, Dr. Gerald Holton of Harvard and Glenn Seaborg, the Nobel laureate, from UC Berkeley.

Milt Goldberg, then the acting director of NIE and a former Philadelphia school official, was named to head the staff of the 18-member commission. In his book, Bell gives this rationale for creation of the commission:

> We needed some means of rallying the American people around their schools and colleges. Educators had to be shaken out of their complacency. More than two decades ago the Soviet Sputnik had spurred us into action to improve educational standards and performance. We needed an equally strong spur today. . . . Our loss of zest and drive and spirit would not be regained until we renewed and reformed our schools. (Bell, 1988, p. 115)

In an interview, Goldberg said that he believed that Ted Bell saw the commission as a way to shore up the department and to keep it from being abolished. Goldberg described the work of the commission over 18 months as consisting of six hearings and four public meetings held across the country, followed by intense sessions to finalize the report. From the start, the NCEE focused on the issues of time, content, and expectations.

Goldberg reports that the first staff-produced drafts were far too stilted and bureaucratic for the commission's members. That view was reinforced when, at an informal meeting with a group of top education reporters in New York City in September 1982, they were told that if the report were to be read, they would have to drop all footnotes and eliminate the education jargon.

The final report, containing rhetoric so powerful that it is still being quoted, was the basically the handiwork of Gerald Holton, the Harvard scientist. The final crafting was done by Gardner, Goldberg, and a handful of others (Milton Goldberg, personal interview, May 8, 2002). In the end, this language emerged:

> Our Nation is at risk. Our once unchallenged preeminence in commerce, industry, science and technological innovation is being overtaken by competitors throughout the world . . . the educational foundations of our society are presently being eroded by a rising tide of mediocrity that threatens our very future as a Nation and a people.
>
> If an unfriendly foreign power had attempted to impose on America the mediocre educational performance that exists today, we might have viewed it as an act of war. As it stands, we have allowed this to happen to ourselves. (Bell, 1988, p. 123)

With 36 pages and an engaging title, *A Nation at Risk*, the bully pulpit for the federal role in education had been elevated to a new height. There would be no turning back. Education had become a national issue and the stakes would only become higher.

The release of the report, according to Goldberg, did not go according to plan. In accordance with cabinet protocol, a copy of the report was sent to the White House in advance of the planned April 26, 1983, release, and the White House staff loved it. The president agreed to receive the report and the media was invited en masse (Milton Goldberg, personal interview, May 8, 2002).

Unfortunately, in what was in many ways reminiscent of the signing of the 1972 Higher Education Bill, the president's statement bore almost no relationship to the report. Much to the delight of White House staff and the dismay of Bell, the Reagan comments talked about school prayer, tuition tax credits, private schools, and abolishing the department—none of which had even been hinted at in the report. These were all positions of the far right, championed by Ed Meese, Reagan's political aide.[2]

Al Shanker, president of the AFT, used his paid column in the Sunday *New York Times* on May 1 to both praise the report and criticize Reagan:

> Clearly, this is language [in the report] designed to make Ronald Reagan sit up and take notice. . . . Nowhere in the commission's report is there mention of the Reagan Administration's major "ideas" with respect to education: tuition tax credits, vouchers, school prayer, etc. The report both rebuffs the Administration by ignoring them . . . and issues a stern warning to the American people and their leaders: Shape up American education, whatever the cost, or pay the consequences of a second- or third-rate power in the world. (Shanker, 1983)

After having been slammed in the media for not seeming to know what was in the report, the White House regained its composure; a number of conferences were held around the country, culminating in a huge session in Indianapolis attended by Reagan. *A Nation at Risk* had become part of the folklore of American education. From that point forward, efforts by the Reagan administration to scuttle the Department of Education dissolved, never to return, even though the Republican right wing—which dominated platform writing—would keep the abolishing of the department an issue for years to come.

In his speech in Indianapolis, Reagan embraced six reforms that he said "will turn our schools around." The first two dealt with discipline and with drug and alcohol abuse; the third item was that states should raise academic standards. Reagan cited his experience as governor of California when he talked with Japanese and West German exchange students studying in the United States: "They would inform me how hard school was back where they came from and what a vacation this has been being here" (Reagan, 1983). The fourth item was that "we must encourage good teaching. Teachers must be paid and promoted on the basis of their competence and merit." Both these issues would remain as national concerns in education for the following 20 years, through several transitions in presidential leadership.

Reagan's embrace of the report gave him a platform to talk about education and had the intended effect of dramatically raising his ratings on this important domestic issue. In fact, in his 1984 State of the Union Message, Reagan actually took credit for having appointed the commission (Reagan, 1984). Notes from a White House senior staff meeting of June 23, 1983, show the significance of this issue to his advisors. On the agenda that morning as item number 4—ahead of an item about the pope and Polish leader Lech Walesa—was education:

> Education: Recent poll results on this issue were mentioned. These show that public opinion on the President's education policies is now favorable by 46%

to 29% (versus 28% favorable to 49% unfavorable in 1981). (Senior Staff
Meeting Notes, 1983)

The White House strategy had worked. A report from a commission that
Ted Bell could not get even the White House to appoint in 1981 was now
being used to create the image that the president was fully engaged in education reform. This was a far cry from the budget cutting and program
consolidation efforts of early in his term, and it set the stage for Reagan
for the 1984 presidential election campaign.

This was yet another example of the use of the bully pulpit as a factor
in federal policy in education. Having worked hard for its creation, the education community, especially the NEA, found that the bully pulpit had become a sharp instrument for promoting reforms that were not of its making.

In addition to *A Nation at Risk*, there were other important reports
released during this time. Under the leadership of Tennessee governor Lamar Alexander, the National Governor's Association (NGA) would issue
Time for Results. Others, like the Carnegie Foundation for the Advancement of Teaching, under the leadership of former commissioner of education Ernest Boyer, would add their voices of concern—usually with detailed prescriptions of what might be done. All these reports served to
influence states to continue the adoption of minimum-competency expectations and assessments. Set at a low level, the entire minimum-competency
movement would fuel the fires of the 1990s for higher standards, more
rigorous assessments, and strict accountability.

It is interesting to note that the NGA's report, *Time for Results*, contains this statement:

> To sum it up: the Governors are ready for some old-fashioned horse-trading.
> We'll regulate less, if schools and school districts will produce better results.
> (*Time for Results*, 1986)

That simple declaration reflected the federal government's philosophy at
that time. The failure of schools and school districts to meet that challenge
would become the rationale for much more proscriptive intervention by
both the states and the federal government, culminating in the 2001 federal
law recognizing that an entirely new approach would be required if significant improvements were to be made.

THE DEBUT OF THE WALL CHART

In the summer following the release of *A Nation at Risk*, Bell again made
use of the bully pulpit. The NGA met that year in Portland, Maine, and

then vice president George H. W. Bush invited Bell and his wife to stay at their home in Kennebunkport and attend a reception for the governors at the Bushes' home. Bell (1988, p. 134) reported that several of the governors, while complimenting him on *A Nation at Risk*, told him that what they really needed was data that compared how their states were doing relative to each other. Bell wanted to make state officials, including governors, feel uncomfortable with how they were doing by showing them their states were not doing nearly as well as they thought.

When Bell returned to department headquarters, he huddled with his staff and created what became known as the Wall Chart. First released in January 1984, the Wall Chart would infuriate educators and politicians and become a sure source of news (Alan Ginsberg, personal interview, October 11, 2002).[3] The chart showed SAT and ACT scores, poverty rates, teacher salaries, average per pupil expenditures, and dropout rates. The church of the bully pulpit had added another pew.

The chart would be used for many years, then be phased out once it accomplished its purpose in the George H. W. Bush administration. By that time, the idea of doing state comparisons had been picked up by organizations like *Education Week*, the highly regarded trade publication. Released each January, *Education Week*'s *Quality Counts* generates hundreds of local stories that pick up on Bell's theme: "So, how are we doing?" The Wall Chart was also a major factor in convincing states they should support the collection and reporting of state-level data by NAEP.

1984 AND REAGAN'S SECOND TERM

Despite all the attention education had received from *A Nation at Risk*, the Wall Chart, and the reports of organizations such as the NGA and the Southern Regional Education Board, education was scarcely mentioned in the 1984 campaign. Walter Mondale was the Democratic nominee and his running mate was the first woman ever nominated by a major party for national office—Geraldine Ferraro, a New York congresswoman. Mondale had served as Jimmy Carter's vice president. (In 2002, a 74-year-old Mondale would see his political career end in failure when he was defeated by former St. Paul mayor Norm Coleman in a bid for the same U.S. Senate seat that he had held more than 25 years earlier. Mondale would be drafted 5 days before the election to replace incumbent senator Paul Wellstone, who had died in a plane accident while campaigning to win a third term.)

The major campaign issues in 1984 were the budget deficit and free trade. Reagan won the greatest victory since FDR triumphed over Alf Landon in 1936. In fact, Mondale carried only his home state of Minnesota and the District of Columbia. Reagan received 54.5 million votes, Mondale 37.6 million. The Electoral College count was 525-13. Reagan had a clear and forceful mandate, and education would not be one of his priorities.

Right after the election, Bell tells about going to the White House to appeal the cuts that he was being told to swallow as his agency was directed to take a greater reduction in spending than almost all other agencies (Bell, 1983, pp. 156–157). Despite assurances before the election that education was a favorite child, it was clear that such was not to be. Bell and his issues had served Reagan well in the election; however, there would be no reward.

In his book, Stockman recalled that at that time he recommended that Great Society education programs be cut 40 to 100% (Stockman, 1987, p. 344). Bell came away from a high-level White House budget meeting very disheartened:

> I left the Roosevelt Room angrier than ever, and I knew that I had incurred the wrath of both Meese and Stockman. But most important, the budget review episode made it clear that the President's second term would not continue the high priority attention that education had enjoyed since April of 1983.
>
> The [Reagan] commitment lasted only as long as the election season: There was no longer a need to "stay out front" on the "sensitive area of education."
>
> We would have changed the course of history in American education had the president stayed with us through the implementation of the school reform movement. (pp. 158–159)

Bell went back to his office and the following day wrote his letter of resignation. He heard not a word from the White House until the president publicly announced his resignation 3 days later. Soon, Bell and his wife packed a U-Haul for the trip back to Utah.

Bell left Washington having created a new role for the federal government in education. Only Lyndon Johnson, and to a degree Jimmy Carter, had exceeded what Bell had accomplished, and Johnson enacted legislation that was as much about poverty as education. Bell had been intent on improving the schools of the nation; he had no new money to spend, so he used the influence of his office to highlight the problem. Arguably, he could not have done that had he remained a "low form of human life," as he had so colorfully put it during the 1978 Ribicoff hearings on creating the department.

Whether because of his personality or because he too lacked the money to fund new ideas, Bell's successor, William Bennett, also used the bully pulpit and took it to even greater heights.

BILL BENNETT: THE MEDIA'S FAVORITE

Bennett would serve as secretary of education for 3 years, until nearly the end of Reagan's second term. He came to that post after 4 years as chair of the National Endowment for the Humanities, a rather obscure federal agency with a tiny budget that Bennett had made into a force in the cultural wars.

During his time at the Department of Education, he became one of the most visible cabinet members, as he refined the use of the bully pulpit. In one of his most memorable actions, during a trip to the Midwest in October 1987, he called the Chicago public schools the worst in the nation. His comments set off a furor that would in 2 years be a significant factor in a decision by the Illinois state legislature to turn control of the Chicago schools over to the new mayor, Richard M. Daley. Whether intentionally or not, by using the bully pulpit, Bennett would have an enormous impact on changing the governance of the third-largest school district in the nation.

Legislatively, the Bennett years were important because of the bill that went through Congress in 1988 to reorganize the Office of Educational Research and Improvement. One of Bennett's major concerns was with the quality, timeliness, and availability of education statistics. At that time, the Center on Education Statistics was a rather little-known agency with a very small budget and had the reputation for being constantly late in publishing its reports. In addition, there were serious questions about the quality of the datum and the degree to which it informed the needs of policymakers. Bennett put money and resources into upgrading this function, making it among the department's best and most trusted resources.

By the time Bennett became secretary in mid-1985, NAEP had been in existence for nearly 2 decades, yet it was known by almost no one outside the small community of people interested in research data. Bennett saw the need for having state-level student achievement data, in more subjects and on a more regular basis. Although created more than 15 years before to provide a national and regional picture of student achievement, NAEP's usefulness if it could not provide state-level data was marginal.

In May 1986, Bennett appointed a commission—headed by Lamar Alexander, then the governor of Tennessee, and J. Thomas James, president emeritus of the Spencer Foundation—to examine NAEP and make recommendations for change.

Since it was first organized in 1969, NAEP had reported data on only four regions of the country, a compromise that had been accepted at NAEP's creation when the nation's chief state school officers objected to state-by-state comparisons, calling them unfair and not useful. Although of some interest, NAEP data showed little more than that children in the South did not score as well as children in the Northeast and Midwest.

Over time, frustration grew over the lack of state-level data. After all, each year The College Board and the American College Testing Service released data by state on college entrance examinations and commercial test publishers provided data showing how students did compared to expected performance. Probably most important, the *A Nation at Risk* report had whetted the public's appetite. How would parents and taxpayers be able to hold officials accountable if they had no accurate data?

The Alexander-James Commission (Alexander & James, 1987). recommended that state-level data be collected and reported in all subjects that were tested. That advice was incorporated by Congress into the 1988 reauthorization of NAEP, with the requirement that it first be done in 1990 on a trial basis, to confirm its feasibility. The trials were successful, and since that point data have been available on a state-by-state basis for those states that have participated.[4] At about the same time, the National Assessment Governing Board adopted a tag line: The Nation's Report Card. It proved to be an excellent marketing tool in making the data important to the media and to policymakers.

Through his actions in the area of data and statistics, Bennett had substantially improved another important component of the federal role: the use of data collected and disseminated by the federal government as a lever for change at the state and local level. Although the importance and contribution of the department's research office had never achieved the promise of the rhetoric that accompanied the creation of NIE, the data and statistics side of the department was becoming a significant resource to states, local districts, federal policymakers, and the media.

Another passion of Bennett's was curriculum reform. He promoted what he believed to be a model curriculum for both elementary and high schools through his James Madison schools, a fictional device that skirted the prohibition against the U.S. Department of Education mandating curricula. By using the bully pulpit, he had great influence without crossing the line of an actual mandate. As had federal officials before him—Allen and Marland in the 1970s—Bennett expressed particular concern about reading skills, with a particular interest in literature. Improving the teaching of reading would remain an interest of federal policymakers for the following 15 years.

Bennett was an interesting figure as secretary. Edward Fiske, Education editor of the *New York Times*, wrote:

> I mean we just loved Bill Bennett because he is so great. He is fun to be with. He is an interesting guy and everyone in the press loves Bill Bennett because

he is so outrageous. He has now given up smoking, I understand. I used to interview him; he'd go out jogging and run around the mall and he'd be in his office. I would be sitting there taking my notes and he was in his sweats, puffing away on his cigarette. He is a big bumbling bear full of contradictions. (Fiske, 1990)

Another writer, Maurice R. Berube (1991), said:

> Bennett ventured where angels feared to tread. Often with inflammatory language, he challenged every public education interest in his role as self-appointed guardian of conservative education values . . . .
> To the public he represented extremes. . . .
> William Bennett also had an added dimension to his role in the Reagan White House. He became the point man in the Reagan Revolution. (p. 103)

Ironically, Bennett, who would never have got the attention he did had he been a third-level official in HEW, said at a Senate hearing in 1988, "A lot of the programs are good, but the department's not necessary." In a heated exchange on his comments with Connecticut Republican senator Lowell Weicker, Bennett said, "I've made a hell of a commitment [to education]. You just don't like the direction that I took" ("Bennett Leaving as He Came," 1988, p. 1329).

THE BATTLE OVER MONEY

For virtually all 8 years of Reagan's presidency, the Hill and the administration engaged in battles over money for education while spending on national defense increased substantially.

The Reagan strategy was to cut federal revenues through tax reductions, thereby reducing the opportunities that Congress would have to either increase spending or programs.

The 1981 Budget Reconciliation Bill, brilliantly engineered by OMB's Stockman, was the key. Not only had it consolidated education programs; it had also included the Kemp-Roth tax cut, thereby assuring that federal revenue growth would slow dramatically. The initial proposed cut in education was severe, $4.5 billion from the Carter proposal for FY 1982, along with rescissions of nearly $2.5 billion for FY 1981 (Verstegen, 1988, p. 78). In every one of Reagan's years as president, he would propose a budget that was significantly below that which would be enacted, sometimes by as much as $5 billion.

In 1983, while the country was in the midst of the worst economic recession since the Great Depression, Reagan proposed what came to be known as the federalism swap. Washington would pick up the full cost of Medicaid while returning to the states responsibility for 40 different programs in education, transportation, community development, and social services. The added fiscal burden for the states would be covered by the federal government in a few years by a "grassroots trust fund" supported by federal excise and windfall profits taxes that would end in 1991; after that date, states would assume the fiscal burden of those 40 programs that they wished to keep. The proposal collapsed because of the failure of governors to embrace the idea (Verstegen, 1988, p. 11).

In his book on the Reagan revolution, *The Triumph of Politics*, Stockman talks often of his passion to cut Great Society programs, especially those in education. Stockman describes a meeting during the first year of the Reagan administration:

> With Social Security and entitlement COLAs [cost of living allowances] now completely untouchable, I proposed to increase the pro rata cut in a number of Great Society–type programs from 12 to 25 percent. These included subsidized housing, urban development programs, education grants, student aid, Head Start, the Job Corps, health and social security grants, and job training. (1987, p. 349)

Although Stockman did not always get his way with the budget proposals, it was largely because the army of education-interest-group lobbyists was working furiously to assure that education did not incur the cuts that were proposed. Table 5.1 shows the relative distribution of funding from state, local, and federal resources, clearly demonstrating that the federal contribution to education spending as a percentage of total spending did dramatically decrease in those years. The 1982 budget was the first one that was totally Reagan's. His last budget was for 1989.

Over the course of the Reagan years, the proportion of K–12 education revenue from federal sources fell by about 30%. The constant battles over education spending were the most significant recurring theme of the Reagan years. Although aid to elementary and secondary education actually increased by 35% during the Reagan years, it fell by 12% in constant dollars.

So concerned was the White House about these cutbacks and the way in which the education world was reacting to Reagan policies that the White House Office of Policy Information produced more than a dozen education "Issue Alerts" aimed at getting better media exposure. One, unnumbered but dated June 6, 1983, 6 weeks after the release of *A Nation at Risk*, dealt with spending. Carefully crafted to avoid mention of the reduction in federal spending, the paper resorted to using data that spanned

Table 5.1. Distribution of School Revenues Among Three Levels of Government, 1980–1989 (percent)

	State	Local	Federal
1980	48.3	41.7	9.9
1981	48.6	42.0	9.4
1982	49.8	41.8	8.4
1983	50.3	41.5	8.2
1984	49.3	43.5	7.1
1985	50.0	42.8	7.1
1986	50.4	42.6	7.0
1987	49.9	43.3	6.9
1988	50.4	42.7	6.9
1989	50.0	43.1	7.0

Note: From *Politics and Policies: Funding Public Schools* (p. 46), by Kenneth W. Wong, 1999, Lawrence, KS: University Press of Kansas. Copyright 1999 by University Press of Kansas. Reprinted with permission

a 20-year time period to illustrate the growth in total education spending that had taken place since the early 1960s. One table does show that in inflation-adjusted dollars, actual per pupil spending had increased from $1,368 in 1961 to $2,690 in 1981, a doubling in expenditures per pupil (*White House Issue Alert No. 14*, 1983).

Another Issue Alert, dated June 23, 1983, is six pages long and titled *Ten Myths About President Reagan's Education Policies*. This paper talks directly about what were perceived as myths about vouchers, tax credits, school prayer, and education quality, among other issues (*White House Issue Alert No. 16*, 1983). There is no evidence that any of the papers received widespread distribution.

A NEW BATTLE OVER REAUTHORIZATION

During this same period of time, support for the Reagan administration's philosophy was eroding; and they were having a hard time holding the line against the creation of new categorical programs. In 1983, Reagan vetoed H.R. 7336, a bill that would have amended ECIA by permitting the Congress to veto department regulations, expanded the definition of migrant children under Chapter 1, and reinstated some program requirements and procedures that had been eliminated in ECIA (Presidential memorandum, 1983).

Four years after passage of the 1981 consolidation act, funding was authorized for several new programs, such as training of math and science teachers, and new authorizations created for old programs such as Follow Through, and Gifted and Talented, programs that had been included in Chapter 2 of ECIA (Jordan, 1996, pp. 20–21).

Because the 1981 bill reauthorized ESEA for 6 years (with an automatic extension for a 7th year) it would be 1988 before Congress passed another major bill affecting ECIA/ESEA. By that point, Carl Perkins, the longtime chair of the House Education and Labor Committee had died, and Augustus Hawkins, one of the senior African American members of the House and who represented the Watts section of Los Angeles, had become chair. The ranking Republican was Jim Jeffords, from Vermont. In the Senate, the Democrats had reclaimed the majority after 6 years of a GOP majority, and Claiborne Pell of Rhode Island again chaired the Senate Education Subcommittee of the Senate Committee on Labor and Human Resources, which was in turn chaired by Edward Kennedy of Massachusetts. The senior Republicans were Robert Stafford of Vermont and Orrin Hatch of Utah.

The major federal aid to education programs, including Chapter 1/Title I were by this time more than 20 years old and even longtime supporters in Congress, like Hawkins, were becoming concerned about the lack of evidence that Title I was making a substantial difference in the education of poor and minority children.

The 1988 reauthorization did represent a breakthrough of sorts in requiring more of districts and schools related to student performance. For the first time, states were required to define the levels of academic achievement that students receiving federal support should attain. The concept of substantial progress also entered the picture with states being told that they must identify schools where students were not achieving as expected (Jennings, 2000, p. 520). In addition, the schoolwide projects idea was broadened so that in schools where Chapter 1/Title I students constituted 75% or more of the children, services could be provided to all students, not just those identified for the program (Jennings, 2000, p. 520).

As had happened so often before, a bill on education became a magnet to attract actions on unrelated social policy issues, in this case amendments banning telephone services that allow a caller to listen to pornographic messages, so-called dial-a-porn ("'Dial-a-Porn' Ban Approved," 1988, p. 1078). North Carolina Republican senator Jesse Helms offered this nongermane amendment in the Senate, and it was adopted 98-0. In two different

House votes, conferees were instructed by margins of 382-0 and 274-17 to either adopt the Helms amendment or find some other solution. In a highly unusual procedure, separate conferees were appointed to deal with just the Helms amendment. Finding no other solution and faced with both procedural complications and the fear of being labeled as voting in favor of pornography, the Helms amendment stuck, and the bill, known as the Hawkins-Stafford bill, became law in early May 1988.

In its earlier stages, the bill had been so relatively noncontroversial that it passed each house with but a single dissenting vote, 401-1 in the House and 97-1 in the Senate. Almost a year elapsed from House passage on May 21, 1987, to final enactment.

As was so often the case, the bill was mammoth, containing sections on Indian education, magnet schools, drug education, bilingual education, adult education, vocational education, drop-out prevention, women's educational equity, and impact aid.

As a result of Bennett's interest in the subject, also included was a title upgrading the department's statistical function, modeling it on the Bureau of Labor Statistics in the Department of Labor, by giving the leader the title of commissioner and making that person an appointee with a fixed term not coincident with that of the president.

Because the gathering and reporting of data was originally a federal role, this change seemed highly appropriate. Unfortunately, making it a fixed term would not insulate the job from politics. A decade later, a sitting statistics commissioner, Pascal "Pat" Forgione, would not get a second term when he crossed swords in February 1999 with Vice President Al Gore over Gore's use of a press conference on the release of NAEP data to preempt its official release by Forgione. After that, the job would remain unfilled for several years.

As the end of the Reagan era approached, it became clear that education was a subject of great interest to voters, one that national leaders could no longer ignore. Polls regularly listed education as among the top domestic issues and almost every governor in the nation believed him- or herself to be "the education governor."

George H. W. Bush had served 8 years as Reagan's vice president and was largely unchallenged for the Republican nomination in 1988. He was, however, viewed with suspicion by the Reagan wing, who believed he was too moderate, especially after he made a comment during the presidential debates in 1980 in which he described Reagan's economic programs as "voodoo economics." Bush promised to bring a "kinder, gentler" administration to Washington.

The Democratic nominee was Michael Dukakis, the liberal governor of Massachusetts. His strongest rival had been Gary Hart, a moderate senator from Colorado, whose campaign imploded when some of his rather high-profile liaisons with women to whom he was not married became public.

The election campaign was lackluster. This would be the last campaign in the 20th century in which education was not a topic of particular discussion or concern. Bush won with 426 electoral votes and 49 million popular votes. He carried all but seven states and the District of Columbia. Although Dukakis did better than Democrats in either 1980 or 1984, he had only 111 electoral and 42 million popular votes.

With the end of the Reagan era, the education focus shifted from being a battle over appropriations to a time of renewed federal interest in the topic. The era of the bully pulpit as a club and the time of turning power and authority back to the states was over. Although the bully pulpit would still exist, it would become a way to help influence policy when combined with funding support, not as a way to create policy absent any funding or legislation.

A new era was about to begin, one in which the federal government would exercise clear leadership through a focus on educational standards. Education reformers were convinced that if the states, with federal assistance, helped establish academic standards and then held schools accountable for having their students meet standards, educational performance would improve.

Rep. Carl Perkins (D-KY), left, chair of the House Education and Labor Committee, and Rep. Al Quie (R-MN), the senior Republican, listen to a Senate proposal during the 1972 House-Senate conference on education.

Two of the leading Senate Democrats, Sen. Claiborne Pell (RI), left, and Sen. Walter Mondale (MN), second from right, during the 1972 education conference. With them are Steve Wexler, second from left, Pell's committee staff chief, and Sid Johnson, a Mondale aide.

▲ During the 1979 conference on creation of the U.S. Department of Education, Sen. Jacob Javits (R-NY), foreground, listens to comments from House members, from left, Rep. John Erlenborn (R-IL), Rep. Frank Horton (R-NY), Chairman Jack Brooks (D-TX), and Rep. William Morehead (D-PA).

Sen. Jacob Javits (R-NY) ▶ confers with Rep. Edith Green (D-OR) during the 1972 education conference. Green was the sponsor of Title IX.

◄ U.S. Education Commissioner Sidney Marland, left, talks with Rep. John Brademas prior to a hearing on the 1972 Emergency School Aid (desegregation assistance) act.

Rep. James Jeffords (R-VT), left, and Chairman Bill Ford (D-MI), during an education conference in 1988. Jeffords later became a senator and left the Republican party in 2001 to become an independent. ▼

President Gerald Ford signs the 1974 Elementary and Secondary Education Act at a ceremony in the auditorium of the Department of Health, Education, and Welfare, one of his first acts after becoming president in the wake of Richard Nixon's resignation. Seated behind Ford are, from left, Virginia Trotter, the assistant secretary for education in HEW, Rep. Carl Perkins (D-KY), Rep. Al Quie (R-MN), Rep. John Brademas (D-IN), and Rep. Alphonzo Bell (R-CA).

Senator Charles Percy (R-IL), left, and Sen. Abraham Ribicoff (D-CN), the ranking GOP member and chairman of the Senate Governmental Affairs Committee, during the conference in 1979 on the bill to create the U.S. Department of Education.

Sen. Claiborne Pell (D-RI), left, leans across the table to confer with Rep. Carl Perkins (D-KY) during the 1978 education conference.

HEW Secretary Elliot Richardson, right, testifies before the House Education and Labor Committee in 1972. On the far left is the author, Christopher Cross; between Cross and Richardson is Steve Kurzman, HEW assistant secretary for legislation.

Rep. Roman Pucinski (D-IL), right, confers with Jack Jennings (Pucinski's staff director) and Rep. John Brademas during the 1972 education conference.

At 5:30 A.M., the conference on the 1972 education bill ended. Sharing congratulations are Rep. John Dellenback (R-OR), back to camera, with Rep. Carl Perkins (D-KY), Rep. Al Quie (R-MN), and Rep. Alphonzo Bell (R-CA).

6

Two Bushes and a Clinton

Remarkable Bipartisanship Expands the Federal Role

GEORGE H. W. BUSH BEGAN HIS TERM in January 1989, the eve of a new decade and a new era. This was a time of remarkable presidential bipartisanship, one that would rewrite relationships between the federal government, states, and local districts. Although the path was never smooth, it was always lively and interesting. Partisanship remained, especially after the Republicans took control of both the House and the Senate in 1994, but underlying it was a strong theme of agreement on the fundamental principles that would define policy over the following 13 years, through the 2001 enactment of the No Child Left Behind Act.

Also remarkable was that for the first time the business community advocated a specific federal agenda and pursued it vigorously with policy leaders at both the national and state levels. There are many, in fact, who credit corporate leaders with having made bipartisanship possible and for holding the policy agenda together throughout some stormy times at both the federal level and in many key states.

There was also an implicit theory of federal action that operated throughout the first Bush presidency and during the two Clinton terms: establish expectations (goals and standards), provide flexibility for states and local districts, then hold people accountable. Often called the "tight-loose coupling" principle, this theory had substantial political support.

Because George H. W. Bush had been Reagan's vice president, a number of appointees were held over into the new administration, including

Secretary of Education Lauro Cavazos. Cavazos had been president of Texas A&M University. When Bill Bennett had stepped down in 1988, Cavazos became the first Hispanic ever appointed to a cabinet position.

The rest of the Department of Education team was mostly new, however, and Bush was clearly looking for initiatives to define his administration as being "kinder and gentler" than that of Reagan. Education was an area where both President Bush and the first lady had a keen interest.

Ted Sanders served as undersecretary of education for most of the Bush administration, and as acting secretary for several months in late 1990 and early 1991. In an interview Sanders said:

> President Bush had a broad view of how education should work. He regularly raised questions about parental choice, vouchers, and markets. He believed that education problems are not the sole purview of the feds—they are shared with states—and that it takes more than government to solve these problems. That was the philosophy behind the Thousand Points of Light. He also believed that leadership is the most important action that the federal government can take and that local governments and states needed flexibility. (Ted Sanders, personal interview, April 19, 2002)

In June 1989, Bush spoke in Washington before the annual gathering of more than 200 of the nation's most important business executives at the annual meeting of the Business Roundtable. He used the occasion to chart a new course for the business community, challenging them to each accept an assignment in a specific state to work with that governor and other state leaders over the coming decade to help improve the schools.

John Akers, chair of IBM, accepted the leadership of a new education task force, which got right to work defining its assignment. Assigned by IBM to work with Akers was John Anderson, a senior IBM executive. Anderson, in turn, worked with David Hornbeck, a former Maryland state school superintendent, to design the Roundtable's nine-point agenda. At that time, Hornbeck was working as a consultant to devise a remedy to the Kentucky Supreme Court decision that invalidated the state's entire public school system because it provided an inadequate education. Hornbeck would later chair a commission that recommended important changes in Title I, then become the superintendent of the Philadelphia Public Schools. Anderson would become president of the New American Schools Development Corporation.

THE CHARLOTTESVILLE EDUCATION SUMMIT

In the meantime, President Bush and White House staff had conceived the idea of holding a summit of the nation's governors to focus on education, particularly what might be done to improve America's international competitiveness, the public schools, and conditions for the nation's children.

Mike Cohen, who at the time of the summit was head of education programs at the NGA, said that at first the White House wanted to use the summit only to showcase states and what they had accomplished, while governors wanted to talk about how they could align federal resources and programs with what they were already doing (Mike Cohen, personal interview, May 10, 2002). According to Richard Riley, who would become secretary of education in the Clinton administration, several southern governors raised the idea of education goals, based upon their work with the Southern Regional Education Board, which had developed its own goals in 1985–1986. That group of governors had included both Bill Clinton and Richard Riley (Mike Cohen, personal interview, May 10, 2002). This same cast, along with Tennessee governor Lamar Alexander, had been involved in the issuance of the 1986 NGA report, *A Time for Results*.

One of the outsiders who met with the president prior to the summit and whose influence would be very significant was Paul O'Neill. O'Neill had just become CEO of Alcoa, after leaving the International Paper Company. Most important, he had been the number-two person in OMB during the Ford administration and was well known to White House staffers and cabinet members. He would later chair an education advisory council for Bush and serve for 2 years as secretary of the Treasury in the administration of George W. Bush.

Symbolically, the summit was held in Charlottesville, Virginia, on the grounds, of "Mr. Jefferson's university," the University of Virginia. Every cabinet member was required to attend, and 49 of the 50 state governors came (the only governor not to show up was Rudy Perpich, of Minnesota). No educators were invited, nor were any members of Congress other than those from Virginia. These were omissions that would cause some serious problems later, especially with members of the House and Senate education committees.

In his opening remarks, Bush said:

This [education] is not a Republican or a Democratic issue. And it's not administration versus the Governors. It's an American issue. And everyone in this room . . . is committed to educational excellence. And we all know too much is at stake to let partisanship get in the way of progress. The call was sounded in 1983 . . . and that report awakened Americans to the situation in our schools, and then those alarm bells began to ring. . . .

There are real problems right now in our educational system, but there is no Federal solution. (G. H. W. Bush, 1989a)

This summit, the first held by a president and the governors since the time of Franklin Roosevelt in the depths of the Great Depression, was cosponsored by the NGA. The NGA leadership of the NGA included the governor of Arkansas, Bill Clinton. Clinton was one of the most important leaders among the governors in attendance and, ironically, Bush went out of his way at several points during the closing remarks to acknowledge Clinton's work.

> I want to single out those on the platform with me now: Governor Branstad, who is head of the National Governors' Association; Governor Carruthers; Governor Booth Gardner of the State of Washington; and of course Bill Clinton, who looks a little tired, but took on an extra responsibility for hammering out a statement upon which there is strong agreement. . . .
>
> I agree with Governor Clinton that this [agreement to set national goals] is a major step forward in education.

Bush then went on to talk about the importance of the summit:

> The press will ask today . . . what really happened here that makes a difference? I would say three things.
>
> This is the first time in the history of this country that we ever thought enough of education and ever understood its significance to our economic future enough to commit ourselves to national performance goals. It has never happened in over 200 years. This is the first time, ever, that any group of public officials have ever committed themselves to a national effort to restructure the schools of the United States—something every educator who studied it says is the single most significant thing we could do.
>
> And this is the first time a President and Governors have ever stood before the American people and said . . . we expect to be held personally accountable for the progress we make in moving this country to a brighter future. (G. H. W. Bush, 1989b)

As Bush's statement implies, one of the major agreements to emerge from the summit was an agreement to set national performance goals in education. This meant that the goals would focus on the outcomes of education rather than the inputs.

The political leaders at the summit, who included Bush's secretary of defense, Richard Cheney; and Lynne Cheney, chair of the National Endowment for the Humanities (NEH), all felt that the education community had remained preoccupied with issues like the number of books, the number of students per teacher, the dollars available for this, the number of that, while failing to look at what the educational system was producing: Are students learning a year's worth of education for every year of teaching?

Are students graduating on time? Do students know how to read? Do graduates have the academic skills they need to succeed in a job or in college? Summit leaders wanted to hold educators accountable, and they said they, too, would be accountable. This was, indeed, a new era—an era in which agreement on the aims and outcomes of education seemed possible.

THE NATIONAL EDUCATION GOALS

Although there had been general agreement on the topics to be included in the goals, they were not written in Charlottesville ("Education Summit Joint Statement," 1989). That task was assigned to a small working group that convened in late October to hammer out the precise language. The plan was that the president would announce them in his State of the Union message in January 1990 and the governors would adopt them at their annual winter meeting in early February.

The assignment for leading the effort for the Bush administration fell to Roger Porter, the domestic policy chief in the White House. As assistant secretary for educational research and improvement, I was the Department of Education's lead person, assisted by Milt Goldberg, head of the research office, and Emerson Elliott, head of the National Center on Education Statistics, a former BOB staff member who had worked with the Gardner task force in 1964. Representing OMB were Barry White, chief of the education unit, and Bayla White of that staff. Goldberg had been executive director of the commission that had produced *A Nation at Risk*.

The lead governor was Bill Clinton. Joining him at various times were Terry Branstad of Iowa, Carroll Campbell of South Carolina, and Booth Gardner of Washington.

The meetings were held in Porter's office on the second floor of the White House—the same office that had been John Ehrlichman's in the Nixon administration and the same office where Elliot Richardson and I had waited on June 23, 1972, to hear whether the president had signed the Higher Education Amendments Act of 1972.

To accommodate Clinton, who never missed a meeting, we generally began our sessions late in the afternoon and often went far into the night; the last session took place in December during a major Washington snowstorm.

The sessions were often rancorous. Whereas there had been agreement at Charlottesville on having goals that focused on outputs, such as the number of women and minorities receiving graduate degrees in math and science and student performance on exams, there had also been agreement that goal number one should be about school readiness. However, no one had any idea about how to write that in a way that did not focus on inputs, such as the number of low-birth-weight babies—since there was also agreement that testing 4- and 5-year-olds was not yet feasible and that school readiness was a complex issue.

Part of the strategy was to have a set of objectives that would accompany each goal, to give substance and form to the brief statements of the goal itself. Goal number one had only 12 words—"By the year 2000, all children will start school ready to learn." However, there were three objectives, totaling 100 words and covering everything from prenatal health to parents as first teachers to the availability of preschool programs. Because none of these objectives really dealt with outcomes and Clinton was determined to have these elements in the first goal—with the White House equally committed to not having them—the arguments went on for hours. Clinton would come with mounds of information about what input measures were needed; Porter would object on the basis of the summit agreement about performance measures. Both Clinton and Porter had been Rhodes scholars, and watching them debate was highly entertaining.

For a time, we just went in circles. Finally, weary of hearing the same old arguments, the group decided to move on, leaving goal number one to the end. That worked; we made fairly rapid progress throughout the other five goals.[1] We finally returned to the first goal and the compromise made to include the input items as objectives but not to enumerate them in the goal itself.

The other difficult goal was the second, on math and science. At Charlottesville, the agreement had been to have a goal on student performance on international achievement tests, especially in math and science. This issue was front and center because of interest generated by the Second International Math and Science Study, where U.S. students far underperformed students of many nations that the United States considered economic competitors.

The arguments on this item, although lengthy, were not as polarized as those around goal number one. In the end, it came down to whether the goal could be anything other than that U.S. students would be first in the world in math and science. After all, how could one say that the president and the nation's governors had agreed to settle for having U.S. students be third/fourth/fifth in the world? To do so would invite even more ridicule than saying first in the world. Everyone also agreed that goals are something that one strives for but may not always achieve; we all comforted ourselves that this was like Kennedy announcing that we would land a man on the moon when, at that time, there was no plan for how to do so.

The objectives were very crucial. They called for substantial increases in the numbers of math and science teachers, especially minorities and women, and for strengthening math and science education in the schools. Everyone felt that by our linking the objectives and the goal, people would see the complete picture. As it turned out, we were, of course, fooling ourselves. Once the goals were released, little attention was ever paid to the objectives, both because they did not lend themselves to slogans and because the goals panel paid them little attention.

Over the course of the following decade, no goal was more controversial than the one on math and science: it seemed both unrealistic—the United States was so far behind other nations in many areas—and jingoistic. However, as a result of this goal, the NSF made a substantial investment in improving the quality of academic programs and increasing the number of qualified math and science teachers. Although the United States still fared badly in the Third International Math and Science Study in the mid-1990s, it is significant to note that over this same period, performance on the math portion of the SAT exam for college admission improved, while verbal scores dropped. In August 2002, the *Wall Street Journal* attributed the increase in math scores in part to the actions taken by the NSF ("Math Score on SAT," 2002, p. B2).

The summit agreement about the third goal—student achievement and citizenship—was rather unclear: "the reduction of the dropout rate and the improvement of academic performance, especially among at-risk students." By the time it emerged from our crafting sessions it was a 68-word sentence calling for all students to learn challenging subject matter in "English, mathematics, science, foreign languages, civics and government, economics, arts, history, and geography." This goal was substantially expanded during one of our sessions, when Porter interrupted the meeting to take a call from Lynne Cheney, who wanted to weigh in against the use of the term *social studies,* because the term was imprecise and moreover, one could have a social studies curriculum without ever learning much history. The language was changed, and we substituted "civics and government, economics, history and geography." Art was added because there was, after all, a National Endowment for the Arts, an agency that paralleled that headed by Ms. Cheney.

In January, in his State of the Union address, Bush announced the goals. Clinton was present as his special guest. Shortly thereafter the goals were adopted by the NGA. The question then became, What do we do about them?

Part of the solution was the creation of the National Education Goals Panel, created in July 1990 through an executive order of the president. The panel comprised 14 people, four from the administration, six governors, two senators, and two congressmen. Several years later, four representatives of state legislatures were added.

The first chair of the goals panel, selected by the NGA, was Colorado Democratic governor Roy Romer. At that time, Romer was not well known for his interest in education. In fact, at the time of the appointment, there was another governor with a similar name, Buddy Roemer, of Louisiana, which caused some initial confusion.

Roy Romer's passion for learning and the interest he developed in education carried over when he left the governorship after three terms. In 2000, at the age of 71, Romer would become the superintendent of the Los Angeles Unified School District, the second largest district in the nation. After taking the job, he would say that it was the hardest job that he ever had (Roy Romer, personal conversation, fall 2000).

The job of the goals panel was to monitor and report on the goals to the American public. During its early days, the goals panel generated a great deal of interest: Its meetings were regularly broadcast on C-Span and were routinely attended by a sizeable audience, mostly Washington-based education association lobbyists, staff from various federal agencies, and reporters for the education trade press.

The goals panel established task forces for each goal, and many distinguished educators and policymakers served on them. The task forces functioned to educate the goals panel and those who reported on its activities. The panel itself also served as a valuable link between state and federal officials on issues related to the goals. Eventually, and despite strong early leadership, those who had been in office at the time of its creation moved on and their successors did not have the passion, interest or commitment to the panel, or in time, to the goals themselves. By 2002, the panel seemed to lose function, purpose, and direction and went out of existence when Congress refused to appropriate any money to fund it.

Despite the history of the goals panel, the goals were an important development in national policy. First, the goals were the device that brought Republicans and Democrats together around a common agenda. This had never happened before, aside from some rather superficial agreement at the time of the NDEA in 1958.

Second, the education summit and the goals served to change the education focus from inputs—books, student-teacher ratio, dollars—to outcomes: What is the education system producing? At what cost? How well prepared are those who graduate?

The national goals were the common agenda around which the business community and other civic organizations could rally. In fact, the mobilization of the business community during this time had a remarkable impact in a number of states, as well as at the national level. Business leadership, when exercised by people like Kent "Oz" Nelson of United Parcel Service

(UPS), John Hall of Ashland Oil, Lou Gerstner of IBM, Frank Shrontz of Boeing, and Ed Rust of State Farm Insurance, often provided the glue that held a common agenda together. This kept political leaders on task to finish what had been started.

The goals also provided a common agenda to which all those who influenced and governed the education community were committed, and convinced the education community that this was not a passing fad that would disappear with the next election.

In many states, (e.g., Maryland, Texas, Washington, Georgia, and Kentucky), the business groups kept new governors committed to the reforms. In almost every state, the fact that there were noneducation groups interested in a specific agenda for education reform changed the power equation, often providing a needed counterbalance to the influence of the teacher unions, school board associations, and superintendent groups and organizations like the Eagle Forum, which strongly objected to almost any state or federal curriculum direction.

The 1989 Charlottesville summit and the creation of the goals brought a national focus to education. The goals also were both the seeds of a new direction for the federal government and as yet another way to use the bully pulpit.

However, one could also argue that the goals themselves failed. Barry White, the OMB official who had been part of the goals-drafting group, said that the goals ultimately failed to achieve their promise because there was no implementation plan (Barry White, personal interview, May 7, 2002). Although they did gain public attention and provide a focus for education reformers, there was no coherent plan for how to achieve the goals. How, indeed, would the United States become "first in the world in math and science?" Who would play what role? Who would be accountable for what, with what resources?

THE GULF WAR AND A CHANGE IN EDUCATION LEADERSHIP

In July 1990, President Bush announced the creation of the goals panel. On August 2, Iraq invaded Kuwait, thereby forever shaping the course of the Bush presidency. For the following 6 months, the president's focus was on mounting a counterattack to force Iraq out of Kuwait, which began in February 1991.

In December 1990, in the middle of war preparations, Bush removed Lauro Cavazos from the secretary's job at the Department of Education and replaced him with Lamar Alexander. Cavazos had been an ineffective leader. He had not used the bully pulpit and had not grasped hold of the power and importance of the goals. His role at Charlottesville had been minimal.

Then president of the University of Tennessee and a former two-term governor of that state, Alexander had been an education leader in the NGA. Alexander was sworn into office in April 1991. He came in with a plan called America 2000, which aimed at building on the goals by establishing national academic standards in the subject areas and by creating national tests, all of them voluntary so as not to challenge the primacy of local control.

Alexander was the fifth education secretary and each had been unique. Shirley Hufstedler, Carter's choice, was a scholarly, somewhat removed, judge; Ted Bell was a wily ex-fed and ex-state official with the ability to operate below the radar to get things done; Bill Bennett was a bombastic, flamboyant person who loved the status and attention; Lauro Cavazos was miscast, an ex-university president with no taste for the pace and detail of Washington policymaking. Alexander had all the right credentials: political leader, academic leader, and as personally ambitious, although less theatrical, than Bill Bennett.

Alexander put together the Bush plan, which was also influenced by a recommendation of the President's Education Policy Advisory Panel (PEPAC), chaired by Paul O'Neill. In January 1991, PEPAC recommended to Bush the creation of national examinations for students in both elementary and secondary schools.

The Bush plan was very comprehensive. It called for establishing national—but not federal—standards in five core subjects; a system of voluntary examinations in the five core areas in grades 4, 8, and 12; and report cards on school, district, and state performance (Jennings, 1998, p. 19). Also included was the concept of school choice and the creation of "New American Schools." This last idea would, under the leadership of David Kearns, CEO of Xerox Corporation, become the basis for the development of the New American Schools Development Corporation. Kearns would become the deputy secretary of education upon his retirement from Xerox late that year.

The plan was announced with great fanfare by the president at the White House on April 18, 1991 ("Excerpts from Bush Administration Plans to Revamp Schools," 1991). It was hailed by those within and outside the education field. Al Shanker, president of the AFT, called it "bold and comprehensive. More so than any President or Secretary has come up with yet" ("Educators, Analysts Hail Strategies as Bold Departures," 1991). William Kohlberg, president of the National Alliance of Business, said, "The whole idea of getting business involved in funding new research and development efforts, not bound by past restrictions, is a very good notion" ("Educators, Analysts Hail Strategies as Bold Departures," 1991). Kohlberg was referring to the plan's idea of having business make a substantial investment in the development of new school models through the New American Schools Development Corporation.

Congress was not quite as enamored of the Bush plan. One part of the plan called for establishing a "New American School in 535 locations around the nation: one in every Congressional district; and an additional two, representing each state's two senators, in every state" ("White House Fact Sheet," 1991). It was attacked as blatantly political. Also, in the Bush plan was a proposal to use Chapter 1 (Title I) and Chapter 2 funds to provide certificates (read: vouchers) to disadvantaged students to use to attend private schools (Jennings, 1993, part 1).

A month later, Alexander announced a plan to appoint a council on national standards and testing to advise the administration. Representative Dale Kildee, a Democrat from Michigan who chaired the House subcommittee, convinced Alexander to create the National Council on Education Standards and Testing by congressional action. Alexander agreed, and, remarkably, in 5 weeks the bill passed through the House and Senate and was signed by the president.

Although the Bush administration sent its America 2000 legislation forward, the bill was not enacted. Hearings were held in the House and the Senate, with liberal Democrats on the House committee expressing great concern about standards and testing and school choice, conservative Republicans about the potential expansion of the federal role (Jennings, 1993, pp. 25–27).

During the hearing phase, Democrats in the House became interested in the concept of "systemic reform," put forward by Marshall Smith and Jennifer O'Day at Stanford and the Consortium for Policy Research in Education, a policy research center supported by the Office of Educational Research and Improvement (OERI).

Systemic reform had also been endorsed by the NGA, among others (Jennings, 1993, p. 26). It was based on the sound observation that the nation would not achieve significant advances in student performance unless the system aligned curriculum with standards, assessments, teacher training, and resource allocation. Systemic reform also contained another idea that would prove divisive, the concept of school delivery standards, later to be renamed opportunity-to-learn standards.

The logic behind opportunity-to-learn standards was that neither schools nor students should be held responsible for learning if schools did not have the resources to teach their students the material that would be assessed. Although this seemed a simple, commonsense concept, critics across the political spectrum saw it as being something that schools would use to evade accountability, as they believed it would be fiscally impossible to provide every resource required for every standard.

The controversy over this provision, and another that called for "certificates" (vouchers) for students in poorly performing schools were enough to slow House and Senate committee passage of the bill until the following year, 1992.

ANOTHER PRESIDENTIAL ELECTION: ANOTHER VERSION OF REFORM

More than 2 years had passed since the 1989 Charlottesville event and the announcement of the National Education Goals, yet there had been no action by Congress. An important factor in the failure of Congress to act was because no Senator or Representative from the congressional education committees had been invited to the summit. Even though the damage had been somewhat repaired by placing four congressional representatives on the goals panel, this did not erase the earlier slight. All politics are based to a large degree on personal relationships, and education is not exempt from this reality.

Then there was the matter of philosophy and politics. Congress was controlled by Democrats, and the idea of vouchers was just not acceptable to the teachers unions and other mainline public school education groups who provided much of the Democrat's political support.

In the second session of Congress, the Democrats countered with their own bill, the Neighborhood Schools Improvement Act, a somewhat sanitized version of the Bush proposals. The Senate version, S.2, was the first bill passed by the Senate in 1992 (Ambach, 1993, p. 43). The bill authorized $800 million in the first year for schoolwide restructuring, codified the National Education Goals, authorized the development of voluntary national content tests in math and science, and created authority for a number of states and districts to waive certain regulations in the administration of federal programs. It contained no authority for vouchers. Just prior to the August recess, the bill passed the House by a vote of 279-124.

For this bill, the fatal blow was struck in the Senate—where it failed to get the 60 votes needed to close debate on the conference report—rather than in the House Rules Committee, the graveyard of so many earlier bills. Conservative senators worried about expanding the federal role, and the Bush administration was peeved that the final bill contained neither the school choice nor the New American Schools provisions (Jennings, 1998,

p. 31). With the session ending so senators could go home for elections, the bill died. In the end, there was little enthusiasm for its passage.

Three years after the Charlottesville summit, there still had been no legislative action to codify or implement the goals. The bipartisanship that had been present at the summit had not carried over to Congress, largely because the agenda had become distorted. Vouchers—called "baby Pell grants," by Alexander—and the rest of the America 2000 baggage was simply more than people had bargained for. Although America 2000 had been cloaked in the National Education Goals, it had merely used them as a stepping stone to achieve other objectives—objectives seen as too partisan and inconsistent with the spirit of the summit.

THE EMERGENCE OF STANDARDS

Absent any legislation, Alexander pushed ahead using his discretionary fund to develop standards. With noted education historian Diane Ravitch leading the effort in OERI, grants were made to a number of organizations for the development of voluntary national subject matter standards. Some were more successful than others.

A grant that had been given to the National Council of Teachers of English was canceled when it became clear that the council would not produce what the administration sought in specificity and rigor. The history standards, originally funded by Lynne Cheney at the NEH through a grant to the National Center on History in the Schools at UCLA, were extremely controversial when released in 1994; so controversial that the U.S. Senate voted 99-1 to condemn them for being biased and not containing enough American history. Grants were made by the Pew Charitable Trusts and the Ford Foundation to the Council for Basic Education to convene expert panels to recommend changes for a revised second edition. The American history panel was chaired by Al Quie, a CBE board member, who had earlier been a key House education leader, a governor, and a member of the panel that produced *A Nation at Risk*.

The first set of voluntary standards had been produced in 1989 by the National Council of Teachers of Mathematics. For months after he became secretary of education, Alexander would invariably take a copy of the NCTM standards with him when he made a speech, to illustrate that it was possible to create good standards.

As each set of standards was produced, it was widely distributed and came to be frequently used by states and local districts as they adopted their own standards. A few million dollars—a relatively small federal in-

vestment—had produced an enormous impact. The fact that these standards were voluntary and not produced directly by the federal government
allowed them to be accepted with few political repercussions.

The federal role had taken on a new dimension.

THE 1992 ELECTION: BUSH IS OUT, CLINTON IS IN; CHANGE, BUT NOT MUCH

The 1992 presidential elections were unusual in many ways. When the Gulf
War ended in 1991, Bush had an approval rating above 80%; Clinton was
governor of a small, impoverished southern state, and was far less liberal
than most of the leadership in his own party. And then there was Ross
Perot. An independent, Perot would be a spoiler, a loose cannon in the
race. Perot was a veteran of the education-reform wars, having chaired a
reform commission in Texas that proposed, among other things, that high
school athletes who failed courses should not be permitted to play football.

Education was a topic of discussion at the second presidential debate
at the University of Richmond, which was, ironically, only about an hour's
drive from Charlottesville, where Bush and Clinton had praised each other
in 1989. Both major party platforms contained sections on education, neither side taking especially radical positions. During the campaign, all three
candidates endorsed the development of voluntary national standards and
voluntary national examinations.

In the end, Clinton's charm, the fact that Republicans had held the
presidency for 12 years, Bush's inability to shed his New England reserve,
an economy viewed as being in deep trouble, and the incumbent's inability
to project a vision led to Clinton's victory. Although Clinton received 45
million popular votes, the combined total of his opponents—Bush with 39
million, Perot almost 20 million—meant that almost 15 million people had
voted for someone other than Clinton. The Electoral College vote, however, was more than 2-to-1 for Clinton, 370–165-0. Perot would run again
in 1996, but would get only 8 million popular votes.

Whereas Clinton's election changed the occupancy of the White House,
the education agenda remained committed to the National Education Goals
and the ideal of high standards of learning for all children. Issues like
vouchers were dropped, but Clinton and Bush agreed on ideas such as
merit pay for teachers. Clinton also liked the idea of the New American
Schools Development Corporation—although as a private nonprofit, not
one funded by the government—and supported "EdFlex," the ability of
states to waive most federal program regulations if doing so would better
deliver of an education program and improve student achievement. This

was exactly in step with the NGA's position in its 1986 NGA report, *A Time for Results*, issued when Clinton and Lamar Alexander, Bush's education secretary, had been members of that group.

To make the point about agreement with the Bush proposals even stronger, the Clinton proposal was called the Goals 2000: Educate America Act. To head the Department of Education, Clinton, like Bush, named a former governor, this time Richard Riley from South Carolina. Riley had served two terms in that state, where he had convinced the voters to add a "penny for education" to the state's sales tax. In fact, he and Clinton were two men for whom the title Education Governor really fit. They had worked together in the NGA on education reform. Riley, a close Clinton ally, would serve the full 8 years as secretary, far outlasting any of the others, including Ted Bell, who had served just over 4 years.

There were three other key people on the Clinton education policy team who would play significant roles in helping designing the Clinton proposals. The first was Marshall (Mike) Smith, dean of the school of education at Stanford University. Earlier, Smith served as assistant commissioner for policy under Ernie Boyer (the last appointed commissioner of education) and as chief of staff to Shirley Hufstetler, the first secretary. As previously noted, Smith was coauthor, with Jennifer O'Day, of the landmark paper that had laid out the concept of systemic reform (Smith & O'Day, 1991, pp. 233–267). The second key person was Thomas Payzant, the department's assistant secretary for elementary and secondary education. Payzant came to that post from the superintendency in San Diego and would leave after 3 years to become the Boston superintendent.

The third was White House policy person on education, Mike Cohen. Cohen had been at the NGA at the time of the Charlottesville summit. Cohen would become assistant secretary for elementary and secondary education near the end of the Clinton presidency. While Clinton and Riley were both very much involved in the development of the Goals 2000 plan, Smith, Payzant, and Cohen handled matters on a daily basis.

As a strong sign of the importance of education to Clinton, the Goals 2000 bill was the first legislative proposal sent forth by the new administration, a phenomenon that was repeated 8 years later, by Clinton's successor.

In little more than a decade, education as a national issue had gone from being slated for elimination to becoming the first priority of a new administration. No longer were there any serious attempts to eliminate the federal agency; no longer was the education budget targeted for major reductions. In fact, by the end of the Clinton presidency, Republicans and Democrats were vying to see who could add the most money to programs like special education, with a Democratic president being put in the position of urging restraint.

Clinton's Goals 2000 proposal ran headlong into opposition from the left side of his own party and from conservatives in both parties who saw Goals 2000 as the devil incarnate for advocating proposals, such as the creation of the National Education Standards and Improvement Council (NESIC). The situation reached its zenith in both zealotry and humor when a Montana newspaper ran a story about a woman who had appeared at a meeting about Goals 2000 claiming to have been "a Goals 2000 sex slave."

Most of the congressional Democrats were being pushed hard by civil rights organizations and the teacher unions to back away from the concept of outcomes as the measure of success, by placing less emphasis on tests and a greater focus on opportunity-to-learn standards.

In classic political terms, the issue made for some pretty strange bedfellows. Hill Republicans were aligned with both Phyllis Schlafly of the Eagle Forum and Al Shanker of the AFT. The issue was so hot politically that *Roll Call*, the Capitol Hill weekly newspaper, devoted a special section to it, with articles authored by Riley, Ravitch, Goodling, and others.

In his article, Riley noted that it had been 10 years since *A Nation at Risk*, and suggested that Goals 2000 would give the nation a new plan. Riley also mentioned that the bill promised $400 million in aid to states and local communities to develop action plans and implement reform strategies" ("Secretary of Education Richard Riley," 1993, p. 15).

Goodling said, "President Clinton and Secretary Riley's school reform vision has been shanghaied by those who think the school reform movement is not worth our support and that all we should be concerned about is making sure schools get the resources they are due. . . . [S]ome Democrats on the Education and Labor Committee have brought us the same old wine (all we need is more money) in a new bottle (opportunity to learn standards)" ("Secretary of Education Richard Riley," 1993, p. 16). Ravitch commented that NESIC would "function much like a national school board . . . dominated by professional educators" (p. 21).

Another complication arose when House Democrats decided that they were going to tamper with the original goals by adding two more—one related to teachers, the other to parents. The administration, the governors, and the business community all opposed the move, as a great deal of time, effort, and expense had been devoted to having people know and understand the first six. Their objections were to no avail; in the end it was simply too politically difficult to argue against goals for parents and about teachers.

The degree of discord between the president and congressional Democrats was best illustrated by the rather extraordinary letter that Clinton sent to Congressman William Ford (Michigan), who had become chair of the House Education and Labor Committee upon the retirement of Augustus Hawkins. In the June 3, 1993, letter, just prior to committee markup of the bill, Clinton urged rejection of all amendments that would modify the goals, require states to adopt opportunity-to-learn standards or alter the composition of the goals panel. This followed an even more unusual letter sent to Ford by 11 committee Democrats urging that he slow consideration of the bill—a very odd request coming, as it did, from members of his and the president's own party (Jennings, 1998, p. 46).

The letter to Ford was initiated by Representative George Miller, a California Democrat, who was a senior member of the committee and the chair of another House committee. The letter was in clear violation of the informal rules of the House and a direct slap at both Clinton and Ford. Eight years later, Miller, then the senior Democrat on the committee, would end up playing a very different leadership role in the consideration of the No Child Left Behind Act.

The Clinton Goals 2000 bill finally reached the House floor in October 1993, after the administration and Democratic leaders had agreed on a package of amendments. Passage was by a vote of 307-118; the primary opposition was from Republicans, who advocated vouchers. In the Senate, the bill passed on February 8, 1994, and the conference report was adopted in both houses and signed by the president in late March.

The bill had nearly been derailed by amendments to permit school prayer, offered in the Senate on several occasions by North Carolina Republican Jesse Helms. When the conference report came back to the House, conservatives attempted to recommit the bill to conference, since it did not contain the Helms amendment requiring that districts permit "constitutionally protected" prayer. The Helms amendment was adopted by a vote of 75-22 in the Senate and the House had instructed its conferees by a vote of 367–55 to accept the Senate language (Jennings, 1998, p. 102). Because House motions to instruct conferees are not binding, the conferees altered the Helms language to meet the concerns of civil rights and education lobbyists.

The attempt to recommit lost by 37 votes, 195-232, and the conference report was adopted, 306-121. Here, yet again, the interplay of social issues—in this case religion—had become a major factor in the consideration of an education bill. Although this time not a fatal amendment, as it had so often been in earlier years, education was once again a magnet, drawing social issues in a predictable manner.

Thus, 3½ years after Charlottesville, the goals became law, though in a different form than that adopted by the governors. Their tortured path was marked by two contested bills and a presidential election that produced a change in administrations. By the time the goals became law, several new governors had been elected and the rather contentious battles over

America 2000 and Goals 2000 had dimmed the luster and the promise of that 1989 summit. Still, the goals were genuinely bipartisan and they were having an impact. Every battle had come when attempts were made to festoon the dignity and grace of the goals with loosely related political agendas, such as the Bush-Alexander 535 new schools and Clinton-Riley's NESIC.

The Goals 2000 bill did encourage states to develop voluntary plans to adopt goals, as well as standards and assessments, by sweetening the pot with $420 million in grants, most of which was to be passed down to local districts based upon their improvement plans.

THE 1994 ESEA AMENDMENTS: THE CLINTON STRATEGY UNFOLDS

Delays in the enactment of Goals 2000 were also causing complications for the coming cycle of ESEA reauthorizations, as the Clinton strategy called for linking these two efforts.

The greatest danger was that the Congress would choose to further delay the Goals 2000 bill and then include it in whole or in part in ESEA. That would have meant the loss of any special attention for the goals and the possibility that money for reform would have simply been used to increase Title I grants.

Another danger was that failure to sequence the bills might eliminate the mechanism to virtually force states to make mandatory the standards, assessments, and curriculum changes that were "voluntarily" contained in Goals 2000 by linking them with the receipt of Title I funds. As policy analysts Michael Kirst and James Guthrie said:

> The Clinton administration, in its Goals 2000 legislation, suggests that states "voluntarily" establish curriculum and performance standards. However, that is not the main news. The blockbuster headline is that administration policy wonks have also invented a means for gaining powerful federal government leverage in the education reform movement.
>
> The lever to enforce state and local school district compliance with national standards is embedded in proposed amendments to (ESEA) Chapter 1. States that are either unable or unwilling to adopt curricular and performance standards will risk losing their Chapter 1 funding. . . .
>
> If successful, the Clinton plan will alter Chapter 1, minimizing its long-standing regulatory and fiscal accounting outlook and transforming it into a powerful administrative instrument for fundamentally changing the U.S. public school system. (Kirst & Guthrie, 1994, p. 158)

As we will see, however, the theory would be put in place through the link that Kirst and Guthrie describe, but the plan would never achieve its promise.

The plan was to get Goals 2000 enacted in 1993 to clear the way for the ESEA reauthorization. This was vitally important to Clinton and his administration, since Goals 2000 was the framework for all that was to follow.

As action on Goals 2000 dragged on throughout the summer and into the fall of 1993, pressure mounted for the administration to unveil its plans for ESEA. Finally, on September 14, the administration released its plan, which included the link to Chapter 1 (renamed Title I in the proposal). The announcement came just a few weeks before the Goals 2000 bill went to House floor; a move that might have backfired had criticism of the link and the potential for withholding Title I money been too great.

Fortunately, the way had been cleared by a number of reports, which added weight to the administration's efforts to focus on student achievement. Most important of these efforts was the Commission on Chapter 1, chaired by David Hornbeck. Its report had been critical of the fact that most Chapter 1 programs focused on low-level rote learning and that there was no accountability in the programs for improving student learning.

The report of the Hornbeck-led group began by saying:

> It is time to reinvent the Chapter 1 (Title I) program. . . . It is time to align the Chapter 1 program with larger reforms in developing higher standards for student performance and accountability. Chapter 1 must be a strong partner in promoting systemic change. (U.S. Department of Education, undated, p. 1)

Phyllis McClure, a member of that commission and a staff member for the NAACP Legal Defense Fund, was quoted in *Congressional Quarterly* as saying the administration's "whole approach is very much like the commission's approach, focusing on outcomes and results" ("Clinton Would Tie Federal Aid," 1993, p. 2394).

Representative Dale Kildee, a Michigan Democrat and chair of the House subcommittee on elementary and secondary education, called the Clinton plan "the most well thought-out reauthorization proposal that I have seen in my 17 years in Congress" (Pitsch, 1993).

Most surprising was the reaction of Representative William Goodling, from Pennsylvania and ranking Republican on the House committee. Not only was Goodling among the 17 cosponsors of the bill, saying that he "particularly liked the link to school reform concepts. "The whole idea of excellence is one that I've been pushing for ages" ("Clinton Would Tie Federal Aid," 1993, p. 2394). In fact, all the major Republican congressional education leadership supported the bill—at first. In a joint letter sent September 24, 1993, and signed by Senators Jeffords and Kassenbaum, as well as Representatives Goodling, Cunningham, and McKeon, they noted that Clinton shared their goals of high standards, flexibility, and program consolidation.

The Clinton proposal was quite sweeping, incorporating as it did several other major changes. The eight primary elements of the Clinton proposals for Chapter 1/Title I were as follows:

1. Require states to develop content and performance standards for all children. These standards were to be for the same academic subjects as those enumerated in Goals 2000.
2. The replacement of generic multiple choice tests for Chapter 1 students with ones that were aligned to the standards, creating coherence between standards and assessments.
3. Lower the threshold for "school-wide" Chapter 1 programs from schools where 75 percent of the population is low income to schools where 65 percent [is low income]. This change would further minimize the use of "pull-out" programs.
4. Forbid use of Chapter 1 money to teach low-level skills.
5. Change the distribution formula so that schools with 75 percent or more poor students would get funded before money was distributed to other schools.
6. Require schools to screen children for health and nutritional problems in schools where at least 50 percent of the students are low income.
7. Target money on districts with the highest poverty rates, increasing the percent of Title I money so allocated from 10 percent to 50 percent.
8. Require that districts allocate dollars to schools on the basis of poverty, rather than student achievement, so as to remove any disincentive for schools to raise student performance, thus losing Chapter 1 money. ("Clinton Would Tie Federal Aid," 1993, p. 2395)

The bill was called the Improving America's Schools Act (IASA). Even though it was signed into law in October 1994, about a year after Clinton sent forward his proposals—a relatively fast pace for such a major bill—and one month before the Democrats would lose control of both Houses of Congress for the first time since the 1950s—the battles that ensued in getting it enacted were often bitter.

To most members of the House and Senate—committee members or not—the major issue of IASA were the changes that would result in concentrating more money in school districts with higher concentrations of low-income students. Because that would mean a loss of money to most Congressional districts, it was doomed in its original form from the start. In politics, as House Speaker Tip O'Neill used to say, "All politics is local." Voting for a bill that might take money away from some or all of the schools in one's congressional district or state was not going to happen. The requirements related to high standards and accountability were little debated, perhaps because of "standards fatigue" from the Goals 2000 legislation that had just passed, and most members of Congress simply did not understand the Clinton strategy.

When the House began consideration of the bill in 1994, the administration's funding formula was quickly defeated by a vote of 12-14. As John F. Jennings noted in his book on Goals 2000 and IASA, that was the high point of support for the Clinton formula change (Jennings, 1998, p. 121).

While the grants consolidation proposal had been removed in the House subcommittee, it was restored in a vote in the full committee in an attempt to win Republican support. Representative Major Owens, a New York Democrat, checkmated that move when he proposed his successful amendment to require that states develop opportunity-to-learn standards in addition to content and student performance standards. That split the committee right down partisan lines, and the bill was reported out on an absolute partisan vote, 29-14.

Goodling and several colleagues launched a major attack on the bill and succeeded in getting the Owens amendment watered down so that the sting was gone. That change was enough so that on March 24, 1994, 45 Republicans joined with 243 Democrats in final passage of the bill, 289–128, in the House—one month after floor debate had begun (Jennings, 1998, p. 125).

During that month, most of the time on the House floor had been consumed with debates over the usual variety of social issues having little or nothing to do with education: prayer, illegal immigration, sex education, smoking, and homosexuality. As *Congressional Quarterly* noted in its story on House passage, a smaller percentage of Republicans—19%—voted for the ESEA reauthorization in 1994 than had supported the bill at the time of its passage 30 years earlier, 27%. In fact, 99% had supported the bill at the time of the last reauthorization in 1988 (Jennings, 1998).

In the Senate, the fight was all about the formula, although Kennedy never pushed the administration's proposal. An attempt by Minnesota Democrat Paul Wellstone to adopt an Owens-like opportunity-to-learn requirement was defeated; Kennedy led the opposition, arguing that inclusion would assure a major floor fight in the Senate.

When the bill came to the floor in late July, the fight was about money. High growth states, like California and Texas, wanted more and claimed that the committee bill favored the Northeast—not surprising given the roles of people like Kennedy and Jeffords.

Kennedy acquiesced, knowing that he would lose a floor vote, and a formula was adopted to give 38 growth states an increase (Jennings, 1998, p. 131).

As was the case in the House, the Senate spent a great deal of time on social issues, with Helms and his school prayer amendments being most prominent. Also proposed were the usual array of other issues for which an education bill served as a convenient platform. Few other pieces of legislation allowed so many people to raise so many social issues in so short a time with so much visibility.

There was one Senate amendment, actually germane to the bill, which provoked a great deal of attention. John Danforth, a Missouri Republican and a former Episcopalian priest, offered and had adopted an amendment to permit single-sex schools in the belief that many teenagers functioned better academically in these settings. Because Danforth was a liberal, his sponsorship meant a great deal and caused great consternation among civil rights lobbyists, nearly all of whom adopted a "camel's-nose-under-the-tent" approach to any amendment, no matter how sensible (Jennings, 1998, p. 136).

The bill passed the Senate just prior to the August 1994 recess, 94-6; only a small band of conservative Republicans did not support the bill.

Conference agreement and final passage were once again racing the clock toward adjournment; 1994 was an election year and a potentially difficult conference on the Title I formula was still ahead.

Surprisingly, the conference lasted only one week. The compromise formula was that only new money would be concentrated on high-poverty districts and there would be a separate authorization to reward states that more equitably distributed their core school funding. Stripped from the bill were amendments on gun possession, school prayer, condom distribution, and homosexuality. Also eliminated was the weakened form of the Owen's opportunity-to-learn amendment and a Kassebaum amendment limiting Title I standards to reading and math (Jennings, 1998, p. 136). Retained was the single-sex school amendment, an amendment on unfunded mandates, and a weak school prayer compromise.

On September 30, 1994, the House passed the conference report after an effort to recommit the bill to conference on the school prayer issue failed, 184-215, a margin very close to that of an earlier attempt earlier that year to recommit the Goals 2000 bill. Final passage was 262-132, with only 31 Republicans voting for it—a reduction of more than 30% in the number who had supported the House bill. Although the formula fight had certainly cost the bill some support, social issues were prominent in the final vote and, again, religion (school prayer) was the most important issue of all.

The following week, the Senate took up the conference report and, after a cloture vote, passed it, 77–20, with the Republican vote being almost evenly divided—21 for, 20 against (Jennings, 1998, p. 148).

On October 20, 1994, President Clinton signed the bill at a school in Framingham, Massachusetts. Kennedy was in a tough reelection campaign and this was a real boost for him, coming as it did 2 weeks before the election.

OPENING A NEW ERA IN EDUCATION REFORM

The significance of the 1994 bill is hard to overstate. A major corner had been turned; the federal government was now firmly involved in the education program of what was happening in almost every district in the nation through Goals 2000 and the ESEA requirements for new standards and assessments.

Significantly, a new, yet surprisingly simple, framework had emerged from the federal government, one that linked standards, testing, teacher training, curriculum, and accountability in what was termed systemic reform. The theoretician driving this reform was Mike Smith, deputy secretary of education and a veteran of the education policy wars for over three decades.

Working with Mike Cohen of the White House staff and with his own extensive set of contacts in the research and policy worlds, Smith had crafted the concept and had done a thorough job in selling the approach far and wide.

It was a very straightforward concept: Adults in the system must be held accountable for performance, but performance must be based on academic content and performance standards developed and adopted at the state level. Curriculum must be developed that ensures that the standards are taught, and teachers trained to teach that material. Finally, new tests must be developed that are carefully aligned to the standards, which in turn must be reflected in the curriculum, and adults (and students) must be held accountable for children's learning the material. Even the latter element was new to many educators, who had previously felt responsible only for teaching the material, not for whether children were in fact learning it.

Although the federal government provided only about 7% of the total spending on elementary and secondary education, the Clinton strategy is a perfect example of how that relatively small contribution can be used to leverage major change. States and districts were under tremendous pressure not to lose the federal revenue since it often accounts for all or most of the money not obligated for regular teacher salaries, overhead, and facilities.

In the wake of the passage of Goals 2000, some states, including Virginia, said that they would not accept funds under that act because of the requirements set forth in the law. Their opposition crumbled fairly quickly so that within 2 years, 48 states had accepted Goals 2000 grants.

Whereas the 1965 passage of the ESEA in the Johnson administration had broken the logjam that had heretofore prevented the enactment of any truly significant programs for elementary and secondary education, the 1994 law placed the federal government in the position of setting the agenda for almost every school district and every state in the nation. The federal government had moved from being a passive actor, providing resources, research, and some guidance, to being a partner that provided the intellectual framework for school reform and education improvement.

This change, one that would be magnified in the No Child Left Behind law in 2001, happened because federal policymakers were observing consistent erosion in student performance, especially by students who were poor and racial minorities.

Although states would often say that they did not pay much attention to the federal law, in reality they did—even if ever so slowly. In fact, the failure of states to move in a more expeditious manner would lay the basis for what would transpire when George W. Bush was elected and forged a bipartisan agreement in support of his plan.

THE CLINTON REFORM HITS THE GINGRICH WALL: CLINTON BOUNCES BACK

Within weeks of the passage of the 1994 amendments, a sea change in politics took place in Washington when the Republicans swept to victory in the off-year Congressional elections, putting both Houses of Congress in the hands of the GOP for the first time since early in the Eisenhower administration.

Newt Gingrich, a firebrand member of the Republican House leadership and a representative from suburban Atlanta, Georgia, was the architect behind the Republican "Contract with America," which consisted of 10 bills that signers pledged to enact within the first 100 days of the 104th Congress. The contract also contained several provisions that would significantly alter the way that the House operated, limiting committee chairs to three terms, cutting the number of committees and staff, and banning the use of proxy voting in committees.

Clinton had been lucky. Both of his major bills for elementary and secondary education were safely enacted before he lost his congressional working majority, but that did not protect those now-enacted programs from attack.

Coming on the heels of Goals 2000 and the 1994 ESEA amendments, the momentum for repeal was strong, especially among Republican conservatives, who were now in the driver's seat with Gingrich's ascendancy to Speaker of the House. Appropriations for education were cut below what

Clinton requested by the House. Twice, block grant bills passed the Senate on a bipartisan vote—as well as once in the House on a more party-line vote—and attempts were made to repeal Goals 2000. Almost all these efforts failed, largely because Clinton either vetoed or threatened to veto these bills. One that did become law over Clinton's veto was a tax code amendment creating education savings accounts with the same tax advantages as retirement savings plans.

Another bill that passed in 1995 was the repeal of the Goals 2000 section that established the NESIC, the organization created to review the voluntary submission of state standards. The bill was pushed through by Representative Bill Goodling, chair of the House Education and Workforce Committee, after a number of conservatives called it a potential "national school board." The Clinton administration had supported the repeal, in no small part as a way to save Goals 2000, which was also a target for repeal (Jennings, 1998, p. 159).

The real action and controversy during 1995 and 1996 was, however, over the budget, and not just the education budget. Clinton and Gingrich led warring armies of supporters, each side intent on having the last word. Appropriation bill after appropriation bill was sent to the White House, with most returned with veto messages attached. So contentious was the situation that on several occasions virtually the entire federal government was shut down—offices, national parks, research labs—everything save a few exempted services.

At one point in 1995, the House eliminated all Goals 2000 funding and moved to make other major cuts in education funding. Although a moderate coalition of Senate Republicans, many in key leadership roles, prevented that from occurring, the partisanship on education in the House was as severe as anything seen in decades.

"THIS IS A POLITICAL ISSUE, NOT A RATIONAL ISSUE": THE ROLE OF THE BUSINESS COMMUNITY

The business community turned out to be a major moderating force in policy circles. Since being challenged and energized in 1989 by President Bush, the organizations representing business simply refused to play partisan games. They had an agenda for reform; they were committed at the state, local, and national levels, and they insisted that the political leaders stay the course. Especially influential at this time was the Business Coalition for Education Reform, which included the Business Roundtable, the U.S. Chamber of Commerce, the National Alliance for Business, the Hispanic Chamber of Commerce, the National Association of Manufacturers, and similar national organizations.

The business leaders—people like Oz Nelson of UPS, Joe Gorman of TRW, Lou Gerstner of IBM, and John Pepper of Proctor & Gamble—found sympathetic listeners among moderate lawmakers at the national level and among governors of both parties.

In the summer of 1995, Gerstner spoke at the NGA meeting in Vermont. As a result of that appearance, and the fact that there had been a major turnover in governors since the 1989 summit, plans were made for a new summit, this time, a joint effort of the business community and the governors. Wisconsin Republican governor Tommy Thompson became Gerstner's cochair and the meeting was set for March 1996 at the IBM training facility in Palisades, New York. Thompson was chair of both the NGA and the Education Commission of the States.

Governors' attendance at this second summit was strong—40%—although the governors of both New York and California were absent. Forty-nine business leaders also attended, a testament to Gerstner's prestige among his fellow CEOs ("Summit Accord," 1996).

Educators were there, unlike at Charlottesville, but as "advisers," not as equals. Although there was a rift when a small band of conservative Republican governors, led by Pennsylvania's Tom Ridge, demanded changes in the final document, a joint statement did emerge, calling for continued progress in the area of standards, assessments, and—given Gerstner's influence—the use of technology in schools.

Whereas Charlottesville had been a creation of the Bush administration, Palisades I (there were to be summits in 1999 and 2001), was anything but White House driven. Riley attended but he did not speak. Clinton came on the 2nd day and used the meeting to talk about the need for national tests, although he had no specific proposal to advocate.

At the opening of this summit, a rather extraordinary exchange took place between Paul O'Neill, the CEO of Alcoa and Gerstner. Having gained recognition, O'Neill, in his tell-it-like-it-is style, asked why the United States could not have national standards, rather than having each state create its own, noting that Alcoa had employees in many states and that "nine times nine should produce the same number in all states." Trying to quiet him, and in an unguarded moment of candor, Gerstner said, "Paul, this is a political issue, not a rational issue."

Although Gerstner's statement provoked laughter, it was an apt description of what was taking place in Washington at that time. It was all about politics, all about positioning for political advantage. As later events would show, O'Neill's candor and openness would undo his effectiveness when he became secretary of the Treasury in 2001.

THE 1996 ELECTIONS AND CLINTON'S NEW PROPOSALS

Nineteen ninety-six was also a major election year. Clinton was seeking a second term and the GOP was trying to hold on to its majorities in Congress. The Republican candidate was Bob Dole, a Senator from Kansas and majority leader. For education, 1996 was a defining year on the national level.

The GOP platform again called for elimination of the U.S. Department of Education, and for federal support of private school vouchers, paid for through a reduction in spending on programs for public schools. The Democrats talked about the importance of education and slammed the GOP for cutting funding.

Public opinion polls were remarkably consistent in showing that voters favored the Democrats on education, often by as much as a 2-1 margin. In the first debate between Clinton and Dole, on October 6, education was an issue. Clinton talked about how the Republican budget would cut programs—he mentioned 50,000 fewer kids in Head Start—while Dole talked about doing away with the education department.

The election was not close. Clinton got 49% of the vote in a three-way race, Dole 41%, and Perot 8%. The Electoral College margin was 379-159. It was a clear victory for Clinton and education had been his issue.

Although the GOP retained control of the House, its margin was reduced. The GOP gained slightly in the Senate. This election marked the high point of Republican opposition to federal spending on education and removed the elimination of the education department as an issue. Every analysis showed that Republicans had lost votes because of their position on education, which simply did not play well with "soccer moms," the business community, or vast numbers of Americans who saw themselves as centrists. In fact, within a year, Republicans were vying with Democrats to add money for education programs and Clinton was faced each year in his second term with appropriations bills for education larger than the ones he had proposed—a fate that had heretofore had usually been reserved for Republican presidents.

Clinton's ideas about national testing were mentioned in his State of the Union message in 1997. He proposed the creation of voluntary national tests—reading in fourth grade, math in eighth grade. In fact, in this speech, Clinton laid out a 10-point education program, including tutoring assistance, after-school programs, and the addition of 100,000 new teachers so that class sizes in the lower grades could be reduced.

The testing proposal was based on the concept that all children should be able to read well by the fourth grade and that a mastery of math by the eighth grade was essential if a child was to succeed in postsecondary education or in a well-paying job. Clinton's proposal was apparently sparked at least in part by his January visit to a school in suburban Chicago. Schools in that district and several adjacent ones had voluntarily taken the Third International Math and Science Study (TIMSS) international math and science tests, and done quite well. Clinton became convinced that it was vital that educators and parents be able to benchmark the education they were receiving (*Education Daily*, February 5, 1997, p. 1).

Educators were reported to be "energized and anxious" about Clinton's reforms. The *Washington Post* reported:

> Yesterday, school officials nationwide said that they were dazzled by the extraordinary emphasis that Clinton put on improving education in his State of the Union address. His call for tougher standards, an army of reading tutors, tax breaks for college tuition, and heaps of aid for school repairs and classroom technology is precisely the kind of support many educators have been longing for from Washington.
>
> But key parts of Clinton's plan could give the federal government a role in education that states, which revere the distinctly American tradition of controlling schools locally, tend to treat suspiciously. Even the pace at which Clinton is seeking to accomplish his agenda poses risks of disappointment. School reform is notoriously slow, and it often falls short of the great expectations parents and educators have. ("President's $51 Billion Dollar 'Crusade,'" 1997)

The Clinton proposal on testing set off a firestorm among conservatives who saw this as yet another Clinton attempt to exert federal control over the schools. This was especially ironic because George H. W. Bush had talked about a similar plan a few years earlier.

Congressional Republicans, led by Goodling, were in fierce opposition, refusing to even consider the legislation. This was the same Goodling who had cosponsored Clinton's ESEA bill in 1993. On March 11, 1997, Goodling was quoted in the *Washington Times* on this testing proposal: "It would be a big mistake. They are going to need Congress to sell their constituencies on anything having to do with national tests or standards, and if they don't go that route, what happened in health care will certainly repeat itself" ("GOP Warns Clinton," 1997, p. 1). In fact, a Wall Street Journal–NBC News national poll published on March 14 found that on the question of whether the federal government should be involved in a national reading test, the public was almost evenly split: 49% in favor, 47% opposed. This was in striking contrast to 81% of adults who generally favored the Clinton proposals ("Clinton's Initiatives," 1997, p. R3).

Part of what was going on was directly related to the pressure on Goodling from Gingrich and the right, which controlled the House Republican leadership; part was an effort to position education as an issue for the next election, as both parties saw it as important even if their positions were often in polar opposition.

By April, Goodling was locked into virtually total opposition to Clinton on the idea of testing individual students, the core of the Clinton proposal. *U.S. News & World Report* said that Goodling "now objects to testing that would produce results for specific students and school districts. He wants results compiled only on a state level" ("Testing," 1997, p. 40).

This was also having an impact on the administration of Goals 2000 and the ESEA. Because NESIC had never been created—largely because of Republican opposition—and to avoid a firestorm of opposition to all of Clinton's efforts, officials in the Department of Education began to adopt a posture of liberally interpreting the two 1994 laws. Rather than judging the quality of standards—a role that NESIC would have had—the department basically allowed any state submission to pass as long as the process steps had been followed, or states were granted waivers to give them a long period to comply.

The 1994 amendments had set forth a long time line to allow states to come into compliance with the statute's implementation requirements for standards and assessments. For example, new aligned assessments were not required to be in place until the 2000 school year. Even with that deadline, in January 2001, more than 6 years after the law had been enacted, Mike Cohen, then the assistant secretary for elementary and secondary education, reported that only 17 states were expected to be in full compliance. The slowness of states to act, combined with the long time line for compliance, would become the fuel to feed the push in 2001 for an even more radical overhaul in federal education programs.

Again, the business community swung into action. More than 200 high-tech business leaders met with the president in April 1997 to express their support for his program (Jennings, 1998, p. 179).

This time, however, the business community's support was not enough. The governors were divided, although not always by party, and conservative interest groups, like Phyllis Schlafly's Eagle Forum and the Concerned Women of America, drew a line in the sand that most Republicans were unwilling to cross; this time opponents held the upper hand in Congress. In September, the House passed an absolute ban on test development by a vote of 295-125. Shortly thereafter, the Senate voted to allow development to continue, but under the control of the National Assessment Governing Board.

Finally the impasse ended with the agreement that test-item development could occur, but that actual testing—even pilot testing—would be delayed. These delays went on for several years until the earlier appropriated money was spent and Clinton was out of office.

Clinton had taken a bold step by establishing a mechanism whereby states could be compared on a level playing field. Although he lost the immediate battle, he helped put in motion a discussion that would culminate in a substantial change in federal education policy 5 years later. As has often been demonstrated, in education, as in other fields, it often takes time for political leaders, those affected, and the public to understand and eventually embrace a change in direction.

THE FINAL CLINTON ATTEMPTS AT REFORM

After the furor in 1997, 1998 was relatively quiet. By this time, the Monica Lewinsky issue had surfaced and the White House was almost totally consumed with damage control and with trying—unsuccessfully—to keep the president from being impeached. Moreover, in a major change of heart for the GOP, appropriations actually rose 38% between 1996 and 1999 to a level in excess of $33 billion, with double-digit increases each year. By the end of 1998, Republicans were boasting that they had put more money into education than Clinton had asked for. The Republican leadership had realized that playing Don Quixote and tilting against public opinion was a losing proposition.

Congressional Republicans were undoubtedly also influenced by the fact that Republicans now held the governor's office in 32 of 50 states, and that being seen as an education governor would help them stay in office. Clearly, having a national party that was associated with a position that they did not share, was not a winning strategy for Republicans.

Also in 1998, one of the Republican governors running for reelection was George W. Bush in Texas. Bush prided himself on his education record. In fact, education would be a major factor in his succeeding Clinton in 2000.

The next reauthorization of the ESEA was due in the 105th Congress, which convened in January 1999. In his penultimate State of the Union address, Clinton laid out the broad strokes of what he called the Education Accountability Act; 4 months later it was sent to the Hill. Among other things, Clinton called for an end to social promotion, a theme that was more popular among Republicans than among liberal Democrats. Clinton also called for an end to the use of paraprofessionals providing any instructional assistance, unless they had at least 2 years of college; this issue was not popular with the two major teacher unions, both of which numbered teacher aides among their membership. Clinton also called for raising funding levels high enough to complete the goal of hiring 100,000 new teachers to reduce class size in the early grades; this goal was very popular with teachers unions and parents.

Another major component of the Clinton proposal, one that would prove very popular with almost every constituency, was an expansion of authority to allow states to waive certain federal regulations not related to civil rights, health, and safety in the administration of certain federal programs.

House Republicans dealt with the Clinton proposal by breaking it into seven separate bills. Senate Republicans chose a single bill. Given the parliamentary rules in the House, every bill could then become a magnet for amendments of all types. A single Senate bill was also more in keeping with the style of Senate action where, because senators have so many committee assignments, they prefer fewer and larger bills to save time.

Six of the seven bills in the House actually did pass during that Congress. Only one, that dealing with state authority to waive federal regulations, known as Ed-Flex, actually became law, largely because of the support that it had from governors, state superintendents, and others.

In the Senate, committee chair James Jeffords, a Vermont Republican, managed to get a bill through his committee by the barest of margins, 10-8. The bill reached the Senate floor, but after several days of debate was pulled from the schedule, and it died. The bill was pulled largely because Senate Democrats had adopted the Republican approach of using it to carry other social agenda items—in this case, gun control.

Another bill in that session, one that would help set the stage for 2001, was known as Straight A's; it was put forward by House committee chair Bill Goodling. Based on the notion that was first introduced by the NGA 15 years earlier that states should be required to improve achievement in return for the ability to combine federal program funds, the bill quickly became a symbol of partisanship. Straight A's passed the House by the close vote of 213-208, but was never taken up as a separate bill in the Senate. The Jeffords bill contained some elements of it, however, largely advocated by New Hampshire Republican senator Judd Gregg, who would succeed Jeffords as the top Republican on the committee when Jeffords left the party in 2001.

Democrats had opposed the Straight A's bill as a threat to the special and targeted programs that had been created over the years. Moderate Republicans in the House modified the original Goodling proposal to limit it to a 10-state pilot program, much to the consternation of conservative groups such as the Family Research Council and the Eagle Forum.

In the Senate, the concepts behind Straight A's led a group of centrist Democrats, led by Indiana's Evan Bayh, a former governor, and Joseph Lieberman, of Connecticut, to offer a bill they called the Three R's—Public Education Reinvestment, Reinvention, and Responsibility. Largely the work of the Clinton-oriented Progressive Policy Institute, the bill also promised greater accountability and reduced regulation. But when it was finally offered as an amendment to the Jeffords bill, only 13 senators supported it.

Although an otherwise minor footnote, the bill was significant as a demonstration of how close was the thinking of important factions in both parties on many issues, a fact that would help pave the way for the large bipartisan majorities that would emerge in 2001 in support of George Bush's No Child Left Behind proposals.

Another sign of the emerging consensus, as well as the fact that Republicans now feared being labeled anti-education, was that Republicans took the lead in pushing through a $6.5 billion increase in education funding (U.S. Department of Education Budget Tables, 1990–1999), the largest in history and $2 billion more than Clinton had requested. This was an increase of more than 16%, the greatest increase in any cabinet-level department. Since 1996, when Bob Dole ran against the U.S. Department of Education, the tables had turned dramatically, partly because of the success that Clinton achieved in appealing to soccer moms, and partly to the pressure from Republican governors, who saw education as an issue that gained them votes.

THE 2000 ELECTION: A NEW PRESIDENT, A NEW ERA IN FEDERAL EDUCATION POLICY

The question of who would lead each party's ticket in 2000 was not a matter of much suspense. By virtue of his service as a loyal and active vice president for 8 years, Al Gore was the prohibitive favorite among Democrats. For Republicans, George W. Bush had earned his chance by virtue of his success in Texas and his efforts on behalf of other Republicans. Both Gore and Bush were challenged for the nomination; Gore by former New Jersey senator Bill Bradley, Bush by publisher Steve Forbes, former education secretary Lamar Alexander, and Arizona Senator John McCain. By the time of each party's convention, the outcome was clear; the 2000 election would pit Tennessee against Texas, the stiffness of Al Gore against the casualness of George Bush.

Education was a major factor in the election and Bush soon had Gore on the ropes. Bush capitalized on his education record in Texas and aggressively promoted his ideas during the first debate, on October 3, at the University of Massachusetts in Boston.

Although Gore talked about the "Clinton-Gore" record in education, it was a mixed blessing, since by using Clinton's name he inevitably also invoked memories of Monica Lewinsky and the impeachment vote and Senate trial. The nation seemed to be ready for a change, and the election was one of the closest in U.S. history.

When it was finally over, long after the November election and then only with the intervention of the U.S. Supreme Court in disputes about vote counting in Florida, Gore had won the popular vote and led in 20 states and the District of Columbia. Bush had won 30 states. Gore had 50,996,000 popular votes and 267 electoral votes, Bush 50,446,000 and 271 electoral votes. The Republicans lost two seats in the House and four in the Senate, throwing the Senate into a tie with Vice President Dick Cheney casting the deciding vote. However, that bare majority was undone within a few months when Vermont Republican Jim Jeffords became an Independent and voted with the Democrats, giving them a one-vote edge.

On January 20, George W. Bush was inaugurated as the 43rd president of the United States. Three days later, at a ceremony in the White House East Room, he announced that his first major initiative would be in education and labeled that initiative No Child Left Behind.

NO CHILD LEFT BEHIND: A REMARKABLY BIPARTISAN EFFORT

Although Chapter 7 is a case study of the passage of No Child Left Behind, there are several aspects of this legislation that merit separate attention.

The fact that the president made this bill the first order of business in a new administration is especially striking. Even more striking is that the president was quite personally involved in shaping the proposal, with Reid Lyon, head of the reading program at the National Institute of Child Health and Development, a career official who shaped much of NIH's research program on reading (private conversation with Reid Lyon, January 23, 2001).

Especially noteworthy is that although President Johnson surely played a part in 1965 in shaping Title I, he was doing so as a part of the War on Poverty. In 2001, President Bush was intimately involved in shaping the instructional elements of the proposal; the 1965 legislation lacked much of the detail, especially around accountability, that dominated the 2001 proposal.

Presidential involvement illustrates how the federal role in education policy has evolved. From a time when education programs were seen as a funding stream where it was hoped that more dollars and getting a better education would mean getting out of poverty, by the turn of the century the issue was how reading would be taught, with what program and by whom. In both instances, the driving force behind the strategy was the president, as it had also been in the Clinton administration.

The remarkable bipartisan consensus that emerged in 2001 was largely fueled by political leaders' frustration over the slow response by the education community to the changes put in place in the 1994 reauthorization. Although No Child Left Behind did contain several new twists on the federal role, much of the groundwork had been laid in that earlier legislation, even though 7 years after the 1994 law had passed, only one third of the states were in compliance with its requirements.

ACT IV OF THE FEDERAL ROLE IN EDUCATION RESEARCH

Ten months after the president signed the No Child Left Behind Act, another bill slipped quietly through the Congress without fanfare and was signed on November 6, 2002, the day after the midterm elections.

Entitled the Education Sciences Reform Act of 2002, the bill called for the re-creation of the department's Office of Educational Research and Improvement (OERI), itself a re-creation of the National Institute of Education (NIE), and that in turn a re-creation of the Bureau of Research in the old Office of Education.

This bill creates an Institute of Educational Sciences, headed by a presidentially appointed director who serves a 6-year term. This new position is at the same level as that of the director of the National Science Foundation, a significant and symbolically important positioning.

Of all of the potential federal functions, the research role remains the most unrealized in the course of the past half century, despite being one of the few roles that almost everyone agrees is uniquely appropriate for the federal government. Since there has been no viable constituency to lobby for education research, the research agenda in the U.S. Department of Education has never really taken hold. By contrast, vast federal investments have been made in medicine, science, and agriculture, to name but a few.

In the second half of the 1990s, the concept of "scientifically based" programs, specifically in the area of reading, took hold largely because of the studies done since the early 1980s at the National Institute of Child Health and Development in NIH. That work had been quite well funded, because NIH had declared that the inability to read represented a health crisis, especially among poor and minority citizens.

Once the NIH work gained attention and showed that a balanced approach to reading was required, phonemic awareness was identified as an

essential component. This mention of phonics caused conservative educators and parent activists, many of them Republicans, to embrace the NIH
work and to use it as a springboard to advance two causes: the need for
scientifically validated reading programs, and the need to refocus federal
research on scientifically based work, with an emphasis on random-assign-
ment, controlled-experiment methodologies.

In 2001, a cadre of followers of these developments was appointed to
high-level positions in the Bush administration. The president had come to
know and respect Reid Lyon when he had advised Texas policymakers on
how to improve reading instruction.

The new White House asked Lyon to assist the Office of Presidential
Personnel in identifying key staff for the U.S. Department of Education.
Lyon did so, and three assistant secretaries—Susan Neuman in elementary
and special education, Robert Pasternak in special education, and Grover
(Russ) Whitehurst in research, were all confirmed within a few months. All
three had worked with Lyon and were both deeply involved in the NIH
reading work and committed to a new paradigm for federal support of
education research.

On the Hill, Delaware Republican Mike Castle, a former governor
and former member of the National Assessment Governing Board, had
long been an advocate for a greater federal role in research. Although he
had not been successful in getting any significant action on his OERI-
reform bill in the 106th Congress, he reintroduced it in early 2001 and
worked closely with Whitehurst in crafting legislation acceptable to both
the administration and House Republicans.

On April 11, 2002, this bill passed out of the Committee on Education
and the Workforce, then passed by voice vote in the House on April 30. In
mid-October, as the Senate scrambled to finish its business before recess
for elections, Senator Kennedy called up a similar bill on the Senate floor
and it passed by voice vote.

The research bill Kennedy brought forward was the product of several
meetings between House and Senate staff, who negotiated a bill the House,
Senate, and administration could all accept. The bill's advocates—Whitehurst, chief among them—believed that sending the bill to a formal conference would mean that it would be very unlikely to be enacted until after
the new Congress was formed in 2003, a delay that could easily stretch to
a year or more.

Just prior to Thanksgiving, the president appointed Whitehurst to be
the first director of the Institute of Education Sciences. Key to whether or
not this new reincarnation will succeed is the level of financial support
requested for it by the president and appropriated by Congress. At this
writing, January 2003, it is too early to evaluate this latest attempt at reform.

7

Leaving No Child Behind

By Paul Manna

Candidate George W. Bush made education a top priority during the 2000 presidential campaign. On the stump, Bush frequently promised that his education reforms would leave no child behind and would defeat what he called the soft bigotry of low expectations. Those two campaign themes illustrated how concerns over racial and educational equality, which animated the first ESEA of 1965, would continue to influence the education debates of 2001.

PRESIDENT-ELECT BUSH AND THE TRANSITION

President-elect Bush hoped to emerge from his transition and present an education reform plan almost immediately after taking office. To lay the groundwork for that effort, Bush and his transition team courted three key constituencies between November 2000 and January 2001.

First were members of Congress. Bush outlined his education vision with Republicans and Democrats at a transition meeting in the Texas governor's mansion. At the urging of Republican representative John Boehner of Ohio, chair of the Education and the Workforce Committee and Bush's key lieutenant on education in the House, the president included at this meeting the ranking Democrat of Boehner's committee, Representative George Miller of California. That olive branch proved valuable for the president because Miller found Bush sincere and persuasive. The Texas meeting did include Republican senator James Jeffords of Vermont, chair of the Health, Education, Labor, and Pensions (HELP) Committee, but it omitted Democratic Senator Edward Kennedy of Massachusetts, the committee's ranking Democrat. Bush did, however, invite Kennedy to the White House to discuss education the day before Bush announced his plan (Gorman, 2001b; Oppel & Schemo, 2000).

Recognizing that the success of his vision depended significantly on implementation efforts beyond Washington, Bush also courted state officials during the transition. Shortly after New Year's Day, the president-elect convened 19 Republican governors at his Texas ranch. At that meeting, Bush articulated his view that annual testing was required of any reform plan that promised to leave no child behind. Bush promised states greater flexibility with federal dollars, which he believed would ameliorate concerns that he was taking a top-down approach to reforming the ESEA. The new president held a similar meeting with Republican and Democratic governors shortly after taking office (Gorman, 2001a; Salzer, 2001).

The business community was the final group that Bush consulted between November and January. The president-elect's meetings included several members of the Business Roundtable, a group of chief executive officers from some of the largest companies in the United States. Encouraged by the president's attention to education, corporate leaders at Intel and Texas Instruments sought advice from Milton Goldberg, executive vice president of the National Alliance of Business and former executive director of the commission that produced A Nation at Risk. Those initial conversations with Goldberg spawned the Business Coalition for Excellence in Education, an ad hoc organization formed explicitly to influence the shape of the next ESEA, but not simply to cheerlead for Bush's (or anyone's) particular approach.

PRESIDENT BUSH ANNOUNCES HIS PLAN

Bush named his plan to reauthorize the ESEA the No Child Left Behind Act, a title that observers noted mirrored the slogan of the Children's Defense Fund. He presented it at a press conference on January 23, three days after his inauguration, and offered some of the traditional rationales that had justified past federal efforts in education. An argument for educational equity played prominently. "We must confront the scandal of illiteracy in America, seen most clearly in high-poverty schools, where nearly 70 percent of fourth-graders are unable to read at a basic level," he said (Federal News Service, 2001, p. A14).

Bush simultaneously stressed the need for all students, no matter what their backgrounds or racial heritage, to achieve at high levels. Educational excellence in math and science, "the very subjects most likely to affect our future competitiveness," required reforms to "focus the spending of federal tax dollars on things that work" (Federal News Service, 2001, p. A14).

In his relatively short speech, Bush also mapped out some important political ground. He stressed the need for bipartisanship, and in a line that no doubt made some conservatives flinch, the president noted that "change will not come by disdaining or dismantling the federal role in education" (Federal News Service, 2001, p. A14).

Substantively, the plan that Bush and incoming Secretary of Education Rod Paige, former Houston superintendent of schools, presented was a 30-page blueprint that embraced four main principles centered on testing, flexibility, assisting failing schools, and choice. The first principle required annual testing in reading and math for students in grades 3 through 8. This would become the only nonnegotiable part of the plan. Two days later, the president called annual testing "the cornerstone of reform" (Blum, 2001). In February, Bush's key White House education advisor, Sandy Kress, a fellow Texan and a member of the centrist New Democrats, stated that testing is "central to the President's thinking. . . . His interest in, and support for, all the other initiatives depends on this particular reform being approved" (Gorman, 2001b, p. 549).

The second principle—providing greater flexibility to state and local leaders to innovate—meant shifting authority and accountability to the local level so that schools could not blame their failings on distant educational bureaucracies. If federal money came with fewer strings attached, the plan argued, then the people closest to children and classrooms would have a better chance to improve learning.

The third and fourth principles concerned failing schools. Bush recognized that some schools faced difficult circumstances, and therefore needed additional help (principle three). He promised to provide that assistance, but not as a blank check, and he noted that children should not remain trapped in schools that do not work. To provide an out, Bush proposed that parents whose children attended schools that did not improve should be able to choose their children's schools through vouchers, which would provide greater public and private school choice (principle four).

NAVIGATING THE THICKET OF THE LEGISLATIVE PROCESS

During his first week as president, Bush maintained that bipartisan education reform would be "the cornerstone of my administration" (Fletcher,

2001a, p. A21). Still, it was not a foregone conclusion that Congress would pass a bill by session's end that the president would sign. The legislative process that eventually produced the No Child Left Behind Act of 2001 was characterized by four distinct themes that emerged nearly every step of the way.

Theme 1: Bush and Boehner Tame the GOP's Right Flank

President Bush and his congressional lieutenants faced terrific challenges from Republican conservatives, who were wary of a greater federal role in education. Conservatives remained committed to key goals, such as expanded federal block grants and greater school choice options for parents. From the beginning of the 107th Congress, it was clear that conservative legislators would not accept the president's plan blindly, or with too much compromise. This opposition created headaches for President Bush because of his willingness to give on school vouchers and block grants in exchange for securing the testing and accountability provisions that he favored strongly.

On vouchers, Bush made it clear that he supported them but would also consider other ideas, especially if it meant preserving a bipartisan coalition for his overall plan. In his first weekly radio address, Bush conceded that "there are some honest differences of opinion in Congress about what form these [parental school choice] option[s] should take. I have my own plan which would help children in persistently failing schools to go to another public, private, or charter school. Others suggest different approaches, and I am willing to listen."

Despite the president's general support for choice, conservatives, including several groups representing religious educators, felt betrayed when the House education committee voted to remove vouchers from the bill. (To avoid this scenario in the Senate, HELP Committee Chair Jeffords and Kennedy agreed to put off debate of the most controversial provisions in the bill for the Senate floor.) Republican representative Bob Schaffer of Colorado argued that "without the ability to exercise real accountability, real choice, this testing is nonsense" (Alvarez, 2001a, p. A21), while Republican Representative Peter Hoekstra of Michigan concluded glibly: "This is no longer a George Bush education bill. This is a Ted Kennedy education bill" (Alvarez, 2001b, p. A15).

Voucher supporters fared no better on the floors of each chamber. On May 23 in the House, Texas Republican and Majority Leader Dick Armey's amendment to provide private school choice for students who attend low-performing public schools failed 155 to 273. When Republican senator Judd Gregg of New Hampshire offered an amendment in the Senate on

June 12 to create a low-income school voucher demonstration program, it failed 41 to 58.

Both the Senate and House bills and the conference report that eventually became law did, however, contain a provision that allowed parents whose children attended persistently failing schools to use a portion of their school's Title I money to buy tutoring or other services from public, private, or nonprofit providers. For conservatives who favored greater parental choice, however, that was a hollow victory at best.

A similar trajectory of debate and eventual conservative compromise emerged regarding the Straight A's proposal for block grants. Republican representative Jim DeMint of South Carolina, who twice voted against the education bill (once in the House education committee, and once on the House floor) before finally voting for the conference report, personified this process. During 2001, DeMint was strongly committed to the Straight A's approach, which would have converted to block grants much of federal education aid. He pressed the issue in committee but lost the debate to moderates and Bush's Republican allies.

When DeMint threatened to refight this battle on the House floor, Chair Boehner and President Bush personally intervened to avert a political melee that they feared would have rocked the bipartisan spirit that still prevailed as of late spring. Not wanting to cross his president, DeMint relented, and was satisfied with Bush's promise to fight for other issues, such as tuition tax credits. In the end, DeMint and his allies were pleased that the conference report did contain a version of Straight A's, albeit in a much more stripped-down form than he and other conservatives had proposed.

Even though some Republicans loathed growing federal involvement in the nation's schools, these critics could not complain about the political success on education that Bush had helped the Republicans achieve. In May 2001, for example, Senator Mitch McConnell reminded his fellow Republicans that Bush "has taken us for [sic] a 20-point deficit on education to a point in which we lead on education" (Alvarez, 2001b, p. A15).

In the end, 188 House Republicans voted for the No Child Left Behind conference report, while only 33, including Republican majority whip Tom DeLay of Texas, opposed it. The Senate had only three Republican defectors: Robert Bennett of Utah, Chuck Hagel of Nebraska, and George Voinovich of Ohio.

Theme 2: Centrist Democrats Play Key Roles

On the other side of the aisle, a cadre of New Democrats, a centrist group within the Democratic Party, played important roles in the legislative process. Even though the education plan that Senators Joseph Lieberman

(Democrat of Connecticut) and Evan Bayh (Democrat of Indiana), leaders of the New Democrat coalition in the Senate, had proposed the previous year received only 13 votes on the Senate floor, these men saw two main reasons why 2001 would be different.

First, the Senate's 50-50 split, which in May became 50-49-1 and produced Democratic control after Senator Jeffords, chair of the HELP committee, left the Republican Party, meant that every vote would be crucial. As Lieberman reflected at the end of 2001: "Having 13 votes in an evenly divided Senate meant that we would be taken seriously" (Broder, 2001b, p. A1). And they were. Both Lieberman and Bayh landed seats on the ESEA conference committee, a rare occurrence given that neither sat on the education committee in the Senate.

Second, President Bush's education reform plan extended many of the provisions of the previous ESEA that President Clinton, himself a New Democrat, had championed. Additionally, the Bush plan borrowed liberally from the Lieberman and Bayh proposal, known as Three R's.

Still, it was an open question whether the New Democrats would be able to warm their party to the Three R's framework. Some traditionally liberal Democrats feared that the plan's consolidation proposals were essentially block grants by another name and would eviscerate important programs. That concern provoked some Democrats, civil rights groups, and others to oppose Lieberman and Bayh's ideas.

Democratic Senator Paul Wellstone of Minnesota, then a member of the Senate education committee, articulated some of these concerns early in the legislative process. In an editorial in which he urged his fellow Democrats to remember their party's core beliefs on education, Wellstone outlined his views on key elements that any education reform bill should embrace. In particular, he questioned the wisdom of more government-mandated exams and tying funding to their results. Wellstone feared that without adequate resources the poorest children would simply be set up to fail (Wellstone, 2001).

Senator Wellstone's challenge resonated with subsequent calls from the NEA, which passed a resolution against mandatory testing at its annual meeting in early July. The NEA's measure directed its lobbyists to challenge federal testing requirements and to support state-level groups that advocated giving parents the ability to remove their children from state testing programs ("Teachers Vote," 2001).

Worrying that senators such as Wellstone and Kennedy (who was then ranking Democrat on the HELP committee) would throw the bill off course, and lacking trust in Chair Jeffords to produce a bill to President Bush's liking, beginning in February 2001 the White House, New Democrats, and key Republicans teamed up in the Senate.

The result, confirmed in personal interviews and the accounts of Gorman (2001a, p. 2231) and Broder (2001a), was a two-track process of negotiations. During the day, this rump group of senators would meet with other members and staff of the HELP committee, and at night among themselves. That pattern persisted from late February to early April, and ended when a confluence of factors led the White House and Senate Republicans to overplay their hand.

Startled to learn that these back-channel negotiations were proceeding without his input, Kennedy approached the White House during the Senate committee markup of the bill and expressed a greater willingness to compromise, even on Republican proposals that would allow parents to use Title I funds to pay for supplemental tutoring services for their children. That inspired Republicans to up the ante, and they used Kennedy's overtures to try to push the New Democrats further along toward supporting full-blown vouchers. Lieberman and Bayh said no, and that ended the evening discussions.

Despite their internal disagreements, both New and traditional Democrats remained united in important areas. From the start, they opposed private school vouchers and demanded greater funding for the neediest schools—both third-rail issues for their party. The funding question became especially important as fall arrived and state revenues began to shrink from the weakening national economy and the post–September 11 slowdown.

On student testing, Democrats were actually much more united than Senator Wellstone's comments from February implied. One House education committee staffer, who worked closely with George Miller, said in a personal interview that the substance of No Child Left Behind was very "traditional," and that "progressive liberals are finally able to hold schools accountable about kids actually learning. That hasn't been done before."

Finally, fears that consolidation would eliminate programs and reduce funding never materialized. Constituent politics and members who championed individual programs sustained the lingering programmatic approach of the now standards-driven ESEA. The Senate's bill actually increased the number of ESEA programs from 55 to 89, and the House bill contained 47 programs.

Theme 3: Crafting Federal Law with the States in Mind

The third theme of the legislative process concerned the relationship between the ESEA and the states. Officials on the Hill and in the White House encountered great challenges as they attempted to write a law that held states more accountable for student achievement while recognizing that not all states were equally prepared to meet this challenge.

Shortly before the House-Senate conference began its work in the early fall, Sandy Kress, Bush's point man in the ESEA negotiations, characterized the difficulty of crafting federal law with the states in mind: "What makes this tough is designing something that will work in 50 very different states, and then figuring out how you can leverage change when you're only pay-ing 7 percent of the bill" (Broder, 2001b, p. B7). Two areas were especially difficult: testing and measuring adequate yearly progress.

On testing, Bush insisted that states should test students in math and reading every year in grades 3 through 8, and that those test results should guide reform efforts. This was the approach that Bush had inherited and continued while governor of Texas. Opinions regarding this approach var-ied across the states, and in part depended on the partisan stripes of the particular state official. While state leaders quietly fretted over Bush's new testing proposals, many muted their criticisms and endorsed Bush's plan.

Top among these state-level supporters were members of the Educa-tion Leaders Council (ELC), a group of reform-minded governors and state school chiefs that formed in the mid-1990s. Even though the ELC is techni-cally nonpartisan, its members identify primarily with the Republican Party.

In a letter to Chair Boehner shortly after his committee completed its work in May, the ELC expressed its support for No Child Left Behind, and for Boehner especially, who the ELC said had stood up "to the inside-the-beltway interest groups and their allies in Congress who are attempting to block some of the key provisions of the Bush plan" (House Committee on Education and the Workforce, 2001). That enthusiasm continued into the fall when the ELC's chief executive officer, Lisa Graham Keegan, a Repub-lican and former Arizona superintendent of public instruction, joined forces with other supporters to urge the House-Senate conference not to let organizations opposing what they characterized as real reform distract legislators from their task (Bennett, Keegan, Finn, & Kafer, 2001).

Other state groups, such as the Council of Chief State School Officers (CCSSO), which represents the top state education officials across the polit-ical spectrum in nearly all 50 states (and partially overlaps with the ELC in membership and some activities), argued that annual testing in grades 3 through 8 was unnecessary and possibly counterproductive. In early May, Gordon Ambach, executive director of the CCSSO, agreed that holding states accountable for their use of federal funds was a good idea. However, he also noted that Texas was the only state with annual testing that scored in the top 10 in math or reading on the 1996 and 1998 National Assess-ment of Education Progress (NAEP) tests (Olson, 2001).

As the House-Senate conference commenced in mid-July, many state leaders remained uneasy that a requirement of testing for grades 3 through 8 would undermine their ongoing reform work. Attempting to deflect this criticism, Sandy Kress responded that the federal requirement would not usurp state power, but actually buttress state efforts and ultimately raise achievement of low-income and other at-risk children (Wilgoren, 2001).

In some respects, both Kress and the critics were right. Although nearly all states had made significant progress in developing standards and assessments during the 1990s—some with a great deal of assistance from Goals 2000—the political battles and policy development that remained continued to dog even the most reform-minded states.

As of 2001, for example, 49 states had established content standards and were linking them to testing in key subjects, sometimes even tying results to high-stakes decisions regarding promotion and graduation. Other consequences included increasing state intervention in schools that were persistently failing (Fletcher, 2001b). Those accomplishments notwithstanding, much political and policy work remained. Even though nearly all states had content standards and testing regimes in place, in most cases these elements were not aligned, meaning that each state's tests did not necessarily reflect the content present in its standards (Citizens' Commission on Civil Rights, 2001).

A second major challenge that federal policymakers faced was how to measure student achievement gains to guarantee that schools were making measurable and steady progress. Devising this formula for Adequate Yearly Progress (AYP) was one of the perpetual snags in the legislative process during 2001. It was characterized by numerous false starts and some confusion by the time the conference committee completed its work.

The nub of the problem centered on an admirable goal, which was consistent with concerns about educational and racial equality that had motivated past ESEA reauthorizations: Whatever formula emerged for AYP, the law should require states to show that all student groups—the disadvantaged, minorities, limited English proficient, and others—were making progress. Legislators considered a formula that would define a school as failing if it did not meet AYP targets for all student groups, with the end goal that all students would be achieving at proficient levels after a specified number of years. In practice, crafting this plan illustrated some of the challenges that federal officials face in developing and applying policy across the country.

The trouble began in April, after work on the Senate side revealed a stunning flaw in the AYP formula that the White House and legislators had worked out. (The House's bill essentially put off the AYP debate for the conference stage of the legislative process.) Mark Powden, staff director for Chair Jeffords of the HELP committee, applied the tentative formula retroactively to test it on three states (Connecticut, North Carolina, and Texas) that nearly all observers agreed had made significant progress in narrowing achievement gaps between student groups. The exercise revealed that the formula would label almost all schools in these states as failures.

The AYP problem delayed the Senate bill for weeks, and eventually produced a new AYP formula. To some state groups, the revised approach appeared worse than the original plan. David Griffith, director of governmental and public affairs at the National Association of State Boards of Education, said this about the AYP fix in mid-May: "It's been explained to me, and I still don't understand the formula" (Gorman, 2001c, p. 1418). Bush education advisor Sandy Kress later called the results of this recovery effort "Rube Goldbergesque" (Toch, 2001).

On testing, AYP, and other issues, representatives from the states continued to lobby the conference committee members as their work dragged into the fall and winter. In early October, the NGA sent a lukewarm letter to the conference leaders—Boehner, Miller, Kennedy, and Gregg—pledging its commitment "to providing the best possible education for children." However, the NGA also reminded the conferees that "without conference negotiations yielding results that are workable and effective for states, successful education reform is not achievable" (National Governors' Association, 2001).

In separate September and October letters addressed to the No Child Left Behind conference members and to Senate and House appropriators who were working concurrently on the education budget for fiscal year 2002, the CCSSO advocated for flexibility on AYP and any federal requirements regarding teacher qualifications (Council of Chief State School Officers, 2001a, 2001b, 2001c). It also wanted the conference to preserve the Harkin-Hagel amendment, passed on the Senate floor, which required the federal government to fully fund its commitment to special education.

Although the governors and state chiefs did not pull their support for the bill—and the members of the ELC continued to endorse the original Bush proposals enthusiastically—by October another major state group reversed its initial favorable position (National Conference of State Legislatures, 2001b). In a letter to conference committee leaders dated September 26, the National Conference of State Legislatures (NCSL) criticized the developing conference report on nearly all levels (National Conference of State Legislatures, 2001a). In its own rebuke of the legislation, which appeared during the first week of November, the American Association of School Administrators raised similar arguments (Hunter, 2001). The nation's governors, Republicans and Democrats alike, also had concerns about the bill's requirements, but remained on the fence, refusing to endorse or oppose the bill even into the mid-fall (Mollison, 2001).

Theme 4: Savvy Leadership of the "Big Four"

Because President Bush and his advisors decided to present No Child Left Behind as a 30-page blueprint, not a formal bill, much of the legislative drafting and leadership burden fell on what became known as the Big Four: Representatives Boehner and Miller and Senators Kennedy and Gregg, who worked closely with their key staffers, Sally Lovejoy, Charles Barone, Danica Petroshius, and Denzel McGuire, respectively.

By early summer, the House and Senate had passed their own versions of the No Child Left Behind Act. The bill cleared the House on a 384-to-45 vote on May 23, and the Senate passed its version on June 14, 91 to 8. In July, as each chamber named its conferees, the *Washington Post*'s David Broder (2001b, p. B7) offered a sampling of the challenges that the Big Four confronted:

> From the National Education Association, which passed a resolution saying all these tests should be made voluntary, to the state and local officials who argue against national norms, to the Heritage Foundation and other pro-voucher conservatives who complain that Bush already has allowed the standards to go limp, to the idealists who argue that if you just demand more of teachers and students, they will perform—all these conflicting views and agendas remain to be resolved.

As if those challenges were not enough, the conference's task became even more difficult after the attacks of September 11, 2001. After the devastation at the World Trade Center, at the Pentagon, and in rural Pennsylvania, and the anthrax attacks that temporarily shut down many facilities on the Hill, several observers wondered whether the Congress would pass *any* domestic legislation by December other than measures to increase homeland defense. With President Bush curtailing, but by no means eliminating, his education efforts to focus more closely on national security, the Big Four began carrying even more of the legislative burden.

On the House side, Boehner and Miller were unusual allies, to say the least. In December 2001, Miller reflected on how far they had come by saying that in previous Congresses, he and his Republican colleague "spent most of our careers throwing rocks at one another" (Clymer & Alvarez, 2001). While it became clear throughout 2001 that Boehner and Miller did not always fit hand in glove, it would be difficult to imagine a better collaboration among two legislators with such opposing views in the past.

Boehner provided keen political insight, admonishing President-elect Bush to include Miller at the above-mentioned December 2000 meeting of congressional leaders. If Bush wanted a bipartisan bill, Boehner recognized that he and the president would need Miller's help. More often than not, President Bush concurred with Boehner's judgment on issues such as Straight A's and vouchers to preserve the alliance with Miller.

Unlike in the House, the committee leadership scenario in the Senate involved much more intrigue. When President Bush offered his education plan in January, nobody could have predicted that Senators Kennedy and Gregg would guide the bill in conference. The 107th Congress began with Kennedy as ranking Democrat on the Senate HELP committee, Gregg simply a committee member, and Senator Jeffords the chair.

The early work on the bill from January through mid-May proceeded with Jeffords and Kennedy at the helm of their respective committee caucuses. During the spring, Jeffords continued to press the president to devote much more of the federal government's (apparent) budget surplus to special education, rather than greater tax cuts. Roughly one month into the Senate's floor debate on the bill, it became clear to Jeffords that the White House would not budge on that issue. Largely because of President Bush's position on special education funding, on May 24, Jeffords took the gigantic step of leaving the Republican Party and his HELP committee chair, and in the process, reordering the Senate (Jeffords, 2001, chapters 2 and 3).

When Democrats took control, Kennedy became chair of HELP and Gregg became the ranking Republican on the committee. That reshuffling made Gregg one of the few Republican senators who personally benefited from the chamber's switch. More broadly, it may have enabled the No Child Left Behind bill ultimately to pass.

One interview respondent involved in the legislative process on the Hill reflected that the Congress may not have been able to complete and pass a bill at all had Jeffords remained chair. With Gregg guiding the Republican side in the Senate, the Bush team had a member they could count on to fight for its priorities. Gregg had also been the key intermediary in the Senate who helped coordinate the back-channel discussions between the Bush White House and the Senate New Democrats in the early spring.

Even though Bush had excluded Kennedy from his transition meeting in Austin, he was pleasantly surprised with the results when the Massachusetts senator took the committee's helm. Kennedy's agreement to a scaled-back version of Straight A's led some Democrats to do a double take. On other key issues, however, he remained true to traditional Democratic constituencies and programs. From start to finish, he and other Democrats, including Miller, pushed the Bush White House to produce an education budget to match the promises for greater support for state efforts to leave no child behind.

In the end, without Miller and Kennedy making a strong case to key Democratic groups both on and off the Hill, it is likely that the bipartisan coalition that eventually passed the bill would have collapsed. Their efforts on the Democratic side were as significant as those of Boehner, Gregg, and President Bush, who tamed the GOP's right flank. If it was true, as some interview respondents remarked, that only a Republican president could usher in an era of mandated federal testing in grades 3 through 8 (much as Richard Nixon could open relations with communist China), then an ESEA with portable Title I benefits and a Straight A's demonstration program would have been unthinkable without the endorsements of Kennedy and Miller.

H.R. 1 BECOMES THE NO CHILD LEFT BEHIND ACT OF 2001

With staffers working essentially around the clock, and the first session's end rapidly approaching, the Big Four finally steered the conference committee ship into port. Despite the anthrax scares that shut down several congressional offices for much of the fall, the conference reported out the bill on December 11, and the full House passed it 2 days later, 381 to 41. The Senate followed suit on December 18, 87 to 10.

Given the grueling legislative process and perhaps wanting to rationalize their efforts, members of Congress, the administration, and other observers hailed the bill's passage as historic, as had leaders during past ESEA reauthorizations (Kafer, 2001; Robelen, 2002). President Bush proclaimed the beginning of "a new era, a new time in public education in our country," at the January 8, 2002, ceremony in Boehner's district, where he signed the bill into law. "As of this hour," the president said, "America's schools will be on a new path of reform, and a new path of results" (White House Office of the Press Secretary, 2002).

The No Child Left Behind Act of 2001, summarized in Riddle (2002a, 2002b), contains nine titles and 45 separate authorizations that extend from fiscal year 2002 to 2007. It runs more than 1,000 pages and includes major provisions regarding testing, AYP, teachers, and funding and flexibility, which further deepened federal involvement in the nation's schools.

Testing

The law's testing components mirror the original proposal that President Bush offered in January 2001. By the 2005–6 school year, it requires all states to develop and administer aligned annual tests in math and reading in grades 3 through 8. (States have additional time to develop tests in science.) The law includes a provision that allows states to delay administration (but not development) of their tests if federal funds fall short of the amount promised for test development.

All states are also required to participate, at federal expense, in the NAEP fourth-grade reading test and eighth-grade math test. Previously, state participation in NAEP had been optional. Although the law does not link direct consequences to NAEP scores, all observers recognize that those results will serve as a de facto validity check on state tests. States that report high levels of achievement on their own tests but do poorly on the federal NAEP will certainly be challenged to explain the discrepancy.

An adjustment to the law's testing framework emerged during the important regulation-writing process shortly after January 2002. After soliciting input and convening groups for a process called negotiated rulemaking, the Department of Education decided to allow states to use a mix of state and local tests, and off-the-shelf commercial exams, to fulfill the grade 3 through 8 testing requirement. States could exercise those options provided they could show that the tests they chose were aligned with their state curriculum standards.

That flexibility pleased state officials who generally loathed the challenges of developing new state tests in six grades. Others, especially congressional Democrats, fretted that using a combination of tests would significantly weaken the law's accountability provisions (Olson, 2002a, 2002c). Assistant Secretary of Education Susan Neuman tried to allay those fears. She argued that showing alignment with state standards, a prerequisite for including local and off-the-shelf tests, would not be easy and therefore not compromise the law's potency (Olson, 2002c).

Adequate Yearly Progress

Student test results are directly connected to Adequate Yearly Progress. The broad goal of the AYP provision is to guarantee that all students will be performing at proficient levels or better (as defined by individual states) within 12 years. During that 12-year period, schools, school districts, and states will have to show that students across different groups—the economically disadvantaged and members of different racial and ethnic groups, for example—are progressing toward that goal.

Disaggregating scores aims to highlight and eventually decrease the achievement gaps between these students and their more advantaged (typically White and higher income) peers. The law also recognizes that requiring annual positive movement in scores across all of these groups is essentially a statistical impossibility, as some studies had shown during the legislative debate of 2001. That means that the *Y* in *AYP* does not necessarily imply a yearly calculation of scores. States can show progress if rolling averages, calculated over 2- to 3-year periods, are steadily increasing. Still, that approach remains an imperfect fix to some of the statistical anomalies that studies of AYP uncovered in 2001.

Even though members of Congress wrestled with the AYP formula for almost a year, the final result remains technically complex. That is in part because of the different options that states can use to establish their baseline levels of achievement (from which they would be expected to improve), and the safe-harbor provisions that allow schools to comply with AYP rules even if achievement for all pupil groups does not increase on schedule. These exceptions are potentially important because if a school repeatedly does not meet AYP goals, then the law allows parents to choose to send their children to another public school.

Teachers

Although testing and AYP stole the spotlight during 2001, equally important, and perhaps even more challenging to achieve, are requirements concerning teacher qualifications, some of which took effect in September 2002 when all new Title I teachers were required to be "highly qualified," a concept that Stedman (2002) describes in detail. Among other things, that meant that new teachers hired with Title I funds must have completed at least 2 years of college. Within 4 years, all Title I teachers, past and present, are required to be highly qualified.

The law also stipulates that all regular classroom teachers in core subjects must meet a more rigorous standard no later than the start of the 2005–6 school year. For new teachers that means having full state certification or being enrolled in an approved alternative certification program, which would disallow emergency or provisional waivers of certain requirements. Also, the law requires new teachers to have at least a bachelor's degree and to prove their competence in the subject areas they teach, either by passing a test or having a college major in the relevant subjects. Veteran teachers will have to demonstrate subject matter competence based on standards that each state will determine.

Funding and Flexibility

If the grade 3 through 8 testing plan, AYP formula, and teacher provisions created new federal mandates, how was it that members of Congress and the Bush administration hailed the new ESEA's flexibility? That claim grew primarily out of provisions that allow school districts to transfer into Title I up to 50% of their funds from four separate programs—(a) Teachers, (b) Technology, (c) Safe and Drug Free Schools, and (d) the Innovative Programs Block Grant.

The Straight A's pilot program provided additional flexibility for specific states and school districts. Under its provisions, called the State and Local Flexibility Demonstration Act, the federal government will select up to seven states to combine all their state administration and state activity funds from eight separate ESEA programs. Participating states may use these program funds for any purpose, and possess this authority for 5 years, provided that they continue to meet the law's AYP requirements. This demonstration program also allows a limited number of school districts in these seven states to combine funds from four specific programs and use them for any purpose.

Other important funding provisions in the new ESEA include changes in Title I allocation formulas that increase targeting of funds to the neediest schools and districts, especially those in large cities. The education appropriation bill for fiscal year 2002 also increased Title I spending by 20%, which in dollar terms meant a boost from $18.8 billion to $22.6 billion. Democrats had held out for these significant increases that were roughly $3 billion above what President Bush preferred (Clymer & Alvarez, 2001).

REACTIONS TO THE LAW AND QUESTIONS ABOUT THE FUTURE

During the period after the conference committee reported out the bill but before President Bush signed it into law, various groups offered their assessments of the finished product.

After interviewing officials in 45 states, *Education Week* concluded that most generally supported the law and believed that it "mirrors the push in many states for greater accountability and results in education" (Olson, 2002b, p. 1). These state officials also enjoyed the promises for new funding, especially to support reading in the early grades. Still, state leaders doubted they could meet the requirements for hiring high-quality teachers, and they worried "about how much they will have to change their testing and accountability systems, and whether the federal money set aside for that purpose will be enough" (Olson, 2002b, p. 1).

Two major nonstate groups that lobbied during 2001 differed in their overall judgments of the conference report. The NEA disliked the final product. Union president Bob Chase called it "a tremendous disappointment." Even though the bill's goals were commendable, he said, "it fails to deliver the support required to help children achieve higher standards. We will not oppose the bill, but we cannot in good conscience support it" (National Education Association, 2001).

Conversely, members of the nation's business community were enthusiastic. For example, Edward B. Rust, Jr., chair of the Business Roundtable's education task force and chair and CEO of State Farm Insurance Companies, concluded that "passage of this legislation will show that, at long last, America has gotten serious about providing a quality education for all of its students" (Business Roundtable, 2001). On the day that President Bush signed the conference report into law, Rust pledged that "the BRT will continue to work with the states to ensure that these reforms yield real benefits for America's students" (Business Roundtable, 2002).

Implicitly, Rust's comments identified two related questions central to the eventual fate of the No Child Left Behind Act: Will the states implement it well? And if not, will the federal government enforce the law's specific provisions?

Even though states had made significant progress in developing their standards and testing systems with previous federal help, many still had not yet aligned these systems as the 1994 ESEA had required. That was no small matter, given that the No Child Left Behind Act depends on this alignment in order to work.

On the teacher-quality provisions, some state leaders bluntly concluded that it would be impossible for them to meet the law's timetable. Colorado Commissioner of Education William J. Moloney, while again supporting the overall law, was quite direct in describing his state's situation: "Will we have a qualified teacher in every classroom by 2005? No, of course not. There are [complex] reasons, and those reasons will not be waved away" (Olson, 2002b, p. 1).

The prospect of states failing to meet the requirements of the No Child Left Behind Act raises the issue of whether the federal government will actually force them to comply. The long-term and recent track record of the Department of Education during President Clinton's two terms leaves many observers skeptical (Taylor & Piche, 2002).

Lax enforcement, critics claim, is one reason why states had failed to comply with the testing and standards provisions contained in the 1994 ESEA. In response, others argue this was not because of shirking, but because of the difficult realities that many states faced. Constructing curriculum standards and aligned tests in multiple grades is complicated work. And given the distance that some states still had to travel, federal education officials during the 1990s were reluctant to sanction a state that was making progress, but was not quite up to speed.

The political ramifications of enforcement are also a reality that President Bush and his team will have to confront. In mid-December 2001, just before the Senate passed the conference report, former Clinton deputy secretary of education Marshall Smith identified a general rule that he believed would govern future enforcement decisions: "It's not in the best political interests of the president to come down hard on governors of the same party—or even of the other party. That's not going to be any different for the Bush administration" (Chaddock, 2001).

Bush officials have challenged this view. Shortly after the No Child Left Behind Act became law, Bush's secretary of education, Rod Paige, met with several state chief school officers at George Washington's home at Mount Vernon. At that event, Paige said that the administration would work with states but it would also demand compliance. State officials should not assume that waivers would be forthcoming if they did not meet the law's expectations.

Even assuming that federal officials possess the political will to enforce the law, it remains debatable whether strict enforcement will produce the desired effects. In large part that is because federal officials rely heavily on lower levels of government to make federal initiatives work. Based on the long history chronicled in previous chapters, creative cajoling of the states rather than employing strong-arm tactics may be the most likely and realistic path for federal officials to take as the No Child Left Behind Act moves deeper into the implementation phase.

NCLB REVISITED: A POSTSCRIPT

At this writing, more than eight years have elapsed since NCLB was signed into law and it is several years overdue for reauthorization. More than a year after the Obama inauguration, the administration finally released in mid-March what they termed a "blueprint" for reauthorization. While immediate action is unlikely, hearings have begun even though a draft bill has yet to be sent to Congress by the White House.

The Obama blueprint retains many aspects of NCLB, such as annual assessments and the requirement that data be disaggregated by groups, while doing away with AYP in favor of a system that relies of the measurement of student growth. Most significant from both a policy and political standpoint, it also requires the creation of effective teacher evaluation systems in every state that incorporate data on student growth. This provision has provoked fierce opposition among teacher unions and is likely to be the focus of much debate.

The Obama proposal is also aimed at taking federal policy in a major new direction by rewarding (through the relaxation of requirements) those schools that do best and by making major investments in competitive programs, raising that potential investment from under $100 million in 2009 to over $7 billion in 2011. Given the economic situation facing schools, these proposals will also be met with serious challenges.

8

Lessons Learned from a Half-Century of Federal Policy Development

FROM THE PREVIOUS EXAMINATION of the evolution of federal education policy some lessons have been learned that provide an understanding of what federal policy is today, as well as guidance with respect to future policy development. This chapter groups these lessons into four sections; the first deals with defining federal policy, the second with how policy works, the third with factors that make a difference, the fourth with other factors that affect federal policy development.

WHAT IS THE NATION'S EDUCATION POLICY?

Several themes characterize the development of education policy in the 20th century, and these may provide important guidance for the further development of federal policy.

The Primary Federal Role Is to Ensure Equity

Although the definition of equity has changed over the years, it continues to be the key principle guiding federal aid. In the Great Society of the Johnson era, equity in education was seen in terms of both civil rights and resources. Getting resources to schools was the main objective. It was assumed that educators would do the right thing, and that education was the ticket out of poverty.

By the end of the 20th century, it had become clear that resources alone were not sufficient to ensure equity in education. Federal expectations have become quite specific and amenable to quantitative measurement. One objective is that all children will read at grade level by no later than the third grade, another is that there will be no achievement gap separating children by race, ethnicity, income, or language.

Federal Programs Are Now at the Core of Teaching and Learning

Whereas federal programs once provided only supplementary services, the 1994 ESEA reauthorization set federal policy in a new direction. Today, it encompasses policies at the core of teaching, assessment, professional development, teacher qualifications, and clear systems of accountability for all children.

In a perfect world, the federal government would decide whether its mission is to support the core, as in the Title I focus on teaching and learning, or supplemental programs, such as migrant education or charter schools. However, the political reality is that the government will support both core and supplementary programs, in large part because political support for the core is often obtained by also supporting smaller, supplementary programs. Whereas bipartisan majorities are required to enact core programs, supplemental programs are generally enacted (and, usually, minimally funded) by political logrolling—"I'll support your special interest, if you support mine."

Race and Religion Are Decisive Factors

The emotional, often divisive, issues of race and religion, though redefined over the years, remain. Although public services to children in parochial and private schools through Title I, while minor, are more extensive than ever, and the U.S. Supreme Court has upheld the use of vouchers for students in nonpublic schools, the battle continues. The coming set of battles will be in the states, as they consider voucher programs as a result of the Supreme Court ruling. However, the 2003–4 reauthorization of IDEA and the 2007 reauthorization of ESEA will rekindle this issue at the federal level. Private school enrollment is about 11% of students aged 5–17. Although this percentage is below what it was 40 years ago in the wake of the *Brown* decision, the parents of these 6 million children feel they deserve public support. The original ESEA law would not have been passed in 1965 had there been no compromise on this issue. Further major breakthroughs will require new accommodations and compromises.

Although the issue of race is no longer one of de jure segregation, the achievement gap between White and Asian children and those who are Black or of Hispanic origin will likely remain a major factor in education policy for decades. If our society is not able to raise the achievement levels of those for whom the system has not worked well, then the nation's economy will suffer and it will be unlikely that these children will live full and enriching lives.

The Quest for Excellence Versus the Opportunity for a Second Chance

The notion that people should have a second chance to succeed is in the very fabric of the nation; after all, the United States was created by immigrants looking for a second chance.

Few of this country's competitors or allies in the industrialized world (Canada, Australia, and New Zealand, also nations founded by immigrants, are exceptions) have this "second chance" tradition. Most other countries channel students, usually by testing, into formal tracks that lead to specific career paths. In those countries, once a student finishes high school and goes into higher education or the labor force, the idea of changing one's mind, discovering new motivations, or simply wanting to go back to school to master a new skill is almost impossible to imagine.

The U.S. system, by contrast, offers students many opportunities, from a GED high school degree, to open-enrollment community colleges, to technology-based education and training programs. Second and third careers are commonplace.

HOW DOES THE POLICY WORK?

There are several factors that describe the way that federal policy works, as well as the importance of how the federal government is organized in the education arena.

The Federal System Is "Messy and Cumbersome," but Unlikely to Change

As Alan Ginsburg, a senior career official in the Department of Education, said, "The feds are very powerful, so a system that is messy and cumbersome is not a bad thing" (Alan Ginsburg, personal interview, October 11, 2002).

Many federal agencies have at least a toehold in education, ranging from the NSF, to NIH, to the Department of Defense. Their education functions are aligned with the respective agency's mission and consolidating them into one agency makes little sense. An example is the DOD school system, which was kept out of the Department of Education because of the strong relationship that exists between military commanders and the support systems that enable the schools to function on a military base.

Politically, consolidation into a single agency is almost inconceivable. Congress has a committee structure that ensures that coordination and consolidation are unnatural acts. Interest groups maintain the status quo, as evidenced by President Carter's attempts to move programs to create a new department. In fact, a recent proposal by President George W. Bush to transfer Head Start from Health and Human Services (HHS) to the Department of Education is generating opposition that repeats the arguments heard when Congress debated creation of the department more than 20 years ago.

The Federal Government Deserves a D in Implementing Programs, Building Capacity at the State and Local Level, and Getting Time Lines Right

As Barry White, now retired after a distinguished career in OMB, put it, when things fail, and they often do, it is almost always due to the lack of an implementation plan (Barry White, personal interview, May 7, 2002). A major factor in failure is that making national policy that will handle the differences in 50 states is very difficult.

When there is a major change in federal law, few, if any, resources are made available for technical assistance, training, and support. The political pressure is to add money for direct services, since that is the money that reaches constituents.

Although Frank Keppel and the Gardner Task Force understood and fought for building capacity in ESEA in 1965, funding for these activities is almost always eliminated or severely reduced. This problem plagues almost all human-service programs. How does a politician explain supporting the salaries of "bureaucrats" rather than expanding services, even if the quality of the services suffers from the lack of the capacity to deliver them?

Communications are a constant problem. The United States has more than 15,000 school districts and 80,000 public schools. The information pipeline is inefficient and, as in the old game of telephone, messages are often received—if at all—with the content distorted as it is passes from layer to layer, person to person.

States want to control the message to local districts; local districts want to control the message to schools. Each has its own set of procedures, its own time line. Some states have more than 1,000 school districts;

Hawaii is a single district. Although there are a few states—such as Delaware, Maryland, and Nevada—where there are so few districts that all the superintendents meet together, for most states, the number of districts and policymakers makes communications, hence implementation, unmanageable.

At the federal level, surprisingly little is being done with electronic communications. Some federal Web sites have been set up and some are quite professional. However, these sites rely on someone seeking information ("pulling") rather than automatically sending ("pushing") it.

Time lines are equally problematic. In 1994, the time lines in ESEA were stretched out for years, yet states still sought, and usually received, waivers. In 2001, the time lines were so short that regulations were often issued after the dates when the law went into effect.

When bills are introduced, the time lines often seem fair; but by the time they are enacted, the time lines are often unachievable. In the fine art of political compromise when legislation is negotiated, all the time and energy goes into other issues; time lines rarely take into consideration when schools start, when staff is hired, or what state laws and local practices need to be enacted or amended to carry out federal law. The *New York Times* reported in mid-October 2002, 9 months after enactment, that states still had not informed schools of provisions in the No Child Left Behind Act that took effect about 2 months before the school year began ("Law on Overhaul," 2002, p. 1).

FACTORS THAT MAKE A DIFFERENCE

As seen above, the development of federal education policy was minor and uneventful until after World War II. Only then did enough support emerge to permit the enactment of major legislation. A number of factors have facilitated or hindered the development of federal policy over the course of the years.

Although Presidential Involvement Is Not Essential, It Makes a Huge Difference

The bookends of current education policy, Lyndon Johnson and George W. Bush, illustrate the difference presidential involvement can make. Neither the landmark original Elementary and Secondary Education Act of 1965, nor the dramatic changes made in No Child Left Behind in 2001 would have been possible without the highly personal intervention of these two presidents.

The most important policy change that did not actively involve a president occurred in 1975 with the passage of the Education of All Handicapped Children Act (EHCA), now known as the Individuals with Disabilities Education Act (IDEA). Coming as it did on the heels of Watergate and addressing an issue around which a strong external civil-rights-oriented constituency had formed, this bill had exceptional external legitimacy and momentum. Few members in either house, or party, dared risk voting against children with special needs, and the issue was consistent with the equity mission established in 1965 for poor children.

Further substantial changes in federal policy will only happen if they are initiated by the White House and if the president is personally committed and involved.

Ideas Do Matter, and Powerful Ideas Succeed

Although federal programs seem to have a momentum of their own, new ideas can change the direction of policy. Three such examples are cited below.

Uniform Standards. The first idea came in 1988 from Marshall "Mike" Smith, then the dean of the School of Education at Stanford University, and Jennifer O'Day, a graduate student at Stanford. In their paper (Smith & O'Day, 1991, pp. 233–267), the concept of an aligned system (systemic reform) was laid out with the starting point of academic content standards. The Smith-O'Day paper influenced the 1988 reauthorization of ESEA, the 1989 Charlottesville Education Summit, policies of the Clinton Administration, and states' policies. One of these states was Texas, where Governor Bush incorporated this idea as a part of the theory of action that he brought to Washington in 2000. A powerful, yet relatively simple, idea changed the course of policy.

Charter Schools. In the early 1980s, Minnesota became the first state to have a charter school. Minnesota activists Ted Kolderie and Joe Nathan were among the driving forces behind this idea.

Although it took a decade, President Clinton incorporated support of charter schools in several of his education initiatives, as did many governors. Today there are federal programs to support charters and almost all states have authorized their creation. Charter schools have opened up the system, made it more flexible, and spurred many public systems to improve.

Closing the Achievement Gap. The top priority of the 2001 ESEA amendments is on closing the achievement gap between White and Asian students at one extreme, and African American and Hispanic students at the other, to improve equity in education. This goal was incorporated into the Bush Administration's first education proposals in 2001. The idea also had support from the left and the right, so it was an easy sell to the leadership of the House and Senate committees. Again, a simple yet powerful idea became the driving force behind a major redirection of federal policy.

The Inevitable Link Between Social Issues and Education

Education bills have long been magnets for social issues, most of which are only tenuously related to federal education policy. Since almost everyone in society has a stake in schools, and since education touches almost every social issue—even if only remotely—that is unlikely ever to change. Unrelated social policy issues have killed education legislation in the past and will continue to do so. The political link between schools and societal issues is inevitable.

The Merits of the Issue and Strength of Leadership Outweigh External Political Pressure

It is relatively easy for an interest group to get a small categorical program enacted; dozens have been so created in the past 40 years. However, enactment does not guarantee even minimal funding. Virtually every major directional change in federal policy has been in the face of significant opposition from the organizations representing the K–12 education community, starting with Title I in 1965 and ending with the 2001 law that changed reading programs and created new accountability systems. In the end, sound ideas and political leadership matter more than externally generated political pressure.

More Often Than We Might Wish to Know, Federal Law Is Shaped by Anecdotes

The power of a personal story, the presence of a wronged parent or child, an exposé of an injustice—all motivate political leaders. Often these stories are reported in the press or told by a witness at a hearing, but often they are the result of a lawmaker's personal experience. When research contradicts personal experience or political ideology, research usually loses. The recent experience with federal evaluations showing the ineffectiveness of programs aimed at drug abuse prevention illustrates this clash of ideology and evidence.

The quality of educational research has had a mostly negative reputation since the 1972 creation of the National Institute of Education. As a consequence, funding for research in both real and inflation adjusted dollars has decreased dramatically. Most of the current appropriation is committed to the support of research centers and regional labs; relatively little is available to fund long-term, quantitative research. As a result, research has little credibility, and personal experiences have great impact.

The Creation of the Department of Education Has Advanced the Education Agenda, but Not Without Some Negatives

Patricia Gwaltney, who headed the Carter administration's OMB reorganization study, which led to the enactment of the department, said, "There would have never been a bully pulpit unless there had been a department" (Patricia [Gwaltney] McGinnis, personal interview, September 17, 2002). Although her reference was to Ted Bell and *A Nation at Risk*, it applies equally to the ability of any secretary or senior federal official to take on issues that must be addressed nationally.

Education was, literally, a "rounding error" in the HEW budget, and any potential education budget appeals to the president—only two or three were ever presented by a HEW secretary—were inevitably trumped by welfare, health, and social security issues. An education secretary may have to prioritize among his or her "children," but everything that he or she considers before going to the White House is in that domain; trade-offs with other domestic programs are not an issue.

On the negative side, a separate education agency means that coordinating programs like Head Start in HHS and Title I and Early Reading in the Department of Education is even more difficult than it might have been under HEW.

Research on education and learning is now carried out by agencies as widely disbursed as the Office of Naval Research, the Defense Advanced Research and Projects Administration, the NIH, and NSF. Only a small amount of fundamental research in education is done by the Department of Education, and there are no viable mechanisms in place to coordinate how research in other agencies might be applied to benefit the education of children, despite the existence of 10 regional educational laboratories that are supported by the Department of Education. In recent years, the only exception is NIH's research on reading, but multiple bureaucratic and cultural barriers between agencies have mitigated the effective use of that research. This is a classic case of "if it's not invented here, it can't be that good."

Finally, and contrary to popular belief, the federal government does run schools. Operated by the DOD and the Department of Interior, these schools serve military dependents (primarily overseas), and children on Indian reservations. According to test data, the DOD schools are far more successful at educating a diverse student body than is almost every large stateside school district, as continually demonstrated by test score data.

Members of Congress from "Safe" Districts or States Have Most Successfully Taken on the Washington-Based Education Establishment

Some, like Carl Perkins, needed little campaign money; others refused to believe that laws should be written by lobbyists and stamped by Congress. Leaders like Jacob Javits, Al Quie, Claiborne Pell, George Miller, Gus Hawkins, and John Boehner all fall into this category.

With campaign costs skyrocketing, few elected officials can ignore the link between political support and campaign contributions. Although education organizations are not as skilled in making the link between lobbying and campaign contributions as unions and business organizations, more political action committees will be formed among education-interest groups, and pressure will continue for the support of certain positions in exchange for endorsements and campaign contributions.

Timing Is Crucial

As noted by former House education committee staff member Marty La-Vor, the special education law that was enacted in 1975 could not have been enacted in the 1980s, or before the 1970s (Marty LaVor, personal interview, September 16, 2002), because the political circumstances were not right and neither was the timing. It is instructive to note that NDEA passed on the heels of a crisis in national defense. The passage of Title I was in part a tribute to assassinated President Kennedy, and the resignation of Nixon and the political furor over his pardon by Ford made a veto of the special education law unthinkable.

The circumstances and timing were also perfectly aligned in 2001, when Bush pushed No Child Left Behind through to enactment, and again in 2002 when the new federal education research bill became law. In both cases, the accumulation of events over time, along with having the right people in the right places, ensured the passage of new laws.

Outsiders Sometimes Play a Major Role, but Rarely Those Who Represent Membership Organizations

Although there are exceptions—the Council for Exceptional Children in the enactment of the 1975 special education act and the NEA in creation of the department—most organized groups of administrators, teachers, and school boards have fought against proposed changes, but they lose far more than they win.

Among the interest groups representing the major stakeholders, a pack mentality operates. That led, in the late 1990s, to the creation of the Education Leaders Council (ELC) by a group of chief state school officers and state board members who often did not agree with the positions of organizations such as the Council of Chief State School Officers and the National Association of State Boards of Education.

In contrast, some individuals and think tanks have had a substantial impact. In the case of No Child Left Behind, the Progressive Policy Institute, the Fordham Foundation, the Education Trust, and the Business Roundtable helped committee leaders gain enactment.

Federal Policy Often Follows State/Local Action

State laws for compensatory education and for disabled children existed before the federal laws were proposed. The idea for individualized education plans came from a field visit made by a House subcommittee (Marty LaVor, personal interview, September 16, 2002). Bush's experience in Texas greatly influenced his 2001 education plan. The impetus for the national education goals emerged from the Southern Regional Education Board, a coalition of states.

Congressional hearings do matter, especially those that occur outside of Washington. In addition, every key elected official has a formal or informal kitchen cabinet of advisors on education, many of whom may not realize the potential influence of their informally expressed views. White House officials listen to governors, especially those in their own party, and are influenced by public opinion polls.

Federal Organization Matters, Whether in Congress or in the Executive Branch

Because several different Congressional subcommittees control federal education policy, there has never been an attempt to rationalize or integrate programs like compensatory and special education. Seven major organizational units in the U.S. Department of Education now deal with K–12 education: the Office of Elementary and Secondary Education, the Office of English Language Acquisition, the Office of Special Education and Vocational Rehabilitation, the Office of Vocational and Adult Education, the Institute of Educational Sciences, the Office of Innovation and Improvement, and the Office of Safe and Drug Free Schools. Each office has its programs, loyal staff, and relationships with interest groups and elected officials to protect those programs, creating the "issue networks" studied by political scientists, and the silos that maintain separation between programs.

The salaries of more than half the staff in state education agencies are paid with federal funds. That practice began in 1965 with ESEA as a way to both build state staffs and create loyalty to federal programs. In many states, staff members who work for major federal programs operate separately from the state superintendents and their staff. Most state agencies mirror major organizational units of the U.S. Department of Education. Therefore, states also usually deal with issues based on program fealty rather than from the perspective of a child or parent.

Until and unless the organization of Congress and the U.S. Department of Education changes, it is unlikely that the organization of most states and large school districts—and the way they view issues—will change. Even though new laws permit the transfer of funds among programs, inertia and fear of a federal audit finding, reigns supreme.

The Federal Government's Control Is Indirect, Because It Operates Through State Agencies

Because the federal government operates through the state agencies, there are 50-plus opportunities for interpretation of laws and regulations. There are few tools that the federal government can use to enforce compliance. Cutting off financial support will hurt children more than the state or local bureaucracy and some states may be willing to accept a cutoff of administrative funds during a period of increasing federal support. Going to court takes forever, and often Congressional supporters will pressure a cabinet secretary or the White House to back off in return for support on another issue. Frank Keppel discovered this in the Johnson administration when he tried to force action on school desegregation in Chicago. He soon found himself in a new job with few powers, and even fewer staff.

Unless state agencies are effective in their roles with respect to federal programs, it is almost impossible for local school districts to "get it right." The regional educational laboratories supported by the federal government should be used much more effectively than they ever have been to assist states. That was, after all, part of the rationale for their creation in 1965.

What the Federal Bureaucracy Does Matters, and So Does That Federal Money!

In recalling the more than 20 interviews I conducted for this book, one keeps coming back to mind. Barry White tells of running into a longtime senior career person one day in 2001 outside the Department of Education. In talking about the change in administrations, the career person said, "This is the first time that someone has ever told us that what we do really matters" (Barry White, personal interview, May 7, 2002).

Whether it is writing regulations, talking with educators, or getting money to schools, the actions of federal staff are exceedingly important. Although the federal government contributes less than a dime of every dollar spent on K–12 education, the leverage those few cents have is immeasurable. Federal dollars are often the "leadership dollars" to ensure that needs are met, progress is made, and all children are served. Without federal leadership and federal dollars, it is unlikely that we would see national attention directed to issues like the achievement gap between students of different races and economic conditions, the need to use reading programs based upon research, or the need for teacher aides to have some education beyond high school. Federal aid is no longer marginal.

The Consistency of the Federal Message Is Extremely Important

If the players on the federal policy scene send different messages, confusion is created at state and local levels, giving those who wish to do nothing, the opportunity to do so.

Following the negotiations and subsequent enactment of the No Child Left Behind Act of 2001, the key leaders were united and have remained so on policy issues, even if they differ on funding. The consistency of that message has made a marked impression on educators at all levels. The education systems in this nation are extremely complex and multilayered. Getting a clear message through the layers to the school principal and to teachers requires a Herculean effort. Multiple messages create confusion, confusion leads to uncertainty, uncertainty stifles improvement.

OTHER OBSERVATIONS

There are a number of other observations that can be made about federal policy and its development that do not neatly fit into a category.

The Power of the Federal Court System Is Immense and Underestimated

Although desegregation cases have clearly been the most important and prominent of the court actions, in recent years almost every U.S. Supreme

Court docket has contained other education-related cases, ranging from prayer, to the privacy of student records, to the enforcement of laws on special education.

So prominent have these cases become that almost any potentially contentious law that passes today contains a severability clause, a provision stating that if one element of the law is overturned by court decision, the rest of the law remains in force.

These court decisions affect policy, but they also influence practice. The 2002 decision upholding the Cleveland, Ohio, voucher program may be the most significant in the long run in helping to open up delivery systems, even though its immediate impact was small because it merely permits the voucher program in Cleveland and, by implication, the one in Milwaukee, to stay in effect.

Political Party Distinctions on Education Have Become Less Clear

In many ways, No Child Left Behind represents the reemergence of conservative Republicans as progressive leaders. After World War II, it was Ohio Republican senator Robert Taft who shocked the body politic with his support for general federal aid, in much the same way that George W. Bush did in 2001 by proposing a law that was at odds with the right wing of his own party. Both parties now vie to see who can get credit for the largest increases in education funding. After the 1996 election, polls showed that the anti-education stance of the GOP was a negative for voters. Within 4 years, that stance has disappeared. Polls—and elections—make a difference!

Federal Programs Do Not Meet the Needs of the Brightest Students

Although there is a small program for gifted and talented students, it does not begin to meet the need. By design, the federal role focuses on those in greatest need, leaving to states the question of how to serve these students.

By focusing on issues of equity and on the need for an aligned system, schools often have no way to challenge students once they have mastered the required standards and demonstrated through the assessment system that they know and understand the material. Schools are, therefore, often doing a disservice to these students and the nation.

Advanced placement classes and dual enrollment in college courses can be used to serve these students, but care must be taken to ensure that federal law protects and encourages these options, without creating a system that is racially or economically segregated.

While Federal Policy Has Attempted to Deal With Parental Involvement and Student Motivation, Those Efforts Have Been Halfhearted, Unfocused, and Ineffective

We have learned from the success of other nations—Japan, Germany, Singapore, Korea—that parental involvement and student motivation are vital to creating a culture that values education, and one in which the need for personal improvement is readily understood.

Student motivation, especially at the high school level, is hard to sustain unless real consequences, such as college admission or a job, are at stake. Many other nations maintain that motivation through a sorting system that keeps parents involved and students motivated. Such a system seems contrary to the American value system.

POSTSCRIPT: FEDERAL POWER EXPANDS

While much has happened since I wrote this book, most of the lessons enumerated in this chapter have stood the test of time, though a few beg for revision and context.

One of the major changes centers on how the federal government operates. With the coming of the Obama administration in 2009, many of the old ways of doing things began to shatter and others took on new prominence. We have also seen Secretary Arne Duncan and President Obama turn increasingly to use of the "Bully pulpit," surpassing even Ronald Reagan and Bill Bennett in this regard.

The implementation of NCLB, the terms of the Race to the Top program, and the Obama proposal for reauthorization of ESEA are all indications that the federal government's influence (sometimes to the point of direction) has spread to every public school in the nation. Whether that will continue and how it will affect student success will be seen in the coming decade, but no matter what, it is an enormous change from the limited federal role that has characterized every previous involvement of Washington.

Nevertheless, there is still a focus on support and assistance to improve student achievement, especially areas where poverty or achievement gaps are prevalent. Instead of federal or national standards, there has been renewed focus on common standards derived from state-led efforts, albeit with the encouragement of the federal government.

Another recent development is the influence of the philanthropic community. The Bill & Melinda Gates Foundation has led and supported efforts ranging from core standards to the expansion of charter schools in ways never seen before in the education field; only time will tell whether that investment has been wise and productive.

9

The Future Federal Role

Observations and Ideas

T HE NO CHILD LEFT BEHIND ACT of 2001 transformed the federal government's role in education, moving it, in a musical sense, from second-chair status in the orchestra to the conductor's podium. The government is now almost literally in the position of setting the stage for all the other players. The conductor can call in the string section (highly qualified teachers), cue the wind section (supplementary-service providers), maintain the drama through the percussionists (adequate yearly progress), and conclude with a stunning finish that brings everyone to their feet (accountability).

This imagery is basically correct. State superintendents of education, along with state boards, legislatures, and governors, must now follow the score. They may chose not to play, but doing so means the threat of a substantial loss in (federal) income and the risk of being tagged a "dropout" by the media, peers, and the voting public.

Having seen how the federal role evolved in the past half century, it is intriguing to consider what the coming half century may hold. My observations are based on the interviews and research done for this book, on my study of the literature, and on countless conversations over the years. Whereas I hold no credentials as a futurist, my own experiences, combined with my fascination with the subject, may, in small measure, compensate for that shortcoming.

Speculating what the future might hold is not merely an academic exercise. As a nation, we need to debate ideas and reach some approximation of a consensus before we can move ahead. Education is now clearly a prominent issue on the national agenda. Every future presidential candidate will be asked for his or her position, as gubernatorial candidates have for decades. Candidates for the Senate and House will be questioned about their views, because Congress will play an ever increasing role.

DIRECTIONS ALREADY ESTABLISHED

Some directions have emerged and seem destined to be enhanced, even strengthened. Although any of these may be derailed, each seems to have a strong political base and substantial momentum.

Redefining Civil Rights for the 21st Century—The Role of Education

In May 2004, the *Brown v. Board of Education of Topeka* Supreme Court decision will celebrate its 50th anniversary. As discussed in earlier chapters, this decision was enormously influential in shaping educational policy at every level from the 1950s through the end of the century. However, with the dismantling of many court orders, the continued opposition to forced busing from parents of all racial and ethnic groups, and the relentless trend in city school districts toward enrollments almost entirely composed of ethnic and racial minorities, the concept of equal education remains a work in progress.

Many believe that by focusing on the achievement gap, the 2001 ESEA amendments have changed the argument from integration to measuring program quality by how well students in each racial and ethnic category perform. Secretary of Education Rod Paige said in a speech on November 13, 2002, at a meeting on English-language acquisition, "Learning is a civil right" ("Language Summit Raises Questions," 2002, p. 10). Other prominent African American leaders, such as Hugh Price, president of the Urban League, and Robert Moses, a civil rights leader, have expressed similar thoughts.

Although the accountability provisions of the law are important, by the end of the decade we will almost certainly see successful malpractice lawsuits against schools for failing to provide an adequate education, based on federal law. Although such suits have already come to trial in state courts, none has yet succeeded. Lawsuits would likely be based on failure to close the achievement gap between racial and ethnic groups.

States will also be sued. Having defined what constitutes an adequate education through the establishment of standards and achievement levels, states will now be challenged if they do not provide adequate funding.

Some think that the Bush administration's belief in the obligation to teach all children to read at grade level before the third grade also sets the stage for legal action. This may become part of a new definition of civil rights with respect to education. Federal reading programs are likely to receive substantial budget increases.

In a decade or so, math is likely to be added. The same NIH office that conducted the reading research has begun similar work in math. It will be years before results are available, but it seems likely that once there is a scientific basis for how best to teach math, math will follow the same trajectory we have seen in reading.

Critics of federal involvement in education usually cite the fact that the 10th Amendment to the Constitution reserves for the states all activities not enumerated as federal responsibilities. Although critics tend to ignore the "general welfare" clause in the constitution, it seems clear that the general welfare requires literate citizens. Thus, education and the general welfare clause are linked in ways that federal courts are likely to embrace.

Research-/Evidence-Based Practice

In the 2001 ESEA law, a variation of the phrase *research-/evidence-based practice* appears more than 100 times. In late 2002, Congress passed, and the president signed, legislation transforming the research component of the Department of Education into the Institute for Educational Sciences.

Although substantial uncertainty exists over exactly how to define *research-based practice*, it is clear that federal funds are to be used only to implement programs and policies that are based on "evidence of effectiveness" and, where possible, on research that uses the gold standard of randomized trials involving substantial numbers of participants.

In many ways, this brings research and evaluation full circle back to 1965 when Senator Robert Kennedy expressed doubt that schools would know what programs worked and use them. Kennedy then said that the federal government needed to make a substantial investment in evaluating programs to determine what works (McLaughlin, 1975). Senator Robert Kennedy's early concerns may have been a major factor influencing Senator Edward Kennedy's support for dramatic reforms in 2001, according to one of the key participants in crafting that law.

As each set of federal programs—vocational education, special education, and higher education—come up for reauthorization, it is almost certain that each new bill will contain similar language on research- and evidence-based practice. Although this change in direction seems to have strong political support, many practitioners are less convinced of its value, largely because it seems to limit the ability of educators to make ad hoc decisions. The movement has also become entangled with the "reading wars"—a battle that divides those who favor the whole-language approach to teaching reading from those who believe that reading must be based on phonemic awareness. Despite these disagreements, the move to research-based practice is here to stay.

Second-Chance Options Will Remain

The American system is unique in the way it offers the young and the old a second chance. Flunk out of high school? You can get a GED, but even without it, almost any community college will accept you. Decide you want to learn a new skill and change jobs? You can enroll in a variety of programs, most state-supported, and use state or federal grants or loans to help you pay the cost. You can do this if you are 25 or 60, want to advance in your chosen profession, or need additional education and training. These actions on your part may also be both supported and rewarded by your employer.

In conversations with education officials of other countries, I have found this is usually the part of the U.S. system that they find most remarkable. Many countries send students off into specific "tracks" at various points in their educational careers, some on the university track, some bound for entry into the trades, others to a second-tier academic strata that will assure they do not enter the best universities.

In many of these countries, where you go to high school determines university admission, which largely determines what company will hire you. Things get set at a relatively young (12–20) age and rarely change. The concept of a second or third career—or, indeed, being a "late bloomer"—is unfathomable.

Regardless of changes made in the U.S. system, the American concept of a second chance will remain because we are a nation of immigrants: people who came here because they wanted a second chance.

Conflicts will arise as we see the consequences of accountability systems (federal and state), which, though focused on the school or school district, often affect students by denying them a high school diploma or advancement to the next grade. As long as there are second-chance options, such as a GED or community college entry without a diploma, these systems can coexist. If attempts are made to couple new accountability systems, federal or state, with the removal of second-chance options, we will have a debate well worth having.

POTENTIAL NEW FEDERAL POLICIES

Some federal policy leaders and observers have shown interest in significantly expanding the federal presence in several new directions, or of substantially expending aspects of federal presence already established.

Technology

Technology is seen as an unfulfilled reality when it comes to education. Although recognized for its contribution to fields as diverse as medicine and communications, technology in education has been marginal, and it has not been seen as a tool that educators can use to increase their own productivity. Gordon Ambach, retired executive director of the Council of Chief State School Officers, noted that the Federal Communications Commission through its E-Rate fund has made Internet access affordable for almost all schools. This step has opened schools' access to technology more than any other program funded by any federal agency. Unfortunately, however, access is not enough. Teachers and principals must be trained and learn to overcome opposition to using private-sector products and services. Educators must overcome the fear that teachers will be displaced by technology. The careful use of technology will expand student options, leave teachers free to work with those most in need, and inspire students with new ideas.

Although the federal government has had technology programs for decades, a renewed and focused effort in this area is quite likely.

Early Learning

Federal early learning programs began with Head Start, under the Economic Opportunity Act of 1964, the cornerstone of Lyndon Johnson's program for the Great Society. Today, Head Start incorporates many elements that are not focused on learning, a source of some disagreement between program advocates and Head Start teachers on one side, and reformers and some federal policymakers on the other.

Since 1964, we have learned a great deal about how people learn, especially very young children; however, much of this knowledge has not been incorporated into programs like Head Start. Research has clearly shown that if children have a learning deficit when they begin the first grade, they are unlikely to ever close that gap; moreover, that the gap is likely to widen as the child gets older. A growing body of evidence shows that many children placed in special education were never taught to read properly at an early age, thereby strengthening the importance of early education.

Much has also been written about the need for universal preschools for 3- and 4-year-olds, contrasting the absence of such programs with their presence in most other industrialized nations. Research on this issue has been compelling to many state policymakers and has finally got the attention of a substantial number of federal policymakers. It is likely that whatever form the new initiatives take, they will include a proposal to transfer Head Start from HHS to the Department of Education. In addition, it is quite likely that we will see some new federal initiatives to expand early learning opportunities, especially for children from low-income families.

High School Reform

Another area in which new federal policy may emerge is in reforming high schools. To date, almost all efforts have dealt, intentionally or not, with elementary schools; the 2001 version of ESEA reform barely touches high school issues. Most of the comprehensive school reform models have little to do with secondary schools (High Schools That Work and Talent Development High Schools are notable exceptions), and most Title I money ends up in the earlier grades. In recent years, a number of private sector initiatives have emerged, most notably the efforts of the Bill and Melinda Gates Foundation, to fund small high schools. Others, including the Carnegie Corporation of New York, have funded similar efforts, but adoption has been far from widespread and few have focused on precise outcomes.

U.S. demographics are a major factor in high school reform efforts. The country is becoming increasingly Hispanic (e.g., California and Texas), and drop-out rates in this population, especially in cities, are distressingly high—usually 40% or more. Among African Americans, the drop-out rate is also unacceptably high, though it has improved somewhat.

Meanwhile, the country is losing jobs to other countries in fields that require educated workers. Although labor costs are clearly an issue, employers report that the absence of a competent labor pool is equally important in decisions to move jobs offshore.

Federal policymakers from the executive and legislative branches recognize that high school issues are likely to become a focus for the next ESEA reauthorization in 2007, unless a White House initiative emerges prior to that time.

Teacher Education and Training

Another area where new federal policy may emerge is teacher education. In the last set of higher education amendments (1998) education schools were required to report on their success with educating teachers. Some states, like Texas, have even shut down schools that do not meet acceptable standards. Title II of ESEA contains a massive professional development program for in-service teachers, some of which is conducted by schools of education.

A major battle is raging in Washington—and often spilling over into states—about what type of education is needed for being an effective teacher. This battle has become surprisingly divisive, with one side claiming that having content knowledge is the only real criteria, the other side defending current practice, which requires a substantial number of teacher preparation courses and may not require content expertise.

Each side seems to have captured both a constituency and some political support. Neither side seems willing to analyze what is required to be a good teacher that goes beyond subject matter knowledge, such as the ability to manage a classroom or the skills to identify and either "treat" or refer children with special learning needs. Many reformers would like to see the elimination of education schools as they currently exist. Most educators support their continuance, while acknowledging the need for reform.

Advocates of change, including both the Clinton and Bush administrations, have supported efforts, such as Teach for America, and Troops to Teachers, that bring people into the field through nontraditional routes.

The debate on teachers will be driven by language in the 2001 ESEA amendments requiring a "highly qualified teacher" in every classroom in the country by the 2005–6 school year. As of this writing (January 2003), virtually every state is trying to decide how to interpret and implement that language. It is unlikely that the issue will be settled for quite some time.

FACTORS THAT WILL INFLUENCE FEDERAL POLICY

In addition to the major issues that are likely to emerge, there are other factors that will influence the development of new policies, perhaps in unpredictable ways.

Choice and Market Forces

As noted, the issue of aid to private, especially Catholic, schools has been a factor in federal aid decisions since these discussions began. In the 1990s, the idea of vouchers became somewhat more acceptable—though still highly contentious—as two states, Ohio and Wisconsin, enacted programs to provide voucher options for children attending schools in their largest cities (Cleveland and Milwaukee, respectively). In 2002, the U.S. Supreme Court ruled that the Cleveland program was constitutional, even though almost all the participants attend Catholic schools. The Supreme Court's decision removed one of the last major legal obstacles to widespread adoption of voucher programs, and placed the issue squarely in the political arena of every state. The implications for federal policy are less clear, but the idea of voucherizing Title I, vocational education, and special education has become legally possible.

In the 2001 ESEA amendments, states are required to certify supplemental service providers, and school districts are required to make those services (in the form of tutoring and related assistance) available to children in schools that do not make adequate yearly progress. In addition, the federal law now requires that children attending schools that fail to improve be given the right to attend other public schools, either in that district or even across district lines if the receiving school or district will accept them. Available space in the "home" district is not an acceptable reason for denial of parental rights to exercise this option, according to the program regulations.

The failure of most districts to offer parents and students options to exercise this right to change schools has become a major issue, with advocates on both the left and right arguing that the only solution is to open all schools, public and private, to students who wish to exercise this right. In mid-2002, the President's Commission on Special Education proposed that services for children requiring special education be converted entirely to vouchers. There are already many special education students who attend nonpublic schools on what are essentially vouchers, because the sending district is incapable of meeting student needs.

Despite these small steps, it seems unlikely that we will see in the coming 20 years an educational system like those in Australia and the Netherlands, where the national or state governments support nearly all schools, public and private, while holding them accountable for what is taught and for student performance. Almost every major education association, particularly the teacher unions—as well as some organizations representing private schools that fear federal intrusion—are in solid opposition to the idea, and campaign money talks. In the 2002 congressional elections, the NEA was among the largest contributors to House and Senate races; though smaller, the AFT was equally as active in its geographic areas of influence.

Unions have been shortsighted in allowing themselves to become almost totally partisan. At the national level, it is a rare Republican who has been endorsed by a teachers union. As a result, these unions have little influence with a Republican White House and the Republican leadership in both houses of Congress. Although union strength is greatest in mustering enough votes to block proposals they oppose, the Reagan effort in 1981 provides a road map for overcoming that advantage.

It is likely that we will see successful efforts to further open the system in small ways, such as in special education. If those efforts are successful, we may see further opening of the system over the following decades. The further opening of the education system will not be risk-free for nonpublic schools. To gain financial support, nonpublic schools will almost assuredly be required to offer a curriculum that resembles that taught in public schools, and agree to the testing and accountability systems imposed by the states and the federal government. Many of these schools will consider these concessions too great and will chose to remain independent, although it is likely that Catholic schools will concede, just as they have in other countries. Whatever the specific details, market forces will continue to nibble away at the current system.

Centralization Versus Flexibility

The movement to academic content and performance standards, which began with the Charlottesville summit in 1989, has forced us to decide which is more important in our society: local flexibility or a coherent system that aligns standards, assessments, teacher training, and accountability. As it has been historically practiced in this country in education, local control is simply inconsistent with having a coherent system.

Parents continue to express their belief, through focus groups and public opinion polls, that they want assurances that their children's education will allow them to compete for jobs on a world stage. Parents know, as Paul O'Neill said at the 1996 education summit, "Nine times nine is the same in any state," and that jobs can be exported with the click of a computer mouse.

Despite these facts, politicians try to use "local control" as a rallying cry against the federal government and the states. On the other hand, parents often believe that local control is the right to hire and fire the football coach, vote in local bond elections, and keep objectionable materials out of their schools. I have never heard a parent, taxpayer, or politician say they do not want the very best education for their children—today this means a competitive, truly world-class education.

Yet flexibility will be maintained through, for example, permitting the transfer of funds across programs, as long as this improves the education of children through the use of proven practices. Centralization need not mean a common curriculum, if schools can assure parents that children are being taught content and if this can be verified through tests and accountability systems. We must also ensure that schools and districts that need comprehensive help receive it and are not left without support, especially in the area of teaching and learning.

In recent years, the federal government has supported the adoption of various models for school improvement through the Comprehensive School Reform Program, using models developed, in part, through the efforts of New American Schools. This represents a pluralistic approach. The choice of models is always made at the school level, usually by a vote of the staff. All models have the common objective of improving student learning, though the methods vary widely.

What does this mean for the future? We will probably continue to see the focus on systems that align teaching, curricula, and testing through accountability systems. Other requirements, such as teacher training and professional development, will only receive federal funding for programs that support this alignment.

We also need a new vocabulary that will permit us to talk about issues like local control without the baggage that now accompanies these and other terms.

WHAT WILL NOT HAPPEN

Some things are quite unlikely to happen within the coming decade, and perhaps in the coming half century.

General Aid Is Unlikely; the Federal Share Will Not Exceed 10 Percent

Although some of the earliest attempts for federal support were for general aid (aid that school districts and states could use for any purpose in public schools), it is quite unlikely that the Congress will enact general aid legislation.

The lessons of the past 40 years, as highlighted in numerous evaluation and research studies, have given Congress and the executive branch no reason to believe that money that was "put on the stump" would be wisely used to meet federal objectives.

Policymakers are concerned that most of any general support aid would be soaked up by increased teacher salaries, with no assurance that the expenditure would be accompanied by an increase in student learning. The movement to accountability that began in 1988, was advanced in 1994, and cemented in 2001 is unlikely to be eliminated. Whereas the accountability requirements now refer to all students and affect all teachers and schools, the federal investment remains targeted on areas such as the education of disadvantaged students and the closing of the achievement gap. The 2001 bill came about largely because federal policymakers grew weary of watching states take federal money and then not wanting to be held accountable for its use. A strong accountability mechanism is seen as the best answer to that problem.

Although the federal share of total public school spending has ranged from about 5% to 9%, it is unlikely we will see the share rise much above 10%. At just over 8%, the federal education budget—including higher education—is more than $50 billion in the Department of Education, with other funding coming from NSF, the Department of Agriculture, and smaller agencies. Given the demands on federal spending, federal deficits, and the primacy of the state role, substantial growth in new areas is unlikely.

No Longer Will Federal Education Policy Be Dominated by Washington-Based Education Organizations

Since the 1989 Charlottesville Education Summit, new players—especially the business community—have been energized and have become major players. Prior to the summit, only an occasional business leader would be visible nationally on an education issue, and then most likely as chair of a study group for the Committee on Economic Development.

Today, a half-dozen business organizations operate at the national level and almost every state has at least one active organization. Although initially timid in their participation, leaders such as Lou Gerstner (IBM), Ed Rust (State Farm Insurance), and Phil Condit (Boeing) have become forces to be reckoned with, as have organizations such as the Business Roundtable and Achieve. Individually and collectively, these organizations and people played a major role in 2001. They and their successors will continue in that tradition.

WHAT REMAINS THAT REQUIRES ATTENTION

Despite all that has been done, there are areas that are appropriate for federal intervention but where no action is likely in the near future.

The first area relates to equalizing the financing of schools—a subject often considered a primary reason for federal support—the rationale being that only the federal government can equalize the resources available for school support that result in some states spending half of what others do on a per pupil basis. Advocates point to the fact that when one examines the property wealth available to be taxed to educate a student, one finds that many states are property-wealth poor. Since most schools are primarily financed by property taxes, there will always be schools with fewer resources, or where property will have to be taxed at prohibitive rates. Advocates believe that with its broad and progressive tax base, the federal government should play an equalizing role.

In fact, in Title I, there is some funding that does just that, but the amount is negligible and the funds are restricted in their use. Finance equalization would be a form of general aid, not to be confused with a general aid program that has little or no relationship to taxing ability. Some advocates believe that if a federal program of interstate equalization were achieved, the next step would be an effort for the federal government to assist with intrastate equalization. This seems like a very long stretch from where we are today and is unlikely to happen, especially given the likely price tag associated with this issue.

Another area that could benefit from federal intervention is the development of capacity to support reform at the state and local levels, as well as the expansion of the U.S. Department of Education's capacity to provide technical assistance.

Few state education agencies have the breadth, and especially the depth, to provide the technical assistance and support that schools and school districts need if they are to meet the expectations of federal law. Title V of the original ESEA was directed at this purpose, and it did help. However, in the intervening 30-plus years, many more requirements have been levied on the overwhelmed states—and states have not spent very much on their own agencies. Key state staff is expected to cover multiple areas and funding does not exist to assure that there is adequate depth of coverage.

States have become the front-line players in implementing federal programs and enforcing provisions, such as the accountability sections of No Child Left Behind. Without adequate staff, the implementation of federal law is in jeopardy, and states believe the federal government should finance that effort.

At the same time, the regional offices of the Department of Education have become little more than places where a senior official can be stationed to represent the secretary in regional activities. Although the department's Office for Civil Rights and various higher education programs do maintain staff in the regional offices, there is no capacity at that level to assist states. Various administrations over the years have stripped regional offices, largely in despair of their staffs' capabilities and with the knowledge that states want to deal with program staff in headquarters where they can be assured that they are getting sound advice.

Whatever the solution, it is unlikely that we will see federal goals met unless both state agencies and the Department of Education have, or arrange through contracts, the human resources required to assist states, districts, and schools in meeting federal expectations. Currently, there is little evidence that such an investment has any political support.

A FINAL NOTE AND A PROPOSAL: CONGRESSIONAL ORGANIZATION AND HOW IT AFFECTS SCHOOLS

Congress is organized as a system of committees and subcommittees that ensures that elementary and secondary education is never looked at as a whole. In the House, one subcommittee handles ESEA and vocational education, but never in the same year or in the same bill. Another subcommittee handles special education. The jurisdiction for preschool is split among committees and subcommittees and yet another committee handles science and NSF. A similar pattern exists in the Senate. An entirely separate set of committees and subcommittees decides how much will be spent to operate programs and agencies, and communication between committees on these matters is rare. In fact, in the House, caucus rules prohibit a member from serving on both the education committee and the appropriations committee.

The organization of the Department of Education is based on congressional mandates and the 1979 statute governing its creation; it has seven separate subparts dealing with K–12 education, ranging from the general, the Office of Elementary and Secondary Education, to the specific, the Institute for Educational Sciences. In addition, NSF plays a major role in math and science education.

Such fragmented policy does a disservice to the needs of children, creates unnecessary bureaucracies at every level, and makes it very difficult to hold people accountable.

Although it is unlikely that these congressional structures will ever be dismantled, the situation cries out for the creation of a congressional task force charged with the specific mandate of studying these issues, including the organization of the U.S. Department of Education, and recommending changes back to the relevant committees and the president. Ideally, the task force would be composed of representatives of each of the responsible committees and subcommittees. The task force would have a limited time period, less than 2 years, and would study matters related to fragmentation, coordination, and communication.

In addition to hearing from bureaucrats and interest groups desiring to protect their turf, the task force should also listen to parents, students, principals, and teachers. Not those who represent, say, the PTA or the teacher unions, but those who represent no special interest. The results could prove to be extremely illuminating.

In support of this proposal, and in recognition of the overall value it has provided, OMB should reinstitute the special analysis of federal spending on education that was discontinued in the 1980s. That document was the only comprehensive picture of federal spending across agencies. Although improvements in the old reports are needed, the existence of this document provided invaluable insights into how the federal government supports education.

Whatever course federal policy follows between now and the middle of the 21st century, the story of that evolution will likely be as interesting as the history of the past 50 years.

POSTSCRIPT: RACING TO THE TOP

Several new issues have emerged in the past few years, some programmatic, others of a more fundamental policy nature.

In 2009, the combination of the Obama administration and a poorly performing economy resulted in changes to the rules in several respects. The most fundamental was the presence of a $100 billion education component in the American Recovery and Reinvestment Act, passed by the Congress in the first month of the Obama administration. That law included $37 billion to the states to replace revenue lost due to lower tax collections, money that became, in essence, the first general aid ever authorized by the federal government, albeit under the guise of a response to a fiscal crisis. While this was a largely unacknowledged breakthrough, it came about as a part of an effort to deal with larger societal pressures, not as an education issue, per se.

That same $100 billion appropriation also gave Secretary Arne Duncan a sizeable pot of money from which he created the $4.35 billion Race to the Top competition. This effort is incredibly significant as both because it represented the largest amount of discretionary money ever made available at the federal level and because the law gave Duncan the opportunity to use his authority to create a competition that rewards innovation and creativity, a second way to have the federal government reach all schools. By the end of March 2010, 16 states had been selected as finalists, and awards to the winning states in round one were to be announced shortly, with a second set of winners to be announced in September.

Notes

CHAPTER 3

1. As Samuel Halperin, a key Office of Education official at that time, pointed out in correspondence with the author, Kennedy was losing on almost every issue at this point, mostly because of the opposition of southern Democrats who opposed Kennedy's social agenda.

2. According to Halperin, the full committee chair in the Senate was Alabama Democrat Lister Hill. He let Morse introduce and manage the bill so that Baptists and others who might be anti-Catholic would not be "on his back."

CHAPTER 4

1. Interview with the author, April 10, 2002. Quie tells of a meeting in the Oval Office where, with OMB officials present, Quie explained why the administration should not oppose the bill and of Ford's agreement with his arguments.

2. Under the rules of both the House and Senate, matters pertaining to the creation of agencies are within the jurisdiction of committees on government organization and operations, rather than committees with substantive jurisdiction over the specific area.

CHAPTER 5

1. In his book, Bell notes that he wanted the author as undersecretary at the department, but the formal nomination was blocked by conservatives mad at Bell's appointment (1988, pp. 40–41). William Clohan was then appointed to the job, but the White House forced Bell to fire him within a few months (p. 59).

2. Jack Jennings, key aide to House committee chair Carl Perkins, reported that Perkins surveyed the commission members after release of the report and found that most did not believe that the president's comments were at all reflective of the report.

3. In an interview, Alan Ginsberg, a senior career official who worked with Bell to create the chart, recalls that Bell wanted to make governors uneasy about how their states were doing and not allow them to sit back.

4. The 2001 law, No Child Left Behind, does require that all states participate and provides federal money to assist the states.

CHAPTER 6

1. Although there came to be eight goals, goals 4 (teacher education) and 8 (parental participation) were added when Congress wrote the goals into law in 1994.

CHAPTER 7

This chapter is based on research from my University of Wisconsin-Madison Ph.D. dissertation, "Federalism, Agenda Setting, and the Development of Federal Education Policy, 1965–2001." The chapter draws on more than 60 elite interviews conducted between April 2001 and May 2002 with current and past members of the education policy community in Washington, DC.—P.F.M.

References

Alexander, L., & James, T. H. (1987). *The nation's report card: Improving the assessment of student achievement. Report of the study group.* New York: New York University, National Academy of Education.

Alvarez, L. (2001a, May 3). House Democrats block voucher provision. *New York Times*, p. A21.

Alvarez, L. (2001b, May 2). Senate takes on Bush's education bill as some conservatives grumble. *New York Times*, p. A15.

Ambach, G. (1993). Federal action essential for school reform. In John F. Jennings (Ed.), *National issues in education: The past is prologue* (pp. 33–53). Bloomington, IN: Phi Delta Kappan International and the Institute for Educational Leadership.

Ascher, C., Fruchter, N., & Berne, R. (1996, September). *Hard lessons: Public schools and privatization.* Washington, DC: Century Foundation.

Bell, T. H. (1988). *The thirteenth man: A Reagan cabinet memoir.* New York: Free Press.

Bennett, W. J., Keegan, L. G., Finn, C. E. Jr., & Kafer, K. (2001, October 3). Memorandum to President George W. Bush, House and Senate ESEA conferees, and congressional leaders re: Recommendations for improving ESEA legislation. Washington, DC: Empower America.

Bennett leaving as he came: Guns ablaze. (1988, May 14). *Congressional Quarterly*, p. 1329.

Berube, M. (1991). *American presidents and education.* New York: Greenwood Press.

Blum, J. (2001, January 25). Bush touts education plan at D.C. school. Retrieved February 15, 2001, from: www.washingtonpost.com

Brademas, J. (1987). *The politics of education: Conflict and consensus on the hill.* Norman: University of Oklahoma Press.

Broder, D. S. (2001a, December 17). Long road to reform. *Washington Post*, p. A1.

Broder, D. S. (2001b, July 15). Salvaging real education reform. *Washington Post*, p. B7.

Bush, G. H. W. (1989a, September 27). Remarks at the Education Summit Welcoming Ceremony at the University of Virginia in Charlottesville. George Bush

Presidential Library electronic archives [Online]. Available: http://bushlibrary
.tamu.edu/papers/189/89092708.html

Bush, G. H. W. (1989b, September 28). Remarks at the Education Summit Farewell
Ceremony at the University of Virginia in Charlottesville. George Bush Presidential Library electronic archives [Online]. Available: http://bushlibrary.tanu
.edu/papers/1989/89092801.html

Business Roundtable. (2001, December 11). The Business Roundtable calls conference report a vital step forward for American education. Press release.

Business Roundtable. (2002, January 8). The Business Roundtable commits to help
states, districts make new education reforms work. Press release.

Chaddock, G. Russell. (2001, December 18). Education law biggest in 35 years.
Retrieved January 23, 2002, from: www.csmonitor.com/2001/1218/p1s2-usgn
.html

Citizens' Commission on Civil Rights. (2001, March 1). *Closing the deal: A prelim-
inary report on state compliance: With final assessment and accountability
requirements under the Improving America's Schools Act of 1994*. Washington, DC: Author. Available online: http://www.cccr.org/CTDContents.html

Clinton would tie federal aid to learning standards. (1993, September 11). *Congressional Quarterly*, p. 2394.

Clinton's initiatives gain approval, but people split on a national test. (1997, March
14). *Wall Street Journal*, p. R3.

Clymer, A., & Alvarez, L. (2001, December 12). Congress reaches compromise on
education bill. Retrieved December 12, 2001, from: www.nytimes.com

Coleman, J. S., Campbell, E. Q., Hobson, C. J., McPartland, J., Mood, A. M.,
Weinfeld, F. D., & York, R. L. (1966). *Equality of educational opportunity*.
Washington, DC: U.S. Government Printing Office.

Congressional Quarterly Annual Almanac. (1988). Washington, DC: Congressional
Quarterly.

Council of Chief State School Officers. (2001a, September 26). Letter to House-
Senate Conferees on the No Child Left Behind Act [Online]. Available: http://
ccsso.org/positions/fed-state-archive.html

Council of Chief State School Officers. (2001b, September 26). Letter to members
of the House Labor, Health and Human Services, and Education Appropriations Subcommittee [Online]. Available: http://www.ccsso.org/positions/fed-
state-archive.html

Council of Chief State School Officers. (2001c, October 29). Letter to senators
regarding the FY 2002 ESEA Labor, Health and Human Services, and Education Appropriations Bill [Online]. Available: http://www.ccsso.org/positions/
fed-state-archive.html

Cremin, L. A. (1961). *The transformation of the school: Progressivism in American
education, 1876–1957*. New York: Knopf.

"Dial-a-porn" ban approved as rider to big education bill. (1988, April 23). *Congressional Quarterly*, p. 1078.

The Education Amendments of 1978, Pub. L. No. 95-561. Available online: http://
thomas.loc.gov/bss

Education Consolidation and Improvement Act of 1981, Pub. L. No. 97-35, 20 U.S.C. ch. 52.

Education Daily, 30(24). (1997, February 5), p. 1.

Education policy in the Clinton administration. (1995, Spring). *Teachers College Record*, 96.

Education Sciences Reform Act of 2002, Pub. L. No. 107-279. Available online: http://www.thomas.loc.gov/bss

Education summit joint statement. (1989, September 28). Available online: http://bushlibrary.tamu.edu/papers/1989/89092802.html

Educational policy in the Carter years. (1978, September). Washington, DC: George Washington University, Institute for Educational Leadership.

Educators, analysts hail strategies as bold departures. (1991a, April 24). *Education Week* [Online]. Available: http://www.edweek.org

Equality of Educational Opportunity Report. (1966). Lyndon Baines Johnson Library, Austin, TX.

Excerpts from Bush administration plan to revamp schools. (1991, April 24). *Education Week* [Online]. Available: http://www.edweek.org

Federal News Service. (2001, January 24). Excerpt from Bush statement announcing start of his education initiative. *New York Times*, p. A14.

Fiske, E. B. (1990). George Bush as the education president. In Kenneth W. Thompson (Ed.), *The presidency and education* (p. 121). Lanham, MD: University Press of America.

Fletcher, M. A. (2001a, February 2). Education has center stage under Bush. *Washington Post*, p. A21.

Fletcher, M. A. (2001b, May 29). School accountability remains tough task. *Washington Post*, p. A2.

Gardner, J. (1964, November 14). *Report of the president's task force on education.* Washington, DC: Library of Congress, Congressional Research Service.

GOP warns Clinton against initiating national tests in reading, mathematics. (1997, March 11). Washington Times, p. 1.

Gorman, S. (2001a, July 14). Behind bipartisanship. *National Journal*, pp. 2228–2233.

Gorman, S. (2001b, February 24). Bush's big test. *National Journal*, pp. 549–553.

Gorman, S. (2001c, May 12). When the fine print changes. *National Journal*, p. 1418.

Graham, H. D. (1984). *The uncertain triumph: Federal education policy in the Kennedy and Johnson years.* Chapel Hill: University of North Carolina Press.

Green, E. (1985, August 23). Transcript of oral history interview. Lyndon Baines Johnson Library, Austin, TX.

Halperin, S. (1969, February 24). Transcript of oral history interview (pp. 7, 10, 15). Lyndon Baines Johnson Library, Austin, TX.

Heffernan, R. (2001). *Cabinetmakers: Story of the three-year battle to establish the U.S. Department of Education.* San Jose, CA: Writer's Showcase.

High aide ousted in Education Department. (1982, June 11). *New York Times*, p. B6.

The high price of cheapening the cabinet. (1978). *New York Times*, editorial page.

Hill, P. T. (1979). *Do federal education programs interfere with one another?* Santa Monica, CA: RAND Corporation.

Hill, P. T. (1981). *The aggregate effects of federal education program.* Santa Monica, CA: Rand Corporation.

Hill, P. T. (Ed.). (2002). *Choice with equity.* Palo Alto, CA: Hoover Institution Press.

House Committee on Education and the Workforce. (2001, May 16). State education reform leaders urge passage of H.R. 1 education bill. Press release.

House Report No. 143 to accompany H.R. 2362, the Elementary and Secondary Education Act of 1965. (1965, March 8). Washington, DC: U.S. House of Representatives.

Howe, H. (1969, October 29). Transcript of oral history interview (pp. 4, 5, 12). Lyndon Baines Johnson Library, Austin, TX.

Hunter, B. (2001, November 8). Letter to Representative John Boehner (R-OH) on the ESEA conference. Arlington, VA: American Association of School Administrators.

Implementing standards in schools. (2000, December). *NASSP Bulletin, 84* (620).

Ink, D. (1969, February 25). Transcript of oral history interview (p. 10). Lyndon Baines Johnson Library, Austin, TX.

Jeffords, J. M. (2001). *My declaration of independence.* New York: Simon and Schuster.

Jennings, J. F. (Ed.). (1993). *National issues in education: The past is prologue.* Bloomington, IN: Phi Delta Kappa International and the Institute for Educational Leadership.

Jennings, J. F. (1998). *Why national standards and tests?* Thousand Oaks, CA: Sage Publications.

Jennings, J. F. (2000, March). Title I: Its legislative history and its promise. *Phi Delta Kappan, 81* (9), pp. 516–522.

Johnson, L. B. (1965, April 11). Transcript of remarks by President Johnson on signing the education bill, Johnson City, TX. Lyndon Baines Johnson Library, Austin, TX.

Jordan, K. F. (1996, November 18). *Block grant funding for federal education programs: Background and pro and con discussion.* Washington, DC: Library of Congress, Congressional Research Service.

Kafer, K. (2001, December 13). A small but costly step toward reform: The conference education bill. Retrieved June 13, 2001, from: www.heritage.org/shorts/20011213education.html

Kanstoroom, M., & Finn, C. E., Jr. (Eds.). (1999). *New directions: Federal education policy in the twenty-first century.* Washington, DC: Thomas Fordham Foundation.

Keppel, F. (1972, January 25). Transcript of oral history interview (p. 8). Lyndon Baines Johnson Library, Austin, TX.

Kirst, M. W., & Guthrie, J. W. (1994). Goals 2000 and a Reauthorized ESEA: National Standards and Accompanying Controversies. In Nina Cobb (Ed.), *The future of education* (pp. 157–174). New York: College Board.

Language summit raises questions. (2002, November 20). *Education Week* [On-line]. Available: http://www.edweek.org

Law on overhaul of school standards is seen as skirted. (2002, October 15). *New York Times*, p. 1.

Letter from Daniel P. Moynihan to Neil McElroy. (1970, July 24). National Archives. Nixon Presidential Materials, White House Central Files, FA3.

Letter from Strom Thurmond to Richard Nixon. (1969, February 21). National Archives. Nixon Presidential Materials, White House Central Files, FG13.

Letter from Theodore Sizer to Dr. Daniel P. Moynihan. (1969, April 8). National Archives. Nixon Presidential Materials, White House Executive Files, FA3.

Marinelli, J. (1976). Financing education. In F. Weintraub, A. Abelson, J. Ballard, & M. LaVor (Eds.), *Public policy and the education of exceptional children* (p. 151). Reston, VA: Council for Exceptional Children.

Math score on SAT improves to highest level since 1969. (2002, August 27). *Wall Street Journal*, p. B2.

McLaughlin, M. W. (1975). *Evaluation and reform: The Elementary and Secondary Education Act of 1965, Title I*. Cambridge, MA: Ballinger.

Memorandum for the President [Nixon] from Arthur F. Burns. (1969, August 18). National Archives. Nixon Presidential Materials, White House Staff Files, FG6-11-1.

Memorandum from Arthur Klebanoff to H. R. Haldeman and John Ehrlichman. (1979, March 21). National Archives. Nixon Presidential Materials, White House Staff Files, SMOF, Box 48.

Memorandum from Daniel P. Moynihan to H.R. Haldeman. (1970, October 15). National Archives. Nixon Presidential Materials, White House Staff Files of H. R. Haldeman, Box 48.

Memorandum from Ed Harper to Ken Cole. (1970, April 10). National Archives. Nixon Presidential Materials, White House Central Files, FA3.

Memorandum from Michael Balzanno to Chuck Colson. (1972, June 15). National Archives. Nixon Presidential Materials, White House Staff Files of Charles Colson, FA3, HU2-1.

Memorandum to the President [Nixon] from John Ehrlichman. (1970, November 16). National Archives. Nixon Presidential Materials, Ehrlichman Files, FA3, HU2-1, FG23.

Memorandum from Richard Nathan to Pat Moynihan. (1969, April 18). National Archives. Nixon Presidential Materials, White House Executive Files, FA3.

Memorandum from Todd Hullin to H. R. Haldeman. (1972, June 17). National Archives. Nixon Presidential Materials, White House Staff Files of H. R. Haldeman, ED, PR1.

Miller, R. A. (Ed.). (1981). *The federal role in education: New directions for the eighties*. Washington, DC: Institute for Educational Leadership.

Mollison, A. (2001). State legislators now oppose Bush's education plan. Retrieved October 9, 2001, from: www.coxnews.com

Munger, F., & Fenno, R., Jr. (1962). *National politics and federal aid to education*. Syracuse, NY: Syracuse University Press.

National Conference of State Legislatures. (2001a, September 26). Letter to congressional conferees regarding the reauthorization of the Elementary and Secondary Education Act.

National Conference of State Legislatures. (2001b, January 26). State legislators eager to work with President Bush on education reform. Press release.

National Education Association. (2001, December 11). Education bill: Right goals, wrong means. Press release.

National Governors' Association. (2001, October 5). Letter to Chairman Boehner, Representative Miller, Chairman Kennedy, and Senator Gregg on the ESEA reauthorization.

Nixon, R. M. (1970, May 21). Message to Congress. National Archives. Nixon Presidential Materials, White House Central Files, SP2-3-49, FA3.

Nixon Press Conference No. 24. (1972, June 22). National Archives. Nixon Presidential Materials, White House Central Files.

No Child Left Behind Act of 2001, Pub. L. No. 107-110. Available online: http://www.ed.gov/legislation/ESEA02/

Office of Economic Opportunity. (1970, August 19). Delegation of Authority to Secretary of Health, Education, and Welfare. National Archives. Nixon Presidential Materials, White House Central Files.

Olson, L. (2001, May 9). Bush test plan fuels debate over uniformity. *Education Week*, pp. 23–24.

Olson, L. (2002a, March 27). Negotiators retain heart of Ed. Dept. proposals. *Education Week*, pp. 24, 27.

Olson, L. (2002b, January 16). States gear up for new federal law. *Education Week*, pp. 1, 24–25.

Olson, L. (2002c, March 6). Testing rules would grant states leeway. *Education Week*, pp. 1, 36–37.

Oppel, R. A., & Schemo, D. J. (2000, December 22). Bush is warned vouchers might hurt school plans. *New York Times*, p. A28.

Patterson, J. T. (2001). *Brown v. Board of Education: A civil rights milestone and its troubled legacy*. New York: Oxford University Press.

Pitsch, M. (1993, September 29). E.D. officials begin task of marketing their proposal to reinvent E.S.E.A. *Education Week* [Online]. Available: http://www.edweek.org

President's $51 billion "crusade" has educators energized, nervous. (1997, February 6). *Washington Post* [Online]. Available: http://www.washingtonpost.com

Presidential memorandum accompanying return of H.R. 7336. (1983, January 12) [Online]. Available: http://www.reagan.utexas.ed/resources/speeches/1983/11283d.htm

Proposed federal aid to education. (1961, July 27). Washington, DC: Library of Congress, Legislative Reference Service.

Public policy and the education of exceptional children. (1976). Reston, VA: Council for Exceptional Children.

Quie, A. H. (1969, April 30). Transcript of oral history interview (p. 24). Lyndon Baines Johnson Library, Austin, TX.

Ravitch, D. (1983). *The troubled crusade*. New York: Basic Books.

Reagan, R. (1983, December 8). Remarks to the National Forum on Excellence in Education, Indianapolis, Indiana. Ronald Reagan Presidential Library, Simi Valley, CA. White House staff files of Douglas Holladay, Box 012150.

Reagan, R. (1984, January 25). State of the Union message [Online]. Available: http:://www.Reagan.utexas.edu/resource/speeches/1984/12584e.htm

Rees, N. S. (2001). *Priorities for the president: Improving education for every American child.* Washington, DC: Heritage Foundation.

Report of the National Advisory Committee on Education. (1931, October). National Library of Education, Washington, DC.

Report of the President's Task Force on Education. (1964, November 14). Lyndon Baines Johnson Library, Austin, TX.

Riddle, W. (2002a, February 12). *Education for the disadvantaged: ESEA Title I reauthorization issues.* Washington, DC: Library of Congress, Congressional Research Service.

Riddle, W. (2002b, February 13). *K–12 education: Highlights of the No Child Left Behind Act of 2001 (P.L. 107–110).* Washington, DC: Library of Congress, Congressional Research Service.

Robelen, E. W. (2002, January 9). ESEA to boost federal role in education. *Education Week,* p. 1.

Salzer, J. (2001, January 27). Barnes cuts Bush's grade over vouchers. *Atlanta Journal and Constitution,* p. A1.

Secretary of Education Richard Riley enunciates administration's goals. (1993, May 24). *Roll Call,* p. 15.

Senior staff meeting notes. (1983, June 23). Ronald Reagan Presidential Library, Simi Valley, CA. White House subject files, FG006-01.

Shanker, A. (1983, May 1). Where we stand. *New York Times,* p. E9.

Smith, M. S., & O'Day, J. A. (1991). System school reform. In S. Fuhrman & B. Malen (Eds.), *The politics of curriculum and testing, Politics of Education Yearbook, 1990* (pp. 233–267). London: Falmer Press.

Sproul, L., Weiner, S., & Wolf, D. (1984). *Organizing an anarchy: Belief, bureaucracy, and politics in the National Institute of Education.* Chicago, IL: The University of Chicago Press.

Statement of Sen. Robert A. Taft. (1948, March 24). *Congressional Record,* p. 3347.

Stedman, J. B. (2002, January 24). *K–12 teacher quality: Issues and legislative action.* Washington, DC: Library of Congress, Congressional Research Service.

Stockman, D. A. (1987). *The triumph of politics.* New York: Avon Books.

Summit accord calls for focus on standards. (1996, April 3). *Education Week* [Online]. Available: http://www.edweek.org

Sundquist, J. L. (1968). *Politics and policy: The Eisenhower, Kennedy, & Johnson years.* Washington, DC: Brookings Institution.

Taylor, W. L., & Piche, D. M. (2002, January 8). Will new school law really help? *USA Today,* p. 13A.

Teachers vote to let parents decide on tests. (2001, July 8). Retrieved July 24, 2001, from: www.nytimes.com

Testing, testing—1, 2, 3. (1997, April 21). *U.S. News & World Report*, p. 40.

Thomas, N. C. (1975). *Education in national politics*. New York: David McKay.

Thompson, K. W. (Ed.). (1992). *The presidency and education*. Lanham, MD: University Press of America.

Time for results. (1986, August). Executive summary. Washington, DC: National Governors Association.

Toch, T. (2001, November). Bush's big test. Retrieved November 4, 2001, from: www.washingtonmonthly.com

Transcript, Frank Keppel Oral History Interview. (1972, January 25). p. 8, Lyndon Baines Johnson Library, Austin, TX.

U.S. Department of Education, Planning and Evaluation Service. (1993). *Reinventing Chapter 1: The current Chapter 1 program and new directions. Final report of the National Assessment of the Chapter I Program*. Washington, DC: Author.

U.S. Department of Education budget tables, 1965–2003 [Online]. Available: www.ed.gov

Verstegen, D. A. (1988). *Fiscal policy for education in the Reagan administration* (Occasional Paper No. 5). Charlottesville, VA: University of Virginia, Curry School of Education.

Wellstone, P. (2001, February 6). Bush plan may set students up for failure. Retrieved February 25, 2001, from: www.latimes.com

White House fact sheet on the president's education strategy. (1991, 18 April). Available online: http://bushlibrary.tamu.edu

White House Issue Alert No. 14. (1983, June 6). Spending on education. Ronald Reagan Presidential Library, Simi Valley, CA. White House staff files of Kevin Hopkins, Box 136132.

White House Issue Alert No. 16. (1983, June 23). Ten myths about President Reagan's education policies. Ronald Reagan Presidential Library, Simi Valley, CA. White House staff files of Kevin Hopkins, Box 136132.

White House Office of the Press Secretary. (2002, January 8). President signs landmark education bill. Press release.

White House staff files of Douglas Holladay. (1962, August 7). Ronald Reagan Presidential Library, Simi Valley, CA. Box 12150.

White House staff files of Douglas Holladay and Kevin Hopkins. (1984, February 21). Ronald Reagan Presidential Library, Simi Valley, CA. Boxes 12150, 136132.

White House Task Force on Education. (1965, June 14). [Recommendations.] Lyndon Baines Johnson Library, Austin, TX.

Wilgoren, J. (2001, July 17). Education plan comes under fire by state officials. Retrieved July 24, 2001, from: www.nytimes.com

Wong, K. W. (1999). *Politics and policies: Funding public schools*. Lawrence: University Press of Kansas.

Suggested Reading

Bailey, S. K., & Mosher, E. K. (1968). *ESEA: The Office of Education administers a law*. Syracuse, NY: Syracuse University Press.

Cohen, D. K., & Hill, H. C. (2001). *Learning policy: When state education reform works*. New Haven, CT: Yale University Press.

Committee on Education and Labor, House of Representatives. (1979, February). *Title I of the Elementary and Secondary Education Act of 1965*.

Education Week. Available online: http://www.edweek.org/search/

Excerpt from Bush administration's plan to revamp schools. (1991, April 24). *Education Week*. Available online: http://www.edweek.org/search/

Education Week, Staff of. (2000). *Lessons of a century: A nation's schools come of age*. Bethesda, MD: Editorial Projects in Education.

Federal role in education. (1965). *Congressional Quarterly*.

The federal role in improving elementary and secondary education. (1993). Congressional Budget Office.

Finn, C. E., Jr. (1977). *Education and the presidency*. Lexington, MA: Lexington Books.

The historic and current federal role in education. (1961). Washington, DC: Library of Congress, Legislative Reference Service.

History Central. U.S. Presidential Elections [Online]. Available: http://www.multied.com/elections/

Jordon, K. F., & Irwin, P. (1981). *Education Consolidation and Improvement Act of 1981*. Washington, DC: Library of Congress, Congressional Research Service.

National Education Goals [Online]. (1990). Available: http://www.negp@ed.gov

Public Law 91-380, enacted August 18, 1970, FY 1971 appropriations bill. Available online: http://thomas.loc.gov/bss

Public Law 92-318, enacted June 23, 1972, The Education Amendments of 1972. Available online: http://thomas.loc.gov/bss

Public Law 93-380, enacted August 21, 1974, The Education Amendments of 1974. Available online: http://thomas.loc.gov/bss

Public Law 94-142, enacted November 29, 1975, The Education of All Handicapped Children Act. Available online: http://thomas.loc.gov/bss

Quattelbaum, C. (1960). *Federal educational policies, programs, and proposals.* Washington, DC: Library of Congress, Legislative Reference Service.

Radin, B. A., & Hawley, W. D. (1988). *The politics of federal reorganization.* New York: Pergamon Press.

Republican Contract with America [Online]. (1994). Available: http://www.house gov/house/Contract/CONTRACT.html

Rethinking the federal role in education [Special issue]. (1982). *Harvard Educational Review, 52* (4).

Senate Report 96-326. Conference report to accompany D. 210 (Department of Education Organization Act).

Sherman, J. D., & Kutner, M. A. (Eds.). (1982). Rethinking federal education policy: Strategies for the 1980s [Special issue]. *Peabody Journal of Education, 60* (1).

Slater, R. O., & Warren, D. A. (Eds.). (1983). The politics of education [Special issue]. *Issues in Education: A Forum of Research and Opinion, 1* (l).

Summerfield, H. L. (1974). *Power and process: The formulation and limits of federal educational policy.* Berkeley, CA: McCutchen.

Surfin, S. C. (1962). *Issues in federal aid to education.* Syracuse, NY: Syracuse University Press.

U.S. House of Representatives Report 95-1753. Conference report to accompany H.R. 15 (Education Amendments of 1978).

Index

About the Author

CHRISTOPHER CROSS was involved in federal education policy for most of his 32 years in Washington. During that time, he served in both the executive and legislative branches, as an assistant secretary at the U.S. Department of Education, the Republican staff director of the House Com¬mittee on Education and Labor, and a deputy assistant secretary in the old Department of Health, Education, and Welfare. He spent several years in the private sector, including serving as president of the Council for Basic Education and directing the education initiative at the Business Roundtable. He is currently a Senior Fellow at the Center for Education Policy and a Distinguished Senior Fellow at the Education Commission of the States. He and his wife (and editor), Dee Dee, live in Danville, California, and have two grown children, Charles Lum and Dana Goodall, and a granddaughter, Allyson Marie Goodall, to whom this book is dedicated.